Robert Hemphill

Money for Nothing

Robert Hemphill is the author of three previous business and travel memoirs, *Dust Tea, Dingoes and Dragons*, *Stories from the Middle Seat* and *Goats Ate Our Wires*, all available on Amazon.com.

He lives in Encinitas, California, where he writes occasionally on local and state politics, engages in intermittent philanthropy, and attempts to train two cats to sit on his lap. Not at the same time.

www.rfhemphill.com

Money for nothing and your chicks for free
Now that ain't working, that's the way you do it
Lemme tell ya, them guys ain't dumb
Maybe get a blister on your little finger
Maybe get a blister on your thumb

—"Money for Nothing" by Dire Straits, 1985

Money
for
Nothing

A Story of Wins and Losses in the
Philanthropy Business

R. F. Hemphill

Published in the USA by

Copyright © 2024 Robert Hemphill

EDITED BY
Andrea Susan Glass, www.WritersWay.com, and Shelley Chung

INTERIOR DESIGN BY
Victoria Vinton, www.CoyotePressGraphics.com

FORMATTING, ARTISTIC INSIGHTS, USEFUL INFORMATION,
GENERAL GUIDANCE AND THOUGHTFUL ADVICE PROVIDED BY
Jared Kuritz and Antoinette Kuritz, www.Strategies PR.com

All rights reserved. No part of this publication may be copied, reproduced, stored in or introduced into a retrieval system, or transmitted in any form or by any means (electronic, mechanical, photocopying, recording, or otherwise) without written permission of the publisher.

ISBN

979-8-218-43736-7

Contents

Dedication vi

Preface: Why? vii

Chapter 1: Sometimes You Need a Change, Whether You Need It or Not 1

Chapter 2: Why Not Dabble in Philanthropy—Everybody Else Does 9

Chapter 3: If You Give Away Stuff Instead of Money, Is It Still Philanthropy? 19

Chapter 4: So Maybe You Like Museums—Cause They're Full of Smart People? 39

Chapter 5: Once Bitten, Twice Bitten 63

Chapter 6: The One Thing I Liked about Marketing 69

Chapter 7: UCSD, the University of California for Silly Decisions 81

Chapter 8: Just When You Thought They Couldn't Get Any Stupider, It Turns Out They Had Stupid Friends to Help 91

Chapter 9: It's Not Just the University, There's Dumbness Everywhere 109

Chapter 10: Finally, a Small Success! 131

Chapter 11: The Bird Story Origins, with Apologies to Batman Begins 145

Chapter 12: A Discourse on Philanthropic Strategy 149

Chapter 13: We Debate the Wisdom of Becoming Drug Lords 163

Chapter 14: The Andean Condor (National Bird of Ecuador) Raises Its Ugly Head . 175

Chapter 15: This Philanthropy Stuff Ain't So Easy 179

Chapter 16: Far Above Cayuga's Waters Where Birds Fly, Unless They're Pelagic, In Which Case They Just Sit on the Water 199

Chapter 17: Perhaps We Are Not As Smart As We Think We Are 217

Chapter 18: We Cement Our Partnership with CLO, but Unfortunately Choose Mucilage Rather Than a Better Kind of Adhesive 239

Chapter 19: Harvesting the Rewards of Success 249

Chapter 20: CLO President's Council Story, Second Installment 259

Chapter 21: Can't Anybody Here Play This Game? 263

Chapter 22: A Final Note on Philanthropy 283

Appendix A: Projects 287

Dedication

This book is dedicated to Janet Starwood
who ignited my interest in birds,
and to Pam Kelly who nurtured it.

Preface

Why?

This is a book about failure—failure in a confusing fashion. Human activities fail in an almost innumerable number of ways: stupidity, avarice, bad luck, poor planning, inability to see the future. You can probably think of as many more without spending more than thirty seconds on this task.

One of the most brilliant ways I ever saw of dealing with failure was to avoid admitting that it was, in fact, failure. In my early days at the Tennessee Valley Authority, I was trotted around to a bunch of the offices and programs that made up the institution. It had grown mightily since its founding in 1933 as a key part of the New Deal. Its purpose had originally been to tame the mighty Tennessee River and keep it from inflicting its annual rainfall-based floods and rampages on the citizens living in its valley. The solution was, of course, dams. Dams and canals and impoundments/reservoirs have been the key, and usually the only tools that people had to deal with naturally occurring water, both good water and bad water.

Dams have been built since very early times, as have canals and reservoirs. The earliest dam, archaeologists agree, was constructed in Jordan in the fourth century BCE. Dams and reservoirs have been built for flood control, for navigation, for water supply, and irrigation. Since 1882 when the first power dam was built in Wisconsin (of all places), dams have also been built to support turbines and thus use water, or the energy that comes from the differential height created by the dam, to spin turbines and then generators and create electricity.

The genius of the TVA and of its first chairman, David Lilienthal, was to see that you could put all these purposes together in the same one dam—navigation, flood control, water supply, and power. It wasn't simple and it took more than a little clever engineering, but they did it and this result has been a standard for dam builders ever since. Almost every TVA dam had a set of locks (for navigation), a spillway (for flood control), and a turbine room (for power).

But this is not a book about dams.

In one of my various orientation meetings, I was being briefed by some people in the TVA's fertilizer program. Yes, as it grew, Congress saw fit to add more and more responsibilities to TVA's charge. One of these was the development of new fertilizers. This was not especially related to the river or water, but maybe to power, but really not that much. But this is the government, and when Congress decides your agency should do something, of course you agree, especially as they generally add to this mandate some useful helping of money and people.

Anyway, I was being briefed by an older TVA executive about all the programs of the "fertilizer institute." I think it was called that to make it seem more non-manure like, which was—until the invention of chemical fertilizers—the main "fertilizer" for all of agriculture.

As the list of positives rolled on and on, I finally had enough. "Thanks, Dr. Smith, that is a truly impressive history of progress in the development and application of fertilizers in the Tennessee Valley. But all the programs upon which you have touched seem to be great successes. Didn't you all ever have any failures? One learns as much or more from failures, I have found, as from successes."

Dr. Smith sat back and thought a minute. "Well," he said, "we did have lots of successes in this program, and I wouldn't say we had any failures, but we did have a few poor successes."

I have treasured the concept of "poor successes" for years now, and have been the instigator of my share of same. This is really a book about poor successes in the philanthropy field of endeavor. I hope that the reader finds it at least entertaining. I am not sure if it is educational, or just an interesting journey into a land that I knew very little of, but learned more about as I stumbled down the path.

Watch out for snakes.

1

Sometimes You Need a Change, Whether You Need It or Not

A Discussion of How to Make Friends When You Move to a New Place and You Don't Have Any

It was the end of 2013, the end of six years of being CEO of AES Solar, a job I dearly loved and was good at—more or less.

We had received an offer to purchase the company and my investors were eager to sell—that's what private equity guys do and that was the origin of half our money and half our board. AES was the other half, but for reasons I couldn't well discern, they were happy to sell as well. I had long since been clear with our board members that I would do everything I could to facilitate a good transaction for them, an "exit" where they got back several multiples of the money they had given us to develop and run the company. That commitment included me not being a jerk about who the new owners would put in charge.

It's business school lore that "the social issues" derail more mergers and acquisitions than any other cause. And "the social issues" is a code for "Who's in charge of the new or merged entity?" I wasn't interested in playing any sort of a game of king of the mountain. Besides, I might lose. I was also more than a little tired of the drag of it all. We had closed our last big project, Mount Signal Solar in Imperial County, Calfornia. It was a pretty big deal: 2,000 acres, 3.2 million installed panels, 256 Mw of solar capacity feeding into the new San Diego Gas & Electric (SDGE) transmission line going to San Diego. Oh, and $800 million dollars of financing, mostly debt but also an odd financial variant called "tax equity" that allowed us to transfer the project's tax credits to someone who could actually use them.

Raising the money for the project was about the hardest thing I ever did. A very long road show to visit and pitch to every investor who had ever thought about long duration debt for a solar plant, and several who hadn't. Morgan Stanley "led" the financing, which is what one says but really, they were helpers. They didn't put in any of their own money but identified potential investors, arranged the meetings, and introduced us, but we—me, Tim Montgomery, Becky Cranna, Patty Rollin, the senior leadership—did the presenting and answering of questions and answering of follow-up questions and revisiting issues and all the things involved in corralling close to a billion dollars. This was a terrific project with great partners and technology and a very good sales contract with SDGE. We had already in our five years of existence put together forty-nine projects like this, mostly in Europe and Asia, but nothing near this big. Even before the offer for the company I was beginning to think about the wisdom of "going out on top." And because humans are complex and not always rational, I couldn't imagine how the company could successfully go forward without me.

To cut to the chase, we sold the company, I cancelled my apartment lease, packed my bags, shot the dogs, sold my car, and moved to San Diego after thirty-five years in Washington.

No job, no friends but one, no particular knowledge of the area although I had spent a lot of time 110 miles east of there working on the Mount Signal project in El Centro. Not the same as living there. Not the same as living there with no business card and no business and no office and nothing to explain about my life—to anyone—except "retired."

Of course, there was the tiny consolation that over my AES and solar career I had been generously compensated so I had enough money to live well for a longer time than it was likely that I would remain upright. Plus, the climate was terrific and the beach house and the new girlfriend weren't bad either.

So how do you make friends in a new place about which you know little and in which you have no natural connections? The simple answer is the same one that we used at AES with regard to "business strategy." By the way, this is a much-maligned piece of the entrepreneurial environment. Many words have been written, usually poorly, about the importance of a business strategy: how to develop one, how to change one, how to explain one, and on and on. But no two sources agree on exactly what such a thing is. Some quote the former GE head, Jack Welch, on his famous dictum— that he wanted each of his divisions to be first or second in their market segment, by revenue as I recall, or get out of that line of work. Well, if a "business strategy" is supposed to focus and direct your efforts, this sort of works. It certainly is easy to explain. But it does not point to the future with any adequacy. What if you are number one in the business of black-and-white TV sets? What if you are number two in space tourism? What if you are number three in a business that has fabulous margins, margins much better than the number one and number two guys? Do you sacrifice profitability for volume? What if your business is the target of Chinese regulators? The "number one or number two" mantra doesn't really give managers much guidance in how to manage and grow a business segment.

Every so often at AES we would have a wave of guilt wash over us and we would run around muttering, "We need a strategy." This is easy to say and makes you feel better. But HAVING a strategy is not so easy. We would take two days and spend some travel money and go to a midlevel "resort" or conference center with a couple of tennis courts and maybe a pool and crumby food and all sit around in a big circle in a conference room and have presentations and a "strategic discussion," which was never very helpful and rarely came to any useful conclusions, but it did make us feel like real managers. Possibly mistakenly.

Ultimately we decided that we would try a bunch of things, see which ones worked, and then declare that this was our "business strategy." Silly as this sounds, it seemed to work reasonably well, depending on execution.

And as Bob Waterman, co-author of the classic business book *In Search of Excellence* remarked to us, business was no more than 10% strategy and 90% execution.

After maybe forty-five minutes of deep thought on my "no friends" problem, I came up with a strategy. I took something from the famous Willie Sutton explanation of why he robbed banks: "Because that's where the money is." I decided I needed to physically go to places where I could meet people who might in time become friends. Aha!

Step one: angel networks. In Washington I had joined several investing clubs that started up their activity by calling themselves "angel networks" and proposing to invest in promising start-ups. Somehow none of us bothered to look out the window and notice that we weren't in Silicon Valley, or Kansas either; we were in a very decidedly government town called the nation's capital. Never mind that—we forged ahead.

It worked like this: You rounded up twenty-five people, each of whom contributed $50,000 in two lumps over two years. The manager did all the work in finding and vetting the possible start-ups, usually with the inexpert help of a couple of the club members. You met every month for dinner and reviewed the investment candidates. Majority voting decided where and how much to invest. The goal was good investments and pulling all the money out within two years. The manager got a certain carried interest but did a very large amount of the work. And once your money was in, you had no more control of it other than through the review and voting system. It was a closed system, and no one else could join, nor could you bail out. But you met some interesting people and peculiar business ideas and went to nice places for dinner.

The Tech Coast Angels worked differently. You could join at any time, and the "management" was a couple of fellow investors. No clubby dinners, just monthly meetings at a law office conference room, and reviews of business plans and investor pitch decks. If the club decided to go forward with an investment, then each member was free to invest or not to invest. You made a "commitment" when joining to invest $25K in the course of a year, but there was no way to enforce this. And if you decided you didn't want to play anymore, you could leave. If you had made any investments, you still owned whatever small piece you had put in, but you were on your own to follow up and to keep in touch with the start-up company to which you had given your small amount of money.

This turned out to be neither a good way to do start-up investments, nor a good way to meet new and interesting people. I think I got to know only one person reasonably well during the course of my year-long involvement. I got to know several others by watching them criticize potential investments. There was way too much incentive to show off how smart you were, almost always by peeing on the start-ups that had come before you. It was frankly an unimpressive group of older white men (*quelle surprise*) who were very impressed with themselves. After a year of generally useless and not-even-that-interesting meetings, I gave up. But at least I didn't lose any money. Nor make any. Next try: fall back on your education. And the way to do that was to join the local university alumni club. Fortunately, there are a number of Ivy League grads in San Diego, and several active alumni clubs, including Yale and Harvard.

I went to the first meeting of Yale grads that I heard of, which was fortunately the annual "mixer." It was held at the lovely La Jolla home of a successful biotech entrepreneur named Tim Wollaeger and his very nice wife, Cindy. Tim was a Vietnam veteran, navy variety, a former biotech executive, and then a biotech venture capital person. He was quite good at the latter, especially the medical devices part of the spectrum. And he was even in the same class at Yale that I was, the class of 1966.

Did I know him from Yale? No, of course not. I arrived at Yale as a transfer student. I had spent two years at the Air Force's answer to Xinjiang prison camps for non-Chinese Uighurs: the U.S. Air Force Academy in Colorado. But at Yale I was still one of the Uighurs and there weren't any other Uighurs there.

Yale had an arrangement where all the freshmen were housed together on something called the "old campus" for their first year. This was a series of connected dorms surrounding a large rectangular quadrangle and was in fact where Yale was born in 1701. The history alleges that the name came from a local merchant named Elihu Yale who donated several bolts of plaid

Indian cotton cloth to the school. Fortunately, they didn't name it Madras University. It might have made a nice crest, however.

Once freshman year was finished, the new sophomores were spilt up into twelve groups by some secret method and apportioned among the twelve residential colleges. And then one spent the remaining three years of his (it was all males at the time, sadly) bright college years in these dormitories with their associated history. All the intramural athletics, the room and board, some classes although not many, and the social life such as it was, was conducted in these twelve colleges. It was supposed to be replicating the English college system at Oxford and Cambridge, but having never been there, I am not so sure.

The friend point was pretty simple—your freshman year you met all your classmates, more or less, and then you still knew them when they broke you up and put you in colleges. I missed that important step. To compound this, I was put in a two-person room in Trumbull College, with another transfer student, a very nice but very academic guy named Steve Davidson who was majoring in French and was about as nonathletic and as non-sociable as it is possible to imagine. It probably didn't matter anyway, as I was on a scholarship with significant work requirements, so I ended up working two different campus jobs for a combined twenty hours a week of work. The scholarship, rightly, was not generous. My dad was very, very unhappy that I had traded in being the ranking number one cadet in Colorado Springs to be a nobody at Yale, so he was disinclined to contribute and I was disinclined to ask him. End result: I did not meet or become close to many of my Yale classmates during my three years there—a combination of no time, no money, and no circumstances. Add to that the fact that half of my classmates had gone to prep school—to the few prep schools that sent kids to Ivy League schools—and so already knew other Yalies and didn't really need to know me.

When I went to the San Diego Yale Club mixer and met Tim, it wasn't a big surprise that we hadn't connected in New Haven even though we were in the same class. But we did connect in San Diego. Okay, one friend here, perhaps more to come.

Step three: get involved in local politics. In Arlington where I lived for twenty-five-plus years, I had eventually gotten to know the local political types through a tried-and-true strategy: give them money.

This was a big step for me because of my family training. If you were a career military officer, you lived under a large bucket of rules regarding conduct. One of the most important of them was something called the Hatch Act, named after Senator Carl Hatch of New Mexico and not after the famous chiles of the Hatch Valley of New Mexico. Passed in 1939, it basically said that armed services members were prohibited from participating in political activities. You could vote, but that was about it. My dad, a career Air Force officer, was pretty strict about this and applied it to all his children and his wife as well. For example, when I was a senior in high school in 1960, John Kennedy was running for president against Richard Nixon. One of his local organizers was able to rent the football stadium at my high school for a local rally where Kennedy would speak. The advance man was recruiting high school kids to introduce the candidate by marching across the field, each of us carrying one large letter. When put together, assuming we had the order correct, this would spell out "John F. Kennedy for President." Lots of my friends were signing up and I was eager to do this as well. Must not have been much going on in Alexandria that evening. I think girls were allowed to be letter carriers also, so it had possibilities.

However, when I came home and eagerly told my mom and dad about this amazing opportunity for unpaid labor, my dad was not impressed. So not impressed that he said that I couldn't do it and specified the Hatch Act. At the time I was not smart enough to research the act and see if in fact the children of military members were prohibited from carrying large letters in stadium rallies. As I never had another chance to do this, I still don't know the answer to this important question. First Amendment, right? Who knows. But it was an important lesson that I didn't have to learn again.

Eventually I did get involved in local Arlington politics in a very small way, by connecting with the local Democratic Party and attending modest local fundraisers. As a result, I got to know some of the local political people a bit including Don Beyer, the lieutenant governor who was a wonderful person as well as an excellent executive. And Mark Warner, who became governor and is now one of Virginia's two senators. It helped that they were both business guys first and politicians second, and so we had a lot in common.

It wasn't at all hard to start this same process in Encinitas. In fact, it was even easier than in Virginia because there were extreme limitations on candidate fundraising in California. In Encinitas, the limit per candidate per election was and is $250, so candidates spend a lot of time raising money in small lumps. Fortunately, I could afford this and got more and more involved in the local political scene. This eventually had mixed results, but at the beginning when I wasn't focusing on local issues, it was all sweetness and light. I got to know all of the city council members and slowly got included in larger local political meetings, and even appointed to Encinitas commissions, all advisory but fun.

Finally, the best "make new friends" strategy turned out to be the easiest: get to know your neighbors. In Virginia I never really did this, in part because I was on the road so much that this was difficult. And in northern Virginia, people came and went with some frequency—political types lost elections and went home, military people were assigned for tours at the Pentagon, then their tours ended and they were sent to Alaska or worse places.

L was really the catalyst for this. She had moved to Encinitas fifteen years ahead of me and had made it a priority to make friends with the neighbors. She was good at it and successful, so all I had to do was try not to be a jerk and tag along with people she already knew. After a year or so we had a conversation one evening, sitting on our deck, drinking a good California Cabernet, and the friends issue came up.

"You know," I said, "in Virginia, probably ninety percent of my friends were lawyers. The town is lousy with lawyers, mostly political but also some in all the ranges of activity that lawyers do—wills and estates, real estate, corporate work, intellectual property, and divorce. And here almost none of our friends are lawyers; instead we know business people, doctors, artists, IT experts, UCSD professors, politicians, and the like, but precious few lawyers." And it was true. Probably the fact that we threw big parties and invited lots of people helped as well. Amazing how several glasses of champagne helps you make friends.

2

Why Not Dabble in Philanthropy, Everybody Else Does

The Importance of Reading the Documents, the Sue Hickey Story, the TVA United Givers Fund Story, How We Did It at AES

I was never much for giving away money. It was hard to make and hard to hold on to, so why give it away? Besides, I was busy working and being in the Special Forces reserves and going to George Washington University at night to get an MBA while I was in the government. When I joined AES when it was started by Roger Sant and Dennis Bakke, I had even less time to fool around with good works, and I was not at all sure that I had money I didn't need. Hence I didn't really bother with charitable stuff. I also had a bit of a hangover from the army, where it was "expected" that you would buy a savings bond every month. This galled me, since even then I had figured out that this was a basically crappy investment with a remarkably low rate of return (I did learn something in business school). Then one day I was grousing about buying bonds every month to my boss, a really wonderful officer named Terry McClain. Of course, it was "Major McClain" or "Sir" to me. He looked surprised.

"Hemphill, you just don't get it, do you? I thought you were a pretty smart kid."

"Get what?" I asked.

"When can you redeem your bonds?" Major McClain asked me.

"When the ten years is up, I guess."

"You're smarter than that, Lieutenant. What do the documents say?"

"What documents?"

Major McClain said with some exasperation, "The ones governing purchase and redemption. The piece of paper they sent you along with the nice green savings bond."

"Oh, that, um, gosh, no sir, I didn't read it. I just stuck it in the files with the annoying bonds."

Major Mac said, "Dig it out when you go home tonight, read it, and then let's have a further conversation tomorrow."

"Yes, sir," I said, a useful catchall phrase for all sorts of things in the military.

The next day my boss said to me, "Did you read the documents?"

"Yes, sir."

"And what did they say?"

"Sir, if I understood them correctly, they said that redemption was not allowed prior to the expiration of the bond-holding period."

"Right, and what's the bond-holding period?"

"It's one-twelfth of any non-leap year annual period. Which I suppose means basically thirty or thirty-one days."

"Okay," he said. "So . . . ?"

"Sir, that might mean that I just have to let them sit there and accrue massive amounts of interest for one month, then I can redeem them and get my money back."

"Very good, Lieutenant. Correct. And what else have you learned?"

"That you should always read the documents?"

"Yes, that's much more important than the solution to your bond annoyance. I would state it this way: Always read the documents because no one else does. It's a sort of a completely fair way to play dirty."

I suppose that I believed him at the time, but as a baby officer I wasn't really doing a lot of complicated financial or legally defined transactions. But let's segue to the instance where this was really illustrated.

It was the first Arab oil embargo and I was at the Office of Management and Budget (OMB) running a task force that was creating the rules for gasoline rationing. No one wanted gasoline rationing, but the American public was getting quite fed up with sitting in long lines waiting for their measly gas allocation. A very smart young woman named Sue Hickey from EPA and several of her colleagues had been seconded to this emergency task force that was dealing with all this mess. One day late we were sitting around the office and the subject of documents came up, probably in the context of someone grousing that we had to write such long and complicated regulations explaining what we were doing and how.

"No one is ever going to read any of this junk we're writing," complained one of the less bright guys on the task force.

One of Sue's colleagues, also a smart and naturally undervalued analyst, said, "You don't know what you're talking about. Haven't you heard the story about Sue and the tailpipe emissions standards?"

"Huh?" several of us responded quickly.

"Here's the story, you clods," she announced. "Several years ago, the Clean Air Act Amendments of 1970 passed, setting for the first time the standards and requirements for reducing the emissions of US automobiles, and by the way, for any foreign automobiles imported for sale into the US."

She went on to explain to us what happened then. The law, despite all its grand language, didn't actually set the standards, it simply gave the authority and the requirement to set such standards, along with measurement and enforcement, to the EPA administrator. William Ruckelshaus, the administrator at the time, set up a process to do what the law required him to do. He complied with all the requirements of something called the Administrative Procedure Act (APA) that specified the regulatory process. Key requirements included that the regulatory agency, in this case the EPA, was required to as a first step lay out the case for what they were doing and what numbers they were proposing, and in this case just how these numbers would be enforced. There was not at the time any requirement to measure these emissions, car by car, as there is now. Nor was there an agreed-upon test procedure, which mattered almost as much as the actual set number, usually expressed in parts per million. To further complicate matters, there were six different chemical compounds that were being regulated, as the emissions stream from a car is, in fact, a complicated chemical stew of unburned or partially burned hydrocarbons, combustion products, and other unwelcome gases such as nitrous oxide formed inside the engine because of the heat and pressure of combustion. Nitrogen, an inert gas, doesn't burn as such, but in the right circumstances it can combine with oxygen, and then becomes an unwelcome contributor to smog. This may be more than you really wanted to know.

The EPA task force labored over all the requirements and eventually formulated something called a "Notice of Proposed Rulemaking" to specify all the details of the new rules. This set of rules would apply to all new US passenger cars and light-duty trucks for ever and ever. Since automobiles and associated products and services were about 10% of US GDP and maybe 7% of all employment in the country, these rules were of keen interest to lots of people. We're not talking about nickels and dimes here.

The rules stipulated a comment period of ninety days, three times the usual period, for any interested party to read the document and provide comments and recommendations on how to proceed. The EPA document, counting all appendices, stretched for three thousand dense pages.

The comments, especially from the auto manufacturers—businesses that had the most to lose (or maybe gain)—amounted to more than ten thousand pages. The job of the EPA staff was to analyze all these comments, weigh their merits, and provide a recommendation to the administrator for a final set of rules and regulations that would have the force of federal law. This was not a small task.

Sue Hickey was working there as a baby analyst, a GS-9, the lowest grade you could be and not be a secretary or an admin assistant. She hadn't been at the agency very long. But she was a member of the task force that had to do all this work.

As the review and analysis process continued inside EPA, there were meetings and subgroup meetings and specific issue meetings, as you might expect in an effort this big and this important. Sue was invited to some meetings, and then she was invited to more meetings as it became clearer that she had a quite good command of all the auto company submissions and their arguments, data, and counterproposals. The submissions were varied in quality and in recommendations, and were far from uniform or monolithic. But the analysis had to evaluate the submissions and prepare responses as to why the recommendations were being accepted, rejected, modified, or whether more information was being requested.

As this continued over several exhaustive months, through the fog of paper and discussion and argument, it became more and more clear that Sue Hickey, junior analyst (without even a master's degree), was more and more a key player because she was the *only person who had read all the documents*. It helped that she was smart and well organized and not threatening; maybe it was the long brown hair worn straight, parted in the middle. And the fact that although she was twenty-eight, she still routinely got carded in bars.

The final act of this long play was the public hearings, required by the APA and held by the EPA administrator to let the auto companies and others testify publicly as to their comments and recommendations. The administrator himself actually presided over these hearings, held in a very big conference room at the EPA. It was temporarily arranged like a House or Senate hearing room. Seated at the dais, immediately to the right hand of the EPA administrator, was not the EPA general counsel, and not the EPA deputy administrator for air quality, and not the EPA director of public relations. It was Sue Hickey, GS-9, the only person in the whole world who had actually read all the documents.

This is a true story. Sue went on to a very impressive career in government, eventually becoming chief operating officer of the Bonneville Power Administration in the mid-'90s, the only woman ever to hold this position in the largest publicly owned electric utility in the country. Although I lost touch with her over the years, I am pretty sure that even as a big executive presiding over literally thousands of government workers, she still read the documents.

One more story about governments and "philanthropy." When I moved to the Tennessee Valley Authority in 1981, I was running all the parts of the organization that dealt with distributing and selling the TVA electricity to 180 small local distribution companies. In essence, one executive ran all the power plants, and I ran everything else across the seven-state TVA area. It was a wonderful and challenging job, especially as I wasn't an engineer and I wasn't a Tennessee native and didn't have the right accent or the right academic background—University of Tennessee, that is.

We had an annual rite that I really found abhorrent. It was the United Way campaign. Every TVA employee was expected to make a contribution yearly to this sanctioned extortion. Better than that, the campaign manager also let everyone know what amount they should give, based on their rank in TVA. This was called your "fair share." It was also clear that each office was supposed to hit 100% of its people making contributions, and so senior managers were dragooned into pressuring their subordinates to write checks that were collected and toted up and names checked off. Unlike the savings bonds, you gave them the money and it was just gone. This was for the organization whose national president was eventually forced out when it was disclosed that he was paying himself a salary of $850,000. But that came later.

I really, really hated the whole idea. I especially hated having to get even the poorly paid administrative people to make their contribution. And the "fair share" calculation rankled me even more. After much fulminating and complaining to some of my friends and senior staff, one of them said to me, "They really don't care how much money they raise, they just want everyone to contribute so that they can brag about hitting one hundred percent."

Light bulb! What if I personally funded contributions for each of my team, which was about 125 people in Chattanooga? This didn't count the folks in the seven district offices, each of whom had their own campaigns. I got all the names and I sent in ten bucks of my own money for each person. And I made sure that it was recorded that way, so that presto! We were at 100%! The marvelous part was that nobody at the senior levels of TVA ever said boo about this to me, not that we advertised it. In fact, several folks complimented me for being such a good advocate with my team that they had all contributed, and so quickly. Probably the best $1,250 dollars I spent in Tennessee.

This was my second instance, the army being the first, of seeing that "philanthropy" was a cover for many and various creative interpretations and behaviors. You just had to work the system a bit.

Not every program for giving away money was annoying. At AES, after the first few years when it became clear that we were actually going to survive as a company and we weren't all going to get fired next Wednesday when we ran out of money, we had an internal debate about corporate social responsibility. This was a long and somewhat drawn-out debate that continued over several years. Mostly we concluded that if we lived up to our values, made electricity in accordance with all the environmental rules and limitations, and did it as cheaply as we could, that would be pretty "socially responsible." Despite a few off-label uses like executions, people used our product for valuable services like lighting, heating, cooling, and industrial processes. It was a damn sight better than making cigarettes and probably better than making M16s, although that is more debatable.

Eventually we got around to the issue of corporate charitable donations. One school of thought on this matter was that it wasn't our money, it really belonged to the shareholders. If we paid them dividends, then they could decide themselves what they wanted to do with their money, charitably or otherwise. However, we were in no position to pay dividends as we were busily pouring any "excess" funds into the development and construction of new power plants in odd parts of the world. The follow on to that argument was that if we did our business correctly, even if we didn't pay dividends, then our stock price would rise and our shareholders could take some portion of the wealth we had created, sell their stock, and give the money to whatever activity caught their fancy, again charitable or otherwise.

The competing school of thought has it that companies should make contributions to local charitable endeavors, although the rationale is murky as to whether this should be in furtherance of the aims of the company, and how to judge that furtherance. I don't think anyone argues that you should contribute company money to a charity or NGO who is actively opposed to your line of work. If you are building coal-fired power plants, for example, you probably wouldn't want to donate to the Sierra Club. But then who should you contribute to, and how much? These numbers are generally disclosed in financial statements, but they tend to be small as a percent of profits. Which in turn would argue that this really isn't that good an idea if the company wants to maximize shareholder returns. Nonetheless, most of the Fortune 500 companies do make such limited contributions.

As so often happened at AES, we decided on a different path. We announced to all our people that the company would match, one for one, any money that any AES person gave to a 501(c)(3) charitable organization. And initially that match was without limit, although eventually we had to put in a per-employee limitation as Roger Sant and Dennis Bakke, the founders, were exceptionally charitable and that started to look bad. But the idea was sound. There was no requirement to do any of this. We promised to keep the names and amounts contributed confidential, although we did have to know it at least in the accounting office so we could send out the matching checks.

The program was, once up and running, a howling success. Without pushing it at all, we had approximately 80% of all AES people use it, and the amounts contributed were 2% or 3% of our after-tax income. This was higher than the national corporate average as far as we could tell, but not really a drag on earnings. The best part, of course, was that the selection of charities was not made by the dreaded "senior management," it was made by every employee, to the charity or charities of their choice and in the amounts of their choice.

After a couple of years, I read somewhere that employees liked to know where the charitable contributions went. Seemed reasonable to me, and since I was, as an ancillary duty, in charge of publishing the company newsletter, I decided to find out and put the data in the next issue. Not amounts, and not names of contributors of course. What we expected was that major "official charities" would get the majority of the money—United Givers Fund, Red Cross, Wounded Warrior Project, Humane Society. Boy, were we wrong. About 80% of the entities listed, and it was a list of more than three hundred, were churches or religious institutions. We were philanthropically surprised. But delighted.

During all my twenty-five-plus years at AES, I was at best a routine contributor to charitable causes. I probably gave more money to support political candidates than I did to charities. And I did not do volunteer work or join boards of 501(c)(3) organizations, not only because nobody ever asked me, but also because I was busy and generally never home predictably, so attending board meetings would have been difficult. It should also be added that I never really saw a charity or a cause that struck a chord with me. This was especially true as AES got more into renewables, a drive that the CEO at the time, Paul Hanrahan, asked me to lead. After I told him to ask me. I was pretty sure I was doing the Lord's work every day when I showed up at Arlington and plunked my butt down in my office chair. I didn't see much need for extraneous activities, and frankly I didn't have a lot of time for them either. I wasn't opposed, I just wasn't that interested. I paid my taxes, so I presumed at least some of that money would go to doing good works, even if it was the US government or the state of Virginia that got to decide said works and the money allocated to them.

3

If You Give Away Stuff Instead of Money, Is It Still Philanthropy?

I Become a Famous Author, and Find Out How Publishing Works in the Modern Era

When I moved to San Diego and left the energy world, at least the paid employment energy world, one of the things I wanted to do was become a famous author.

I came by it naturally. My mother, after her three kids reached the point where they were in school and more or less able to take care of themselves, decided to go back to school at George Washington University and get a master's degree in religion or possibly religious education. Fortunately, this did not require devotional activity or self-flagellation. It did require writing papers, so she drew on her experience in Japan where she and my dad had befriended and supported several local missionaries. One in particular had been of special interest, a woman named Thomasine Allen, a Congregationalist missionary who ran a mission north of Tokyo in a town called Kiyosato.

My mom knew nothing about writing books or publishing books or selling books, and I don't believe she had any friends who were in the author business. But she did plow ahead and write a book whose title was *A Treasure to Keep* and got a small Midwestern publishing house called Judson Press to publish it. I do not believe that the royalties from the sales of this book made our family fabulously wealthy. If they did, this fact was carefully hidden from me and my siblings. I reluctantly read the book many years later, and it wasn't bad, if your taste runs to biographies of missionaries. Somewhat to my amazement, you can still buy a copy of this on Amazon, sixty years later. You cannot, however, find the other two books she wrote, also about missionaries in Japan. A specialized niche.

She was as well an avid letter writer and kept in touch with her increasingly far-flung family and friends this way, usually making three or four carbons of each letter. We used to argue about who got the last carbon, although I think it was always me. And we usually wrote back. This was all before cell phones and email and was, therefore, by definition quite primitive. I am not even sure if you can buy carbon paper anymore, or "carbon sets" as they were called. You cannot buy this on Amazon; when you type in "carbon sets" in the search box, you get back "carbon sensor." You can buy carbon paper, but it's now predominantly used for tracing patterns onto other materials like wood or fabric. Since using it in letter writing required a typewriter, and we know what's happened to them, I doubt that carbon paper manufacturing is a growth industry. Now you know.

When I was about to go away to the army, and thence to Vietnam, one of my professors at UCLA, a former fighter pilot named Chuck Reis, said to me, "You are about to have an experience that few of your contemporaries will ever have. You're a good writer, and you should try and capture this experience. The best way to do that is in letters home. But write them not as 'How are you, I am fine, we had peaches at the mess hall for dinner tonight' missives, but explain what you're doing and what the experience is like."

I thought this was good advice, so I took it. I wrote a lot of letters home to my wife, but sadly only about one-third of them survived. Again, this was before computers, so I was never able to keep copies myself.

But when at AES we started doing overseas development of power plants and we were getting bigger as a company, I thought of Dr. Reis's advice again. And I thought about my father, at that point a retired colonel living in Olympia, Washington, not a location that I recommend to anyone who likes decent weather from time to time. He was a smart man and had gone back to school after the war at Denver's Sturm College of Law, his schooling paid for by the air force. But he was not and never had been a business person; he was a flying-airplanes person and then a diplomat as air attaché in the US embassy in Japan.

I decided to write him letters about my AES experiences, especially the ones involving travel as this was an area of great interest to him. And I thought he'd find the business parts interesting and, in some ways, curious. I surely did.

From time to time I showed copies of the letters to my colleagues, and they were uniformly flattering, even if they did work for me. The response was often, "You should publish these in a book." The other good news was now that Bill Gates, or possibly Steve Jobs, had invented computers, I could keep copies of the letters myself.

I did have the slight handicap of knowing nothing about publishing.

I arrived in San Diego, certain that I would soon get an agent and a publisher, be reviewed in the *New York Times Book Review* section, and be selected for Oprah's Book Club. Not to mention receiving a huge advance from whatever publisher won the competition for my first book, then get a three-book deal and relatively soon thereafter sell the screen rights to Hollywood, again in a competition. I didn't expect an interview on *60 Minutes* or a guest appearance on somebody's late-night show. At least not immediately.

I did figure that I would need a full and relatively complete manuscript, so I set to work editing all the letters, arranging them in chapters, giving each chapter an intriguing name, and putting them all in the same font and typeface. I chose Arial 12 point for no good reason other than that it was what I had been using at work. And I could still read it without glasses.

In the course of this desultory knocking around, I was introduced to a local person whose mom was a book publicist. He was Jared Kuritz and he had an undergrad degree from Brown, and a law degree from Brown as well, plus a couple years as a grunt baby lawyer. But he had decided to go into the book business with his mother. He performed three valuable services for me:

1. He knew all the local book industry service providers—each category of whom I ended up needing.
2. He understood the mechanics and related economics of the bookselling world.
3. He was able, carefully but truthfully, to explain to me the facts of life. These had about as much similarity to what I was expecting (see above Oprah ref, etc.) as my understanding of the mechanics of sex did when I was eleven, a point in time when I had bizarre constructs of who did what to whom. None of my eleven-year-old classmates, except probably all the girls but we weren't speaking to them, had any clearer sense of the geography or the necessary procedures either. I am still not entirely clear on some of this but let's not go there.

He was, in short, exactly the sort of Yoda/Guru/Natty Bumppo (the Pathfinder for those of you not schooled in the works of James Fenimore Cooper—the $1,000 question on *Jeopardy*) that I really needed. While he was expensive, he was willing to take some of his compensation on a "success fee" basis.

He also urged me to sign up for and attend the meetings of a local group called Publishers & Writers of San Diego. This cost a massive seventy-five dollars a year and had monthly meetings where "experts" and less-expert people gave lectures to the waiting audience, and then answered questions afterward. Sometimes these people actually were experts, and sometimes they were service providers. But it was okay, it wasn't costing much and some of the speakers were actually useful. Some of the audience was at least interesting. Occasionally an audience member would ask a question that revealed they knew even less than I did. This did not, sadly, happen very often.

What did I learn about the book business, in bits and pieces over the two and a half years that I was almost wholly working on my first book? For starters, it's all different than it used to be. Oh, gosh, I am surprised—no other aspect of life in the US is any different than it was in 1954 when I was in fourth grade. When did this happen?

Here is what had changed. In the "old days," which we shall define as up to when Jeff Bezos got in his car and drove from New York to Seattle with the intent of setting up a website that would sell books, to be called "Cadabra" after "abracadabra," until someone told him this sounded too much like "cadaver." Why Seattle, by the way? Because it was close to the largest book distribution warehouse in the country in Roseburg, Oregon. Now you know.

At the time the publishing industry existed essentially in New York, and there were six big "houses"—Penguin Group, Random House, Simon & Schuster, HarperCollins, Macmillan, and Hachette. These houses published a combined 100,000 books per year. This excludes textbooks or scholarly works or small religious press output.

You could not get your book published by sending it to them, as they got hundreds and hundreds of bad book manuscripts every day and threw away most of them without reading. Yes, that's the ugly truth. Maybe they sent you a rejection letter if you were lucky, but probably not. They hired starry-eyed English graduates from Bryn Mawr and Sarah Lawrence to do the grunt work, of which there was much, like carrying around slugs of books to be thrown away.

To get your book even looked at, never mind published, you needed an agent who specialized in doing this work. But the best agents, if they were ethical, only worked on contingency, usually a fee of 10% of any payments you the author received. So how did you get to hire one? As above, you couldn't just send them your manuscript, as they too got hundreds of such submissions a day. And proceeded forthwith to stuff them into different trash cans than those used by publishers, but still pretty much in Manhattan. These weren't even recycled; how wasteful and non-environmental. The answer is, you had to know somebody. Or you had to already be a published and successful author.

If this all sounds depressing and somewhat circular, sorry, but read on. You couldn't get your book published unless you had an agent, and you couldn't get an agent unless you already had one. Thanks to Joseph Heller for writing *Catch-22*. Amazing how applicable it still is.

What about costs and economics? Once you entered the promised land of having an agent and a publisher, then the publisher would hire an editor to make your book more salable and pay for it. And also an artist to prepare the art for your cover and pay for it. And a book designer to "design" your book's text and pay for it.

This last part seemed especially strange to me. What's to design? It's words in paragraphs on a page of white paper. No, no, no, no. You need to have a page format—page numbers at top or bottom or center or left or right, what size and font to use; how about the title page and the next page and the table of contents and so forth and so forth? Personally, I didn't especially care, but I began to understand that there was real work to be done here.

Once all this work was done, some of which you as author got to approve, some of which you did not, then you finally got to the point where the publisher actually did something that we can all agree was what you expected—he published that book, meaning he actually had it printed. In some number of copies, probably a thousand if you were a new author that no one had ever heard of. Like me. This is not a great number of books.

Then came marketing.

This included, if you were lucky, not just a press release, but sending copies of the book out to the numerous local and regional newspapers and magazines that reviewed books. It wasn't just the *New York Times*. Even the publishing industry grudgingly acknowledged that people outside of New York sometimes actually bought and read books.

If you were particularly hot in the eyes of the publisher, they took out ads for you in some of the appropriate publications. The apex of the system was, natch, the *New York Times Sunday Book Review* magazine, actually a section of the weekend paper. That was heaven and was naturally expensive.

We pause here for a bit of real life intruding on the fantasy world of ideal life.

Authors are generally told that getting reviews of their books is very difficult, especially in the *New York Times* previously mentioned book review section. Authors take this on faith, I suppose. But perhaps taking a moment to view the numbers will make this allegation more believable. The book review section varies a bit, but it runs between twenty and thirty actual reviews, and we mean here one-half to one-quarter page reviews, written by what are probably real people who have actually read the book they are reviewing. After all, they're getting paid. Probably not much.

I don't mean the "new in paperback" section or the "books just published" section. Nor do I refer to the fairly stupid half-page ads quoting several semi-famous persons you will never have heard of unless you live in Manhattan and spend every day reading every word written in the *New York Times*. All you learn from these ads is that these are books with taglines: "A heartrending account about juvenile elephants who survive captivity" or "A remarkable book describing rural teenage loss and despair" or "A book we have long needed [we who?] by a talented author who had an uncle in the Spanish Civil War."

Unless you want to wait until Sunday and run out to the local 7-Eleven and get the only copy of the NYT that they carry, which generally costs more than seven dollars, which is *a lot* for a Sunday newspaper without any comics section I believe, and then count the reviews in the book review section your own self, the number is, on average, twenty-five. Each week. You may then multiply this by fifty-two for what we hope are obvious reasons and get the result of 1,300 reviews each year, more or less. This is called data.

Stop and compare this to the 100,000 books that traditionally were published each year out of New York. Yes, good job, the answer is 1.3% of the published books get reviewed. In other words, you have a far less than 10% chance of getting such a review. If you are a first-time author then that chance has to be reduced again by 90% since most of the reviews are for books by people who have written more than one book. So, not so good odds. Better than being hit by a comet, thank goodness, or bitten by a cobra snake. Your agent is supposed to help you with this, but those are his odds as well.

Just for laughs, let us return to the issue of virtue-driven selection, the ideal governing choosing the books reviewed in the *Times*. While reading this next section, quietly hum the tune "Can't Buy Me Love" by the Beatles, although sometimes misattributed to the Shirelles.

It's about my friend and colleague Dennis Bakke, a very good person and comrade with whom I worked closely both in the government and at AES where he was the number two guy in the company. After ten or so years there, he decided he would write a book about his experiences in starting and building the company. Many senior executives get this affliction, but it is usually not fatal, just debilitating.

So, he did. It was moderately well written, although not gripping, or maybe it was just that I had already heard the company stories more than a few times. It was called *Joy at Work*. It was published but with no particular marketing or reviews. It did not sell well, no surprise there—first-time author, company no one had ever heard of in an industry that was possibly even more boring than watching cricket. But because he had the money, and because he believed he had some interesting ideas about a somewhat different way to run a company, and because he had always had a bit of an evangelical streak, he went to the *New York Times* and bought a full-page ad promoting his book. Note that these ads cost around $50K. It was a nice ad, professionally done, several good quotes from members of our board, etc.

Perhaps it inspired one reader out of a thousand to go out and buy his book just based on the ad. But imagine this: four weeks later, that same book was reviewed with a full-page and mildly positive review in (wait for it, drum roll . . .) the *New York Times Book Review* section! Well, well, well, and well.

Honestly, I thought this was pretty neat. At the end of the day, having a lot of money is okay, but it does have distinctive shortcomings, mostly limited by one's physical inability to consume more than a limited quantity of all physical and intellectual goods. But I was charmed that if you waved ego-driven money at the *Times*, then there was a quid pro quo. I am sure that this was not a contractual obligation and that the two things—he buys add, book gets reviewed—were never discussed. But, somehow, there it was. I never asked him about this, and he never discussed it, so maybe there was no obvious connection, and even if there was, it ain't illegal or immoral. So, good for Dennis.

Back to the main narrative. After the publishing and early marketing stuff is done, there remains a ritual known as the "book tour" where the famous or would-be famous author has a several months-long tour of all the small bookstores in cities and towns that he or she has never visited. These visits are frequently billed as a "reading" although reading a page or two of your book to a small group of people who have never heard of you before is not actually much fun, nor does it seem likely to inspire a positive commercial reaction, as in the listener rushing to the front cash register where many copies of the book are handily stacked, and buying one or several copies. If you are a moderately well-known author with several bestsellers under your belt, you are now more knowledgeable and should take those books at the front desk and put them in your briefcase. Besides, you don't have to do this anymore! The internet has been invented! But more on that later.

Traditions die hard, of course. I asked a friend of a friend about her experience with readings. This is a woman author who specializes in a genre referred to as Christian chick lit. I am not sure what this genre is exactly—bodice rippers where only the top button is ripped off, then everyone kneels and asks forgiveness? Anyway, she was modestly successful, and her publisher decided to put her on a book tour. It should also be noted here that you pay for your own transportation and lodging in this adventure, and you eat at a lot of Howard Johnson's if you can find any.

She was scheduled for a reading in a small Midwestern town. The place of the reading was called Chuck's or some nonspecific name like that. She showed up, checked in to the Days Inn, and went to Chuck's, which was on the main street at least. When she got there it turned out to be a drugstore. The owner, the aforementioned Chuck, actually Chuck Jr., who had inherited the store from his dad, explained that there wasn't a bookstore in the town but that he sometimes carried books. These were usually paperbacks displayed on one of those unstable circular wire racks that fell over when bumped, spewing all the books all over the floor. Chuck Jr. had arranged four chairs in the back, in a one-by-three facing setup. There was a small hand-drawn "poster" in the window announcing her reading and getting the title of the book right, but her name slightly wrong.

It was not an auspicious beginning, but she was a trooper, godammit, and she had paid to be here and anyway she was fifteen minutes early and the crowd would soon arrive, no doubt.

She chatted awkwardly with Chuck Jr.: "So, how's it like running a drugstore in a small Midwestern town?" and elicited the response that he probably should have gone to pharmacy school so he wouldn't have to hire a part-time pharmacist, only there wasn't really that much pill business so what he was doing was okay. Time passed. It was now ten minutes after the start time, and it was still our heroine and Chuck Jr.

At fifteen minutes past the start time, she said to Chuck Jr., "Let's get started." It seemed likely that CJ, as he had asked her to call him, might be her only listener, and since there was no one else in the store that probably wouldn't do much damage to the bottom line. "Just sit down," she said, "and if someone comes in who's not coming to my reading, we'll pause and let you handle him. Or her."

She launched into her reading to the audience of one, sort of a captive audience in reality, and moved through the two scenes she had picked out, one a "meet-cute" scene where her two protagonists intercepted each other at the punch bowl at the CYF (Christian Youth Fellowship—you knew that didn't you?) Wednesday-evening meeting/social hour, which followed the short "lesson" given by the junior minister who was one of several lackluster competitors for her hand.

The second scene was where the heroine's new, recently met, punch-bowl paramour confesses that he was only coming to CYF because of her, but her religious example and devotion to Jesus had inspired him to ask the minister—no, not the junior minister, the real minister—to instruct him further in the faith, with the ultimate possibility that he would stand and make his confession and become a full member of the congregation.

She finished both readings, the second one somewhat more quickly as Charles Jr. was starting to fidget and look around. At least he didn't look at his watch, a cheap Timex from the watch rack up front.

The evening then ended with Chuck Jr. thanking her, and she him, and then Chuck Jr. actually asking if he could buy one of her books. She did not say, "Well hell yeah, big boy, I brought twenty of the damn things with me." Although she was tempted. She thanked him and took his money and proceeded out of the store and down the street to the Days Inn, which unfortunately did not have a restaurant attached. Even more unfortunately it did not have a bar attached. She might be a Christian chick lit author, but at that point she was in need of a serious drink.

The general consensus of both my newfound marketing guru and of everyone else I asked about this was that book tours were a thing of the past and an expensive waste of time. So I didn't do one, except once in Lincoln, Nebraska, at our annual family reunion where I imported my four cousins and their various husbands/wives to come to a reading that my agent had arranged at the local Barnes & Noble. The bookstore didn't really mind; they had space and if someone bought a book, they did it through the store even though I had personally arranged to send the books ahead on my own nickel. It was a nice enough store, and they had set out plenty of chairs, and sixteen of my relatives showed up and stayed the whole time. Well, I had also given each of them a T-shirt with the cover of the book on it, so they were kind of tickled, and besides they were supportive, and it was July and hot and the fireworks weren't until later and the store was air-conditioned. We did have a real, un-bribed, nonrelative woman wander over to where we were all sitting waiting to start and she stayed for about half of my pitch. Then she wandered off to the Christen chick lit section. So it goes.

Now the thing you've all been waiting for, the discussion of book sales economics. It works like this, but please prepare to be depressed. I recently read an article about book authoring, and someone called it "the world's worst business."

Old days economics: If you had a publisher (and as we have explained above that was the only way into the fraternity of "Published and Maybe Even Bestselling Authors") the publisher set the economic terms. Since there were only six of them, there is no doubt that they all colluded. However, remember the basic negotiating posture of the two parties, author and publisher. The author comes to the table with a manuscript, note, not even a book yet, and no money. Sometimes the author has fame and a reputation and has successfully made publisher a lot of money in the past and so can maybe be counted on to do so in the future. That changes the balance of power a little bit but not tremendously. The publisher comes to the table with money and connections and experience and knowledge of distribution channels, and, most important, the willingness to take risk.

The "deal" that is concluded between the two generally works like this: the author agrees to license his manuscript exclusively to publisher, to include the rights to publish, distribute, market, and generally manage the whole process, usually for all geographies and for a long time. Publisher has to pay for everything, except maybe author's book tour, and even there publisher is in charge of the itinerary and setting it all up. Publisher gets author an editor and a cover artist and a book designer and these people work on turning a manuscript into a book. Then publisher pays to get it printed, and publisher pays for all the marketing, however much that is. Author is involved in all these steps with varying degrees of authority depending on what he or she has been able to negotiate. Oprah Winfrey gets a lot, first-time author pretty little. But first-time author doesn't know much about this end of the business, so his opinion probably shouldn't count for much anyway. Author turns over his manuscript to publisher and takes the risk that publisher is not a bozo and will actually do what the contract says that he will do. Author takes no financial risk. Let's say that again: author takes no financial risk. Publisher takes all the financial risk.

Who gets the money? The way the deal works is interesting if you are something of a business nerd. First, there's the distribution. Publisher uses his experience and connections to get bookstores to order some number of copies of the book. But the bookstores do not pay publisher for the book, not even for the postage of having it delivered to their stores or quaintly named shops in Nantucket. And if a copy of the book actually sells, the bookstore gets 50% of the revenue, and sends the rest back to the publisher. Publisher than takes around 25% of the revenue and sends the rest to the agent, who in turn takes 20%. Note that agent has also been working on contingency, because author has paid agent nothing, zero, nada. All the parties on the non-author side of the deal are paying their own costs and expenses, and betting that the stupid book actually sells, and they can make their money back and then some more money.

If you have followed the math, you know that it leaves author with 5% of the revenue. If the book costs twenty dollars, then author gets a buck a book. Magically, a dollar a book for the author turns out to be the general expectation in the publishing world unless you are good, famous, and lucky. The percentages can be and are adjusted, the deals are fiddled with based on volumes sold and time periods, but a dollar a book is the standard. It's what you get as an author for not taking any financial risk on your own book and its travails in the marketplace.

There is one more important piece of the publisher/author deal that applied in the old world—the advance. If you are a first-time author, forget this. But if you are a middling-good author in a popular niche, you can get a cash advance in return for giving up all your rights to the publisher. But you have to pay the advance back by giving up the dollar a book (about what you make when all is said and done) until the advance is fully repaid. No, I don't know if the publisher charges you interest. The good news is that this is yet another cost for publisher and no risk for author, because if author's book is dog poop, despite all the experts who have helped get it published, and the author never "earns out" his advance, he doesn't have to do anything. It's not a debt, or if it is it is not collateralized. The general talk in the publishing world is that most books never earn out their advances. Take the money and go to the Bahamas for a vacation, it is probably the only money you will ever receive as an author from the sale and publication of your book.

Now forget about almost all of the economics we have just covered, because that is the old world of publishing.

The new world of publishing is different in some ways and the same in others. It is only partially the fault of Jeff Bezos.

Most people know how he invented Amazon, starting with books. His insight was that you really didn't need bookstores, you just needed a way to buy books over the internet. You did still need books, physical books, and someplace to keep them, and then a way to take orders and money from customers and in return send them the book they had just ordered. No need to go into detail here but what's baffling is that we have had "mail order" in the US since before the Second World War. Remember Sears, Roebuck and Co. and Montgomery Ward and those big, thick, aquatint catalogs? My dad was based in Japan from 1954 to 1958 and we lived off those catalogs, at least for the things that they sold.

Somehow Bezos determined that you didn't need catalogs if you had the internet and that you could simplify the ordering and delivering process, and if you were centralized, you could afford a larger inventory and warehousing system and you could drive all the small bookstores out of business. And the big bookstores as well.

Remember Borders? Remember Barnes & Noble before it went bankrupt several times? Remember Brentano's and B. Dalton and Crown Books and Waldenbooks? Bezos was right and only a very few competitors remain.

But that's probably not the most important thing that Amazon did, significant as it is. Some smart people in Germany started monkeying around with, of all things, the printing press. Only modest changes had been made since Gutenberg invented it. And the setting up of the type was always the worst and slowest part of the printing process. Once that was done, then you could run lots of copies for only the cost of ink and paper and maybe the odd supervisor in case something broke. But to make a long story short, your printer doesn't seem to need anyone to do typesetting so you can send a memo to your boss who insists he won't read stuff on his computer.

Over the last thirty-five years, those technologies have been applied to printing presses so that they can accept digital content and turn it into analog paper copies. Initially this was difficult, and much engineering had to be done and unions had to be dealt with and new skills had to be learned, but now we have something called "print on demand." Amazon no longer has to have a hundred copies of your book in its warehouse to send out when someone orders it. Instead, they have a special section of the warehouse where some people sit around watching TikTok until an order comes zinging in from the ether.

"Hey," says Merle the foreman, "somebody wants a copy of Charley's book on flintknapping." This is not, by the way, a book about how to take flint and hold it for ransom. One of Merle's workers takes the order and looks up *Flintknapping for Amateurs* and inputs the file into the printing press, and pretty soon out comes an analog book, cover and all. Off it goes to the person who ordered it in Petaluma, one of the flintknapping centers of the US.

This also happens in several other large book companies, but the process is still generically the same. But what about the economics?

First of all, you don't need any inventory. Not at Amazon, not at Barnes & Noble, not at some warehouse in the Central Valley, not anywhere. Surely not in the warehouses of the publishers, since they no longer print books. The inventory is on the cloud. In the cloud? This has several interesting implications. First, your book can never be "out of print." Amazon will not disclose how many books it has in its digital library in the cloud, ready to be printed, but most industry experts estimate that the number is more than seven million. And probably growing every day because storage is essentially free.

Second and equally important, Amazon as "publisher" is still taking some risk in making your book available, but much of those costs have shifted. The author now has to be responsible for arranging and paying for the cover art and the book design and such, or Amazon will not accept the file. The author has to be responsible for arranging and paying for any marketing of the book. But he or she doesn't really have to do any—Amazon don't care. They only print books that have already been sold, so they take no market risk.

The publishers have been essentially disintermediated. They are no longer the gatekeepers they once were. They still survive but in shrunken form. The terrible beauty of democratization has taken over the book writing and publishing business. You want to write a book about the cute tricks of your kitten—go for it. Amazon will publish it if anyone ever orders it.

Several other interesting things have happened. Since overall costs per book have gone down and risk has been taken out of the commercial process, there is more money per book to distribute. One result has been slightly lower average prices, but the other result has been slightly more money per copy to authors. Not a lot, but the dollar a book rule is no longer exactly true, it's edging up to two dollars. Finally, there is an enormous amount of crap out there. Maybe there always was. This is even more true of things published in a Kindle version, where all the costs of analog books have vanished. Amazon sends me a promotional email every day for five to ten Kindle books it would like me to buy, and they are almost all $0.99 to $1.99. And some are even by authors I have heard of! I don't know how much the author gets of this—clearly not two dollars. Maybe a dime?

Despite all this revolutionary change, writing books for a living is not a sure thing. The best data I have been able to find about author incomes indicates that the famous Pareto principle applies here: 10% of the authors make 90% of the money. The author earnings for the latest available year indicate that the average author earns $1,200 per year from book sales. Sobering unless you already have either a ton of money or a day job.

Here is a personal example: My first book, *Dust Tea, Dingoes and Dragons*, was published in 2014. In addition to being available on Amazon in infinite quantities if purchased, I ordered an additional two hundred that I planned to give to a few friends and colleagues. Plus, I would require copies to take with me to sell at all my book readings that my agent was to arrange for me. Things started off very well when I called up Andres Gluski, the AES CEO, and said that my book was published, and wouldn't he like it if I came and gave a little talk about it. AES could buy some books and give them out to all the troops. Andres, bless his kind and caring heart, thought about this, and said that he would have AES buy three hundred—and pay for them!!—and he would introduce me at a morning gathering of all the staff. I could do a talk and then pass out and sign the book to whomever wanted one. I was thrilled and honored. He didn't have to do this, and it also meant that I didn't have to try and sell books to all my old colleagues after my little talk. I did have to pay my own travel but, heck, this was just the beginning! I was on the way to Famous Author Land and was planning on inviting Tom Clancy out for lunch. And then maybe drinks with Ann Beattie.

It also helped that Keith Martin, who ran the Washington office of Chadbourne & Parke, the law firm that had done lots of AES business, wanted me to come by that same day and give all their lawyers a talk at lunch about the book. They did not, however, promise to buy any, but it was free and personal publicity, the best kind, marketing to people I actually knew and who would be interested in the substance of the book.

In addition, my agent/publicist said I should send out copies of the book to people who did reviews, since they did not go out and buy their own copies. So I did. By the way, when mailing a book, you can use what the post office calls the "manuscript rate," which means it only costs you three dollars and change per book. I packed and addressed more than a hundred copies of the book and sent them off. This resulted ultimately in one lukewarm review in a newspaper in the Pacific Northwest. Other authors I spoke to talked about having sent out two hundred books and gotten zero reviews. Well, I did better than that, although not much.

My agent, Jared, did other things for me. He called lots of radio shows around the country, talk show people he knew who from time to time interviewed authors if they had written an interesting book. Not so many in big markets, i.e., none in San Diego, San Francisco, Los Angeles, New York, Chicago, Miami—etc. None of the cities that had either an NFL team or an NBA franchise. But I spoke to "radio personalities" in Huntsville, Duluth, Poughkeepsie, and Truth or Consequences, New Mexico. These interviews usually lasted ten minutes, with a two-minute commercial in the middle. None of the personalities had read the book. None. So how good do you think the questions were? Right, not that good. I eventually got the drill down, which was ignoring the question and simply telling a story out of the book. Worked for both of us. But it seemed pointless, and it was really no fun.

Jared did get me a two-minute live spot on a local San Diego TV station, and that was also no fun, and I didn't do it very well, despite rehearsals.

I pined for the energy business, where the sales cycle was long and the risks were many, but once you made the sale you could build the power plant and sell electricity for twenty or thirty years. And that one sale was worth around $20 billion in eventual revenue. Selling fifteen-dollar items one book at a time was way different and not really in a good way.

After trying all these alternatives, recommended by Jared and others, it finally became clear to me that there was one thing that mattered. As most Amazon customers know by now, you can leave a review, featuring one to five stars plus pithy comments. I always look at the stars, and I frequently read the comments unless I'm buying mayonnaise or something equally complicated. I sent out notifications to all my friends and acquaintances telling them of the marvel of having a book published and urging them politely to buy it. More important, I asked them to leave a positive review—five stars would be good. And bless their hearts, many of them did it. I got sixty-five positive five-star reviews in the six months after it was published. I was very pleased. I also got two four-star reviews from good friends, which was surprising and disappointing. Just wait till they write books and try to get reviews. Not that I'm vindictive and mean-spirited. Well maybe a little.

I ended up selling about 1,200 books, counting the three hundred from AES, although the book is still available on Amazon and occasionally someone buys a copy. Figuring out the math on this is not difficult.

Based on the buck a book rule, I made over the two-year period after publication about $1,200.

Costs:

Cover art: $750

Book design: $500

Purchasing 300 books from Amazon to send out to reviewers (you get a break on the cost): $1,200

Purchasing 300 books to send to potential reviewers: $1,200

Postage for sending out 300 books to potential reviewers at $4 a book: $1,200

Flying to Washington from San Diego to do book talks: $1,200

Staying in cheap motel in Washington as part of book talks: $150

Paying advisor/publicist (who took a risk on half of his fee): $3,500

For anyone reading this who cannot add, shame on you, numbers are important.

This is not an audited financial statement, but it's pretty accurate because it was money, and I was curious. So: revenue $1,200, costs $9,700. And no cost estimate for my time.

There you have it. I am not in the least disappointed in this experience, and Ann Beattie probably wouldn't take my call anyway. There is something really wonderful about finally, after a lot of effort and struggle and cost, holding in your hands a real book that you have written. Not as good as birthing a child although guys only get to take credit for the end product, none of the real effort. But very nice.

What I learned from all this was two things: I don't much like marketing, especially flogging the book to people who I do not know and who are highly unlikely to buy it. Saying the same things over and over to different audiences is not fun. It's a bit like doing an initial public offering for your start-up company, where you fly around the country and make the same presentation over and over. In that case the end result if you're successful is raising hundreds of millions of dollars. In the case of a book, you're raising, um, a dollar? Maybe ten dollars if you sell ten books. Which I never did in any one setting. There does not seem to be any magic bullet that will pay you back more than you spent on it.

The second thing I learned is that sending out the book to potential reviewers is even stupider than talking with talk show hosts, and more expensive. The results are pretty much the same, that is, almost nothing. But what I didn't mind was sending the book out to friends and colleagues, for free. Sometimes they even posted positive reviews on Amazon, even if they didn't read the book. I got lots of nice feedback from friends and relatives, and that was nice. This is not an economically sensible thing to do, but neither is sending out Christmas cards, but we all used to do that. It's part of staying connected to people with whom you share a friendship or a relationship, and that's a good thing in general.

In line with these brilliant insights, on my next two books I gave up on all the costly and time-wasting "marketing" stuff and just made a long list of people. Then I sent out about two hundred copies of each of the books, *Stories from the Middle Seat* and *Goats Ate Our Wires*. I felt better about doing that and maybe it generated some word of mouth and maybe some other people then bought the books on Amazon, but I didn't care. I liked writing them and I liked sending them and that justified any expense in doing it. No, the famous economist of the Chicago School, Milton Friedman, would not approve. I didn't send him a book anyway. I probably won't send him this one either. Anyway, I think he's dead and no longer reading books.

To answer the question in the title of this chapter, it's probably not philanthropy to send out a free book to friends. At least I have been unable to find an accountant who thinks this could be either a charitable deduction or written off as a business expense since I am clearly not doing this for any defensible business reason. Accountants are so negative.

4

So Maybe You Like Museums—Cause They're Full of Smart People?

Ah, If Only It Were So....

In 1985 while I was still at AES, my boss there—Dennis Bakke—got a call from the newly appointed chairman of the Smithsonian National Museum of American History. The caller was a smart guy named Ivan Selin. He had been part of the small group of analysts that Defense Secretary Robert McNamara had put together in 1962 to help run the Department of Defense. They got lots of publicity but actually made a number of improvements, especially in the procurement system. He later went on in 1970 to establish American Management Systems (AMS), a consulting firm that initially did defense-related work, but later all sorts of government-related consulting. Ivan Selin's company was at the time one of the few non-government firms in Washington, DC. AES was one of the few others, and the AMS offices were right across the street from ours in Rosslyn. Ivan had been appointed to the newly formed board of the Smithsonian National Museum of American History.

The Smithsonian had hastily formed such boards after a fiasco where they mounted an exhibition on the B-29 and its role in dropping the atom bombs on Nagasaki and Hiroshima. The show had, in the opinion of many who saw it, come down on the side of the Japanese with how terrible it was to be bombed. Well, yes, said many, but you might have mentioned Pearl Harbor and a number of other aggressive military actions—say Rape of Nanking, for example, that the Japanese government and military perpetrated during the war. And that ultimately led to the US ending the war with two atomic bombs.

The museum scrambled. It was not used to this or any form of criticism of what it did or how it did it. One solution was to create advisory boards in each museum, of which the Smithsonian now has fourteen, which would vet any new exhibits that were to be put up. Somehow Ivan got inveigled into this enterprise as chairman of the board for the American History Museum and was busily trying to fill the board seats. He invited Dennis Bakke to join. Dennis's inclinations for non-AES activities ran mostly to church-related opportunities, so he passed but asked if I would like to do it. I said, "Sure." Dennis told Ivan that I had accepted on his behalf. This is not exactly what Ivan expected but at least he didn't turn me down. I was the number three guy at AES, and I had a fancy title so that was probably what was needed.

You might have thought, like I surely did, that the Smithsonian was one big museum. After all, it's located on the mall in Washington, and you can go into those various buildings and see different stuff—the space shuttle, the X-15, dinosaur bones, pictures of famous people, the original flag made by Betsy Ross, Judy Garland's ruby slippers from *The Wizard of Oz*, and a very large stuffed elephant. Among many, many other things. The Smithsonian is in fact a collection of smaller museums, none of them very small, but each somewhat focused. The Air and Space Museum does not want the ruby slippers but the National Museum of American History sure does. And that is the Board I found myself on.

It was my first real "board of directors" experience and it was quite interesting. But that's not the point of this wordy introduction. I went on to join many other boards, some fiduciary including AES, and some advisory. The difference between the two is that the fiduciary board members have real legal responsibilities to oversee their organizations and can be sued if they do not use reasonable standards of care in exercising these authorities. All the Enron board members were sued personally, and many had judgments rendered against them after the big Enron collapse in December of 2001. Advisory board members have no legal authority, and consequently no real personal exposure or liability for the organization's decisions. This is not a small difference. We will come back to this later.

As I mentioned earlier in the book, shortly after I moved to San Diego, I joined an angel investing group called the Tech Coast Angels. Among the more interesting people I met in that group was a very accomplished woman named Martha Dennis. She is an MIT PhD in electrical engineering and was among the core group that formed the local tech company Qualcomm, which grew from a small start-up to the largest company in San Diego, with a current market value of a modest $240 billion.

I liked her, and we hit it off. It probably helped that her husband, Ed, was a highly regarded professor of biology at UCSD and a Yale graduate, as was I. I mentioned to her that I would like to join some boards now that I was here, and museum/arts boards would be high on my list. Martha was nothing if not a networker. As far as I could tell, she knew everyone in San Diego who was of any consequence. Pretty soon I got a call from Elizabeth Yang-Hellewell, the development director at the La Jolla-located Museum of Contemporary Art San Diego, also known by its initials as MCASD. Elizabeth was a smart and grounded Asian American with, to my surprise, little art history background but an MBA from Temple. She guided me through the resume submission, background and reference checking, and interviewing that generally make up the process for joining such organizations.

The board was a fiduciary one and composed of slightly more women than men. This is not the usual makeup of most boards, even in the era of California legislating 30% minimum female membership on boards of directors. Despite my gender, they seemed impressed by my Smithsonian history and offered me a board position, which I accepted without much diligence on my own part. The museum was in the middle of a fundraising campaign. Several years prior to this they had decided, as organizations are wont to do, that they needed to be bigger.

Let us pause a moment and muse on the nature of museums. With exceptions, the role of museums in US society is to collect stuff and exhibit it. People who join museum staffs are generally called curators, and usually focus on a particular piece of the universe that the museum has taken as its charge. There is some "educational" work but it's usually trivial as museums are not physically set up for this, and we have something called "schools" that are better at this function. The Japanese word for museum, if the characters are literally translated, is "national old things place." Pretty accurate.

Curators are collectors. They buy things and they get things donated to them. The more professional ones are careful about what they buy, which is easy since they rarely have lots of money. They tend to be less careful about what they accept as donations. They all have limited space, so they can only display a portion, in many cases a small to very small portion, of their total collections at any one time. They really do not like to sell ("de-accession" in museum parlance, since "sell" is too pedestrian and low class a word for what a museum might do) any of their stuff.

Early in my tenure at the Museum of American History, I was self-educationing about the museum and its business since I knew bupkis about the whole area. "How much stuff do you have?" I asked the person who was charged with showing me around.

"We don't call it 'stuff,'" she sniffed.

"Okay, what do you call it?" I responded gamely.

"We refer to it as 'items,'" was the reply.

"Okay, how many items do you have?"

"Between three and four million."

I was a little surprised by this answer. If the business of a museum is to attract and maintain items, shouldn't you know how many you have? It was explained to me that this was a difficult question. I couldn't quite understand why. We knew at AES how many power plants we had, and we knew the inventory of spare parts we had, and we knew how many people we employed—32,000 at that point. And I am pretty sure that J.P. Morgan knew how many dollars they had, since they were in the dollar collecting business.

It turns out that the collection had never been digitized—although they knew that they really had to get started on that. And that each curator was in charge of keeping the records of his or her own collection. And that apparently no one ever audited anything, physically audited, as in counting all the stuff. And of course, all the records were in different formats.

If you are a museum, and if you are well run, you have something called a collections policy. If you show up with a box of black-and-white photos from your grandma's attic, all of people whom you cannot identify, and offer to donate them to the Smithsonian, they will take them. Smarter museums, even the Museum of Old Photos We Cannot Identify, will not. The collections policy of the Smithsonian was clearly, "If you want to give it to us, we want to take it." And they did.

Later in the orientation, they took me and several other new board members to the "backstage" part of the museum. This consisted of cramped offices, since this is the government in some ways after all, and some modest space for storing bits—oops, *items*—making up the various collections. In this case we were being shown the patent medicine collection. I will leave out the part about how important in US history patent medicines have been, you can fill that in for yourself. The collection included small- and medium-sized bottles, packages, and tins—many, many of these. Within large, industrial bureaus with deep but shallow drawers were laid all the collected bottles, packages, and tins. Most of them were old but hardly all.

The tour guide pointed out the several drawers devoted to Sucrets tins. If you do not know what this is, you are probably younger than fifty. A "Sucret" was a menthol-flavored, round, green throat lozenge, individually wrapped in silver foil, and sold in small four-by-four-inch tins with navy blue bottoms and gray-green tops that snapped shut. They were invented in 1932 and had been on the market continuously since then. My parents had given them to me when I was a kid if I had a cough. I am sure they were probably 90% sugar.

Our tour guide, seeing us marvel at the opened drawer of small blue-and-grey tins, proudly announced that the museum had and was preserving a copy of *every* type of Sucrets tin ever made!

Right off the top of my head, I had trouble coming up with the scholarly purpose that such a collection would serve. But here's the best part: by simple inspection of the nicely ordered and labeled slug of tins, you found that not only did they have a copy of every tin ever made, but they also had five or six or seven copies of every Sucrets tin ever made. My goodness!

I was slowly coming to realize that my idea that a museum was an asset manager and should maximize the value of its collection was a naïve view of a museum, at least according to the people who were running this museum.

Later, after I had digested and ruminated on what I had been told and what I had seen, I asked one of the senior managers there whether they had ever considered a de-accession sale, a recognized museum practice, at least in theory. The only reason I knew about such things was that the Smithsonian's National Museum of African Art was then housed in a couple of small town houses very close to where I lived on Capitol Hill. They had recently held a "de-accession sale" of excess parts of their collection, and I had gone to it and bought several nice African masks.

The senior manager paused and thought for a while. "Oh, yes," she exclaimed, "we did have one several years ago."

"One?" I asked.

"Yes, we did, we had one, and it was very successful. I think we made close to fifty thousand dollars."

"Very impressive," I responded. "What did you sell off?"

"We sold twenty sets of medieval European armor," she said proudly.

Something wasn't clicking here. I had spent days being oriented to this museum and its collections, both items on display and items not. I had attended numerous meetings on the question of what to do about Betsy Ross's flag that flew over Fort McHenry and had been on display in the grand hall of the museum since 1905. It was, by the way, now falling apart and the issue of how to remedy this was center of mind for the leadership and the board. I had not been taken to the European medieval armor collection, nor had I met the European medieval armor curator. It is, after all, the Museum of American History.

"That's really interesting," I said chummily. "How did you get the sets of armor that you sold?"

"Well, someone gave them to us of course," she replied as if speaking to the retarded. "How else do you think we get things?"

Of course, it was all becoming clear to me. As earlier noted, the official "collections policy" of the museum was, succinctly stated, "If you want to give it to us, we want to take it." And they did.

All this means that the museum was probably out of room—both display room and storage room—on the day that it opened. Subsequent conversations I initiated provided the following interesting facts. The museum had roughly 5% of its items on display at any one time. Because mounting a new exhibition was a bunch of work—taking down the old stuff, redoing the space, repainting, selection of the items and the theme of the display, mounting it, writing the copy for each of the items, writing the brochure for the exhibition, writing the press release and background information for the exhibition and its items, arranging the opening night, and on and on—the average exhibition was up for ten years.

You can do the math on this if you are so inclined. Assume that there is rigorous rotation of the items, so that each item is somewhere in the "to be exhibited" queue. A new 5% of the items go up every ten years. Hence you have one chance out of twenty to be on exhibit, and then it's back to storage for you until your turn comes around again. You have on average a two-hundred-year rotation. Ten years on exhibit, 190 years in the closet. Since there are effectively no de-accession sales, you can't get out of the closet that way.

But it's worse. The display space for this museum is fixed by its handsome marble walls. The two-hundred-year rotation calculation only applies if the number of total items is fixed as well. If the museum keeps adding to its collection, then soon it only has 4% of the items on display, then 3%, and the rotation period increases proportionately. It's just arithmetic.

Armed with all this hard-won knowledge of museum secrets, I approached my job interview with MCASD with confidence. They had all seen my rewritten resume to focus on my many and varied board positions and would no doubt wish to know my opinions of collections policy, de-accessions, and the like.

Not really. They never asked. What they wanted to know, politely and discretely, was whether I had enough money to make interesting financial contributions to the museum. I assured them that I understood the responsibilities of a board member of a 501(c)(3) organization, and I was fully prepared to carry them out. I assured them, although they never asked, that I really did like "modern art" and had even written a term paper on Jackson Pollock when I was a junior in high school. This was in fact true, although when I handed it in my teacher looked at the title and said, "Oh, no, I'm not going to have to read something about that weird modern art am I?" This did discourage further papers on similar subjects.

I noted that I was a long-standing member of the Museum of Modern Art in New York, and always used their Christmas cards. This was actually true as well. They did not appear to find this impressive. In fact, as I read these words, they do sound idiotic. Then the money shot. The La Jolla Museum had decided, in the finest traditions of museums with stuff everywhere, that they needed more space to display their collections. Collections expand inexorably; space does not expand. Until it does. In the ensuing discussion we got down to the issue of construction, finding a contractor, and (*ta-dum!*) raising the money. I agreed that it was important, but it was also important to be diligent on the design and construction process that would get them more space. Especially since they were going to do this by tearing out some of the inside stuff, like a five hundred-seat auditorium, and replacing it with more gallery space. And digging up the garden space between the north wall of the current building and the street and making it into more gallery space. I tried to point out that retrofitting an existing building was always more difficult and expensive than starting with a clean slate or an empty lot, but they were more interested in describing for me how wonderful the space would be when it was all done. Sometimes you talk; more often you make progress by listening. Not that I am always great at that.

But I passed whatever the test was and was voted onto the board. I was put on the investment committee on the theory that raising money for AES and for the solar business should have given me some insight into money. I was also put on the ad hoc construction committee along with a smart architect who was already on the board. But then they were careful never to really ask me anything about the project. The board and the management had long since established how they wanted to work together, and that was how they were going to work together. And how they wanted to work together was the management did everything, and the board watched, occasionally bemused. Far be it from someone who didn't even live in La Jolla to change that.

Let's start with the money. It's always a good place to start. When I arrived, the board was in the middle of a major fundraising activity. The museum had hired a fancy New York architect named Annabelle Selldorf. Her resume included David Zwirner's second gallery; updating and expanding the Frick Collection; reinstalling the High Museum of Art in Atlanta's collections; and a school in Zimbabwe. Curiously she also had designed a waste recycling facility in New York. Who knew that trash needed a fancy architect? She had done nothing in California.

So far in her engagement by the museum, some preliminary/conceptual work had been done, but no real designing, as in plans and drawings that had enough detail that they could be used for real cost estimating. But we had an estimate anyway, and that was a construction cost of $70 million. Because this is San Diego, and because Irwin Jacobs (founder of Qualcomm) and his wife Joan are generous beyond reason, the fundraising had started with a $20 million donation from them. It did come with a matching requirement, but that was just a pesky footnote.

The odd thing was that the fundraising raising campaign had set a target of $55 million. Yes, against a cost estimate of $70 million. I was not there for all this initial work, so I cannot be certain how this came about. Probably they convinced themselves that once they got the real design and the associated details, they could get the costs down without eviscerating the design. Architects have been known to tell clients fabrications like this, and museum directors have been known to tell board members something similar. They were now at the $35 million mark in the money raising, which wasn't even enough to meet the matching requirement.

But we soldiered on. The two board members in charge of the fundraising duly made reports to the board at our meetings about how things were going. Slowly was the usual answer. But Anna the architect and her crew were busily drafting away, and the CFO was doing the complex business of securing the permits from the city and the Coastal Commission. Since the museum sits on the coast in La Jolla with terrific views from its conference rooms and some of the galleries, we were in the jurisdiction of the Coastal Commission, one of the most powerful and most arbitrary regulatory bodies in all of California, and that is saying a lot.

We were also in the middle of evaluating and soliciting several construction companies and accompanying bids for building the plans that Anna was drawing up. I was enlisted to be there for the presentations on capabilities that each of the four selected contractors were about to make. I sat in the museum conference room with the ocean view and listened carefully. When that was done, we went on several field trips to see examples of what each of the contenders had built recently.

If you have not recently designed, permitted, financed, and then built a large project, this may all sound sensible, but it is not. What is sensible is determining what you want or need and doing enough work to get drawings, which allow cost estimating. This means you can do what are called "take-offs." For example, how many square feet is the building you are designing? If you know this number, you can determine how much concrete you need to pour for the base of the floors, and if your building is more than one story, how much you need to pour for the pillars and how much structural steel that will support the second floor you will need. You can also determine how much marble flooring will be required unless you are going to use linoleum, in which case you are assuredly *not* designing a museum. There are standard estimates not only for each of these materials, but also for the installation costs. All in nice units (square feet, linear feet) so that all the estimator need do is multiply, then add all this together. It's more complicated than that but not hugely. We've been building large buildings in this country for a long time, and we know how to do this, despite numerous examples to the contrary. This isn't a nuclear plant, for goodness' sake, which we really do not know how to build.

But that work had not been done, perhaps because it would have cost several millions of dollars. "Design" is not as expensive as construction, but it's not free. If you do it right, then you don't have expensive surprises later. You will have surprises on a daily basis, but that's the nature of construction.

We had not done this, so the nature of our cost estimate was, to say the least, shaky. But what was really not possible to explain was why the fundraising raising target was so much less than even this estimate? I asked a couple of times but got vague answers or suggestions that as a new board member maybe it would be a good idea to be quiet and learn. I wasn't clear who I was going to learn from, because no one on the board had ever built or redone a seaside museum, but never mind.

We forged somewhat blindly ahead. We had nice presentations by the selected constructors. They all knew how to do PowerPoint presentations, and mainly to show off stuff that they had built. That was fine and useful—no sense hiring someone who had only built small outhouses. But these presentations were remarkably short on numbers, even from the projects that they had completed. Ok, I know, I know, all projects are different, so the numbers are never comparable and cannot be used to make back-of-the-envelope estimates. But I, for one, would have loved to have seen such numbers, and I could not understand why my board comrades seemed uninterested.

We eventually selected a construction company. Then a second interesting process item arose. Our designated big-time architect from New York, the careful reader will note from above, had never built a project in California, let alone one on the coast of the ocean. She needed to hire (and we needed to pay for) a local architect who could provide the local permitting and design standards information that is always an important part of any large construction project. Also, little things like soil conditions in the area.

Soil conditions may seem like a curious thing to raise, but in construction, especially in power plant construction, you quickly learn that soil is not soil, it's sand or clay or aggregate or solid granite or some wet bunch of slimy stuff or varying amounts of all of the above as you move across the surface of the site and drill into it for foundations. Your building needs something to sit on. It will weigh many hundreds of thousands of pounds and if you're not careful it will either sink into the ground—think Mexico City, which is sinking about eight inches a year because it is built on the original Aztec capital of Tenochtitlan. As everyone probably remembers—at least in Mexico—this city was an island in the middle of a lake. Classic wet bunch of slimy stuff, but the Spaniards in the 1500s didn't have such good civil engineers, so they went ahead and built lovely big buildings, cathedrals and such, on ground that you shouldn't be playing croquet on. Ditto Venice in Italy. And many other large cities.

We could not even do rudimentary soil borings, which are just what they sound like: you take a big machine with a drill on it, and drill into the soil. The drill has a hole in the middle and when raised it brings up a "core," which is a foot-by-foot picture of what is below your future building. If the core is dripping, this is a bad sign. But if you already have a building sitting on your site, you cannot run big tractors into a conference room and do a soil boring, even if there is no meeting that day. You need local knowledge, very specific local knowledge. We did not have that. So, we guessed, and put those guesses into the estimate.

And then there is the matter of local codes and standards. Southern California is an earthquake zone. The San Andreas Fault, and many other faults, run merrily along under the ground. Every so often they slip against each other and that produces an earthquake. This is not a good thing for a building to be sitting on top of, but faults are large and run for literally miles and miles. They also intersect with each other, which makes predicting their behavior even more difficult.

The remedy for all this is to over-engineer the foundation of the building. Crudely, this means more concrete rather than less. If you put in a whole lot of concrete, then the building will shake less because, well, it's big and heavy and takes way more energy to shake it than your average run-of-the-mill earthquake is likely to generate. The various governments, who in general do not want buildings to fall down in earthquakes, have set the best standards they know how to set, which require that buildings pour enough concrete to stop this.

As an interesting aside, much academic work has been done on earthquake prediction and monitoring, and California has now put in place an earthquake early warning system. Note that despite much publicity, this is *not* really a prediction system, rather it is an earthquake early warning (EEW) system that detects significant earthquakes once they have started. It then quickly provides alerts that can reach many people before shaking arrives. If you are connected to the system, it will now give you up to *ten seconds* of warning that an earthquake is coming. I am not making this up. Ten seconds. And that's if you have your radio or TV on or are deep in meditation with your cell phone (but only if you have the app).

Think about what you would do in that ten seconds before your whole house is going to fall down on your head and crush you like a glass Christmas ornament. Run outside, I guess—don't forget your shoes, there's going to be a lot of broken glass around.

But to get back to the point, you need a local engineer/architect who understands what the codes say you have to do, and how to then apply the general rules to the specifics of your building. Here's a surprise—not all buildings are the same. No matter how carefully and voluminously the code writers have written the building codes, they cannot have written a set of requirements for your building that does not need some interpretation in applying it. The local guys will know that, having done it before, and if they're good, they will have worked with the code-enforcing/interpreting individuals in the city permitting office before, hopefully many times.

It was hard to argue that we didn't need a local architect/engineer firm on the team. We finally selected one and then waited while they reviewed all that had gone before and made recommendations for changes or additions. We watched while the NY guys and La Jolla guys had "discussions" about their changes/recommendations. All on our nickel, of course. The only good part was that we hadn't broken ground or poured any concrete yet, so the consequences of changes were less costly than they might have been.

I soon tired of not being a part of the process and stopped going to those few meetings to which I was (it seemed to me) grudgingly invited. The architect on the board was good enough to deal with all this, and we had already selected the construction contractor and negotiated the construction contract. It was the job of the architects (NY and La Jolla) to make sure that the contractor followed the designs and built the building and its renovations as per the plans. I figured there were enough cooks stirring the pot at this point and I was tired of trying to push my way in to sessions to which I had not been initially invited. The museum staff and the fundraisers did continue to ask me and everyone else on the board and everyone else they knew for money, however.

We eventually got to the point where the plans were done enough to start construction. The cost estimate could now be done with a higher level of precision than previously (see discussion of construction drawings above). Then came the big shocker: We were now looking at not $55 million, not $70 million, but $105 million. There was no especially good argument for why the cost estimate had risen. The truth is that we were building/renovating, which is always, always, always more expensive than just starting over. No sponsor ever believes this. The second law of major construction is that the estimate always goes up, it never goes down. This is sort of like the law of gravity. I have done probably a hundred construction projects in my energy career, and not one, not a single solitary one, has ever come in as estimated, and none for darn sure have ever been built for less than the estimated cost. This museum was no different.

That was problem number one, predictable but nonetheless a problem. Problem number two was that the museum staff and most of the gentle people who were on the board wanted to start construction, even though we didn't have all the money raised. This is never a good idea. Once you start construction, you really can't change the design halfway through and make, for example, the building smaller, and take out the ground floor that is to be dug out. We had a long and pointless discussion in the board meeting where we decided to go ahead about whether in fact we should first change the design to make the place cheaper and closer to our then current funding level. It may come as no surprise that I was on the "take out the ground floor" side of the argument, which was estimated to save some $20 to 25 million. We would still be over budget, but not by nearly as much. There was much debate about "the integrity of the architect's design" and "this is the only chance we will have to make these changes, we can never get things like this past the permitting authorities again." I thought the second argument was interesting and actually not a bad one. But it did not overpower the fact that we didn't have enough money.

"Why is this a problem?" one might ask. Several reasons: first, starting construction removes much of the urgency from the pitch of the fundraisers. It should not, but human nature, especially the human nature of donors, says, "What the heck, you must have the dough, you're building the place." You can swear that you do not, but it becomes a much harder sell to contributors. Second, the construction company is now no longer on the hook to change the design, economize on the materials and the finishes, etc. that he has been being pestered to do. And which he doesn't much like to do. What he wants to do is build the doggone building.

There are worse possible consequences. Once you start and the contractor and his subcontractors begin working and spending money, then you—the sponsor—have a contractual obligation to pay them. There's usually a 5% or 10% deposit up front, but once that is blown through then the contractor is spending his own money and waiting at the end of each month for the museum to pay the invoice that he has submitted. But what if you are halfway through, and have paid all the invoices, and you are out of money even though you were expecting more donations, and the contractor is still working? What if he runs up another monthly bill of $5 or $8 million dollars? And you cannot pay him?

The relationship between you will no longer be one of "teamwork," which both sides will have agreed it should be, and perhaps has been. It will now be frosty and heading to below zero. Pretty quickly the contractor will take the legal steps required to put what is called a "mechanic's lien" on all that he has built. This entitles him to stop work and to seize and sell all the assets, if necessary, even though you have paid for most of them. This rapidly gets ugly as you keep assuring him that your donors are just about to come through, so he should keep calm and (ha-ha!) keep working. He won't. But it gets uglier still.

As a general matter, incorporated entities like a museum can have two kinds of "boards"—an advisory board and a fiduciary board. You can even have both if you want to. The advisory board does what it sounds like, but it has no legal authority over the entity that it is advising, and the members have no legal liability for anything that they have advised. The fiduciary board is quite the opposite: it has legal authority to hire and fire, set salaries and strategic direction, and generally provide binding guidance to the management of the entity. The directors as a result have legal liability for the actions of the entity. This is why most sensible companies and nonprofits of any size have "directors and officers insurance" that protects them from having to pay for the consequences of the entity doing bad things. Like not paying its bills. In the extreme, this can mean that each director can be personally liable for judgments brought against the entity.

Whoa, stop, say that again?

Yep, you as a fiduciary board director in the extreme case can be personally liable for paying any legal judgements lodged against the entity on whose board you cheerfully serve, if and when the entity cannot pay them. Quickly resigning as you get into trouble does not remove this liability other than for bad things going forward. This is also why directors of large companies get paid what may seem like extravagant amounts of money for four meetings a year. It's not the meetings, it's the risk.

For reasons that I never got any clarity on, the museum did not have an advisory board, it had a fiduciary board. When it cannot pay its bills, there is a not-so-theoretical chance that you as a director will have to fork out some of your personal wealth to make up the difference. This is rarely in my experience explained clearly to new board candidates for fiduciary boards—why would it be? To make matters even more interesting, the claimant (the unpaid contractor) can pick and choose which directors to go after, with the result that he always chooses the ones with the most wealth. Why wouldn't he?

Perhaps this is more explanation than necessary as to why it is not a good idea to start a large capital project without having the funds in hand. And why the museum's board seemed blasé about just charging ahead. But, you may say, why not just borrow the money? Get a bank to bridge you over until all those almost-ready donors come through and the funding crisis is averted? Sadly, banks are not really dumb about their money, despite the occasional allegations in the popular press. The bank's officers do not get paid to lose its money.

But can't the museum pledge its collateral to the bank for protection of the loan? It has all those pictures and stuff.

Yes, true, but what are "all those pictures" really worth? A bank, contemplating a loan to the museum secured by its art collection, will first need an accurate and complete inventory of said collection. You would think that any museum worth its salt or white wine in plastic glasses would have a digitized, complete record of what it owns. Not likely at all.

But assume it does—what is all that stuff worth? The bank will demand that the museum hire an outside financial expert who understands modern art things to do an appraisal of the collection and determine its current market value. But we're not talking nice clean things like shares of GE or US treasury bonds, which trade daily and therefore whose value can be determined by reading the second section of the *Wall Street Journal*. You have to look to the records of auction houses as the best market indicator, and even then, this won't give you the exact price of the ten most valuable items in your collection, because each is unique, and none of them have been bought or sold recently. At least very few of them will have been.

Getting a loan from the United Bank of Commerce is not certain, it is not quick, it is not cheap (appraisals cost money and the bank is surely not paying, you are), and it may not give you what you want. Or as much as you want or need.

But enough of this. The board decided to go ahead anyway in the serene belief that the money would show up. *Field of Dreams* redux—"If you build it, they will donate?"

Cut to the chase—the construction commenced and was completed more or less on time and for more or less what had been estimated and the funds were raised, mostly from the same major donors, Irwin and Joan Jacobs and some others. I clearly didn't understand how the La Jolla system worked. How could I? I live in Encinitas, an hour to the north, and I never went to La Jolla Country Day, the primo private school to which everyone in La Jolla sends their kids.

The whole funding/construction process unnerved me. Maybe I am too conservative, but I had no interest as a board member in putting my net worth at risk for a museum for which I didn't care a great deal and whose activities I had only one out of twenty-eight votes to direct. Eventually I decided that my best defense was to "act as a prudent man" and bring my concerns to the board chairman and the museum director. It's probably not much of a defense, but it's something.

This involved writing down what bothered me, politely, and suggesting what changes needed to be made. When in Washington I had served on several advisory boards including, as mentioned above, one for the National Museum of American History, a Smithsonian museum, as well as the AES board, unquestionably a fiduciary board. I had also been on a number of boards of small start-ups, again fiduciary boards. Some had survived and prospered, some had not, which is the nature of the start-up business.

I made appointments with Paul Jacobs, the board chairman , and with Kathryn Kanjo, the museum director, to discuss my concerns. Paul was the son of Irwin, the major Museum donor and Quallcom founder, which may help explain his board position. For each meeting I provided a written outline of what I considered to be best practices and where the museum was falling short. The document was polite and not accusatory, but it was clear. Otherwise, it would be of no benefit to me in case a legal defense was necessary. Here is what the outline looked like; it was the same for both Paul and Kathryn.

18 July 2017 Meeting with Kathryn Kanjo
1. Fiduciary relationship and responsibilities
2. Board orientation
3. Hygiene—
    a. Minutes of all meetings, especially finance and investment committee
    b. Board material ahead of time—for all meetings
4. Financial matters
    a. Quarterly review of investment results
    b. Financial and investment results distributed quarterly
    c. Better focus on forecasts, esp. shortfalls
    d. Endowment management
5. Construction program

a. Regular item on board meeting agenda
b. Monthly progress reviews
c. Construction contract approval
d. Invoice approvals

In both cases, I was politely received and listened to, with few questions asked. I wasn't being accusatory; I was just sharing what I knew about how to set up and run a fiduciary board. In each case, the day after the meeting I documented what had been said and saved that document on the off chance that this whole thing descended into a big legal mess.

Here is a copy of my notes on the Kathryn Kanjo meeting, but they are almost the same as my meeting with Paul Jacobs.

19 July 2017 Memorandum for the Record

Confidential

Meeting with Kathryn Kanjo at Valencia Hotel

18 July 2017

I met with Kathryn in the bar of the hotel after the MCASD board meeting. The purpose of the meeting was to discuss certain board and management procedures that I believe are necessary to adopt to move the organization toward best practice in a number of important areas. I gave her the outline below which we discussed for several hours. My record of our conversation is interspersed in italics. She was in general very open to suggestions for improvements as discussed.

1. Fiduciary relationship and responsibilities

    We discussed the difference between an advisory board and a fiduciary board. The MCASD board is the latter, and therefore there are higher standards of recordkeeping, diligence, decision-making and the like that are applicable. Failing to follow these basic rules puts the executives of the organization and board members at potential personal financial risk if something goes badly wrong. I have now been on the board for one year, and there are items that I think need attention.

2. Board orientation

   There should be a new board member orientation and each new board member should receive a "board book." In addition to descriptive material about the museum and its history and role in the community, the book should contain an explanation/discussion of the legal requirements of board members and what is expected of them. It should also contain the basic organizational documents, and each new board member should execute a document testifying that he or she understands the requirements of board membership. The new member should also disclose certain personal financial parameters so that potential conflicts of interest can be avoided. A record of board orientations and participants should be kept. The conflict forms should be refreshed and re-executed annually. I did not receive such an orientation or material on joining the board, or up to now.

3. Hygiene

   a. Minutes of all meetings, especially finance and investment committee

      All board meetings, and all board committee meetings (building committee, finance committee, etc.) should have minutes taken. The minutes should be subsequently circulated to all members and approved at the next committee meeting. A record should be kept of all minutes of all meetings.

      I have been told that this is being done but I have never seen such minutes of any of the committees on which I serve. And full board minutes are not always circulated promptly.

   b. Board material ahead of time—for all meetings

      Current practice is to provide board meeting material, including minutes of previous meetings, budget, and financial material, etc. at the board meetings but no sooner. This does not allow for any meaningful preparation by board members. All such material should be prepared and circulated at least one week ahead of the relevant meeting.

4. Financial matters

    c. Quarterly review of investment results

An investment committee has now been established and had a meeting with the investment manager, Northern Trust. These meetings should be held quarterly in person, after the preparation of quarterly results of the financial status of the endowment. The current practice is to have them semiannually.

    d. Financial and investment results distributed quarterly

Prior practice has been to distribute such results semiannually. This should be changed to quarterly distribution, with space reserved on the board meeting agenda each quarter for discussion of these results.

    e. Better focus on forecasts, esp. shortfalls

The operating budget and results vs. budget should be more clearly presented to board members, and budget shortfalls should be more carefully explained and alternatives for fixing shortfalls laid out. The most recent $100K projected shortfall was not handled in this manner.

    f. Endowment management

There is concern that we are not managing our endowment in accordance with state rules. The problem may be that we are taking a larger draw than we can replenish through growth. There are differing opinions as to how serious a problem this is, but it should be called out and the investment committee asked specifically to look at this and report to the full board. This examination should include a review of the terms of each of the endowment contribution documents—limits, restrictions, etc.

5. Construction program

We are about to embark on a $70 million, three-year construction program. This is quite different from managing an ongoing organization with a $6.5 million annual budget. There are a number of steps that should be taken to make sure that all board members are fully reviewing and appropriately participating in the construction process, particularly as to its financial aspects.

    a. Regular item on board meeting agenda

> *Construction projects always generate monthly reports covering progress against plan, to include major milestones, and spending vs. budget. Such reports should be sent to every board member every month. There is not any plan to do this.*

b. Monthly progress reviews

> *Well-run construction projects have monthly in-person review sessions with the project sponsor, where the progress and problems laid out in the reports above are reviewed and solutions discussed. I do not know of any plans to have such meetings. There is a "building committee" of the board that was set up for this purpose, and it was used to good effect in the contractor selection process, but it has not been used since.*

c. Construction contract approval

> *The project construction contract has not yet been approved. Once finalized, it should be presented to the full board for review and approval.*

d. Invoice approvals

> *There should be a level of invoice approvals established and approval authority specified for various sizes/amounts of invoices. Invoices larger than a certain amount ($1 million? $3 million?) should require board approval. Change orders above a certain amount should also require board approval.*

> *Other matters: Given the change of leadership at the museum, it might be useful for Kathryn to commission an outside review of management and board practices to determine if these or other matters should be changed or improved upon.*

There were some other things that I did not mention. For example, all the board meetings were lunch meetings—why? At the meetings, board members were trying to review the documents with which they had just been presented and trying to manage eating sandwiches or salads or whatever and participate in the board discussion. This was pure silliness and led to ineffective discussions.

The board chairman attended perhaps half the board meetings. This is a serious red flag for a fiduciary board.

The discussion of proceeding on a major construction program without complete funding was also discussed, per the above.

Both Paul and Kathryn listened carefully and thanked me for taking the time and effort to prepare this information. They also assured me they would give my suggestions full consideration. Everyone was very polite, and we all parted on good terms.

I waited four months for changes to be made in accordance with my recommendations. Any changes at all. There were none.

I am not a big fan of quitting in the middle of an important activity, throwing a tantrum because you don't get your way, going to the press with all your criticisms, or the various ways that aggrieved folks today seem to use to get what they want.

I am also not a big fan of trying to change an organization that clearly does not recognize the need to change. At the end of the four months, I handed in my resignation, again in a bland resignation letter, thanking Kathryn and Paul for the experience and wishing them and the museum all the best going forward.

What's the Kurt Vonnegut line? "So it goes."

5

Once Bitten, Twice Bitten

The Oceanside Museum of Art Experience—Smaller Is Not Necessarily Smarter

I met a quite interesting guy via my service on the La Jolla museum board. His name was Fenner Milton, which I tried hard to remember since there was a strong tendency to call him Milton Fenner. He was an MIT undergrad and Harvard PhD and thus can be considered a serious scientist. He had recently retired from DARPA, the Department of Defense agency that handles all research, much of it both military and secret. It was an impressive credential to have on your resume. When we met him, he was about to go to Europe to receive a pretty big deal medal from NATO for the anti-terrorist work that he had done while at DARPA—something about stopping terrorists from crashing cars or trucks into military buildings or facilities. I was pretty impressed.

He was also a serious connoisseur of modern art, and his house was tastefully arrayed with a lot of pieces, many of them drawings or prints but some sculptures and some oils. I could recognize the Giacometti but not any of the Russian "between the wars" engravings and lithographs. Soon after we met he invited us to his club—Rancho Bernardo Country Club—for their Easter buffet. Fortunately, you didn't have to attend church services to get to go.

He had several other interesting people in the dining group. One was a scientist who worked at one of the big science consulting firms, SAIC. His focus was nuclear power, and he was happy to expound on its benefits and how it was "the answer" and everything else was, in honor of Easter, rabbit poop.

We had just met the guy, and in truth we didn't know Fenner that well, but all the others at the table were nodding vaguely or focusing on their ham and deviled eggs and something potatoes. This went on for a period and then of course I couldn't resist. I suggested that nuclear power was: (1) expensive to build and operate, and (2) dangerous, both for short- and long-term consequences.

He became even more agitated to confront someone who had actually worked at the nation's largest nuclear utility, TVA. I didn't feel it was necessary to add that I had helped Dave Freeman shut down TVA's nuclear construction project (seven plants, a total of seventeen reactors) and start to substitute renewable options instead.

Finally he said, "Dangerous? That's ridiculous! The largest nuclear event in history, Fukushima in Japan, didn't even kill anyone!"

This is true and not true. The immediate results of the reactor meltdowns did not kill anyone—mostly I suspect because when it became clear to the operators that things were going badly south, they all scrammed. Big traffic jam, all those Toyotas streaming out of the plant parking lot. However, all the sources I have seen and read agree that the radiation released in the area resulted in between 15,000 and 20,000 deaths, mostly from various cancers that were radiation related.

This gentle rebuttal only led Mr. Nuclear to more raving. Hence, I turned to the person sitting next to me and asked, "What do you do?"

She was Maria Mingalone, and she had just been hired to be the head of the Oceanside Museum of Art. About which I knew nothing, since my whole exposure had been to the La Jolla museum, and I had been indoctrinated to believe that all culture in San Diego stopped at La Jolla and didn't go any farther north. Oceanside, although a lovely place, is right on the border where San Diego becomes, shore to summit, Camp Pendleton, home of many marines. Marines in general are fine people but not known for a preoccupation with art or museums.

The museum ("OMA") was in dire straits, probably more dire than had been explained to Maria when she was recruited from the Berkshires where she was an officer at a small but well-regarded museum there.

"I have never been to it, I am embarrassed to say, but I just got here myself." This is what you say when you know nothing, which is where I found myself. When all else fails, try the truth.

"Well, you must come visit, you'll be surprised," Maria responded politely.

We did, and we found a well-organized museum, mostly with a focus on modern art and on California art. And no endowment, and hardly even enough money to pay Maria's salary. But she persevered, brought the museum back from the brink, and it is now regarded as a serious facility if not as fancy as the La Jolla museum.

We became members, and joined at the top level, which as I recall was only a thousand dollars. Not that that's nothing. We went to several openings and got to know some of the regulars. We had Maria over for dinner since we wanted to help her meet new friends—I knew how that felt. When it came time for the museum to have its annual gala we bought a table and invited some of our friends to come. I generally hate galas and the fixed seating, and the lousy food served cold, not to mention the cheap wine, so this was a big give on our part. But we did like Maria, and she was working hard to get the ship righted, and we had met several interesting people through our participation in museum events.

At a point probably nine months into our acquaintance, she asked me if I had ever considered joining a museum board. Given my experience with the MCASD I was not in a big hurry for round two. Because I have no tact, I said so.

We had attended a "new members" function where we all sat around a large conference table. The hosting board member was sitting there drinking coffee. This was not, however, provided for the rest of us. Then it degenerated into one of those meetings where the convenor says, "We're really glad that you're here and we really want to hear from you about what you want from the museum as new members. But first, let me tell you a little about the museum." On the off chance, I suppose, that we hadn't been to it before?

An hour and ten minutes later (I was taking notes) the host finally shut up. We decided that we had better things to do than to engage in a conversation with this person. Besides, we wanted what everybody who joins wants—good content, nice receptions, and decent treatment, e.g., a cup of coffee as appropriate. We slid out and left, pleading another meeting elsewhere.

Maria was persistent. "Just listen to our board member, Mrs. X, who does board recruiting, as a favor to me," she responded. "Besides, we'll buy you lunch."

Okay, I am probably too easy on things like this. A lunch was duly set up with Mrs. X, who was a nice enough older woman. We ate at a very good restaurant two blocks from the museum, a discovery that I duly tucked away. We went through all the normal stuff about my resume and experience. The museum did not really have a strategic plan or a dreaded "vision statement," so that was good. It also did not have two nickels to rub together so that was not good. I clarified that I fully understood that board members are supposed to provide donor support to the institutions on whose boards they sit. No surprise there.

Then she said, "Well, I think you would make a wonderful addition to our board, and I would like to go back and recommend you for membership at the next meeting."

"Do you need any references?" I asked.

"Oh, no, your background is really excellent!" she commented, and of course I agreed with her.

"I just need you to sign this agreement and we can move your nomination forward."

"What is it?" I asked.

"It's a confidentiality agreement."

I sat back a moment, sure that I had heard wrong.

"A confidentiality agreement? A binding commitment from me to keep everything you tell me secret or confidential?" I asked in disbelief.

"Yes, all the board members sign them."

I was still trying to get my head around this. Note that the place was on a piece of public land; it was subject to all the regulations of California governing nonprofit entities, and they are many. It was a financial basket case, its assets were questionable because it only did exhibitions where it could borrow the art, and it had a grand total of two employees besides Maria.

"What exactly is it that you need this legal document to enforce the confidentiality of, if you don't mind me asking?" I said as politely as I could.

"Well, board deliberations and things like that."

I more or less lost it. "Deliberations about what, where to go for lunch? I have been on many for-profit boards and start-ups, and a fair number of nonprofit boards, and never in my entire experience has anyone ever asked me to sign an NDA. You have to be kidding."

Thus ended my second experience with museum board membership in San Diego. At least she did pay for lunch.

6

The One Thing I Liked About Marketing

We Set Up Sunshine Soldiers and Run Around Giving Talks

I maybe overstated my position, above. There was one thing that I only kind of liked about marketing my books, and that was meeting with small- to medium-sized groups and talking about renewable energy. Since my career was in energy, the topic always came up, and we'd have fun discussions. So, after some stumbling around, I went back to my agent/publicist and said, "What if we hired you to promote us as speakers on renewable energy? We really do know this stuff, and we're good presenters, and it's a subject that is becoming more and more important. Besides, we can make PowerPoint slides and we can find clever pictures and we can do graphs and slides and keep people interested for at least thirty-five minutes. This is an ideal length for a presentation to almost any interested group interested about anything."

We put together a slide show and showed it to him. Instead of having him do all this work for us for free, we said those three magic words: We'll pay you! We also suggested that this could be a new line of business for him, and if we ever got to the point where we weren't doing it for free, we'd give him a split of whatever we earned. We didn't have to write a book, just put together about thirty slides. Who couldn't do that? Our resumes were good enough that we were believable as energy experts.

We tried this out on some of our friends who were kind enough to listen and help us. Most of their advice was to make it shorter. We had grand ideas of where this could go: presentations to Fortune 500 boards headlining their strategic planning retreats, speaker fees of $5,000 a pop, guest starring on talking head energy policy shows, maybe even a shot at *60 Minutes*! No telling what was in our future.

The other nice part, and the part where we got it completely right, was that we could organize ourselves as a nonprofit, which is not very hard. More important we could become a charitable nonprofit with an education mission. If we did that, then whatever we spent to cover our costs before the big fees started rolling in would be deductible as a charitable contribution to our new organization. We didn't do anything stupid like paying ourselves a big salary, which would have been taxable anyway so what was the point? We had to follow the rules and not be stupid. This is also a pretty good idea in any commercial activity.

Boy, were there rules. What you needed was to hire a lawyer. Gosh, how is that for a not-very-wonderful beginning? Fortunately, we knew one who was a tax guy, but not quite the right kind of tax guy for what we needed. But he had a partner who was the right size and shape for nonprofits. We connected with him and got the lowdown on how to become deductible. It amounted to setting up the organization, which takes maybe five minutes and a two-page form and requires a filing with the state attorney general. But he's not the one who matters, it's the IRS commissioner who hands down the 501(c)(3) designation, the ruling that your organization has filled out the IRS application form that says essentially who you are and what you plan to do. If you're smart and if you have a good lawyer, you say all the correct magic words about your charitable purpose. "Education" counts as one of these, and that's essentially what we were doing. Then your lawyer files and you wait nine months, at best, for an IRS letter saying, essentially, okay, go ahead, but don't forget to file the annual forms with us.

While you are in this no man's land of having filed but not having been anointed, you can and should keep track of any contributions you receive to your nonprofit entity, as you can subsequently deduct them as charitable contributions, assuming that you get blessed by the IRS. This is better than nothing, but not much.

Once the IRS application had gone in, based on significant substance from us and legal crafting from our lawyer, we settled down to wait. We were assured that the IRS on average took nine months to approve this type of application and could take as much as a year.

We got going on the rest of the work of becoming profitless. Besides having some vague idea about what your organization is going to do, you need a name. Not that the IRS cares, but anyone who engages with you probably won't be impressed if you call yourself "Bob Nonprofit," suspecting that this is something of a scam. We thought and discussed and tried to figure out a name that wasn't taken and that at the same time made sense.

This is not as easy as one would think. Especially because when we were doing this, solar energy and even wind were becoming more and more mainstream. "Sun" and "solar" and "sunny" and "sunshine" and many, many other combinations of these words were already taken. "Taken" in this case means that you could not get a URL and thus a digital identifier for your website because someone else had already paid the GoDaddy people to secure this for at least a year. This at least makes sense because without this discipline, if there was more than one "Amazon.com" then how would the internet know where to send your request for a dozen white running socks or a copy of *Lady Chatterley's Lover*? Or even if your chosen name just happened to also be the name of a poorly received rock song from the late '60s, it might still be copyrighted and the aged guitarist with the copyright would come after you. Having your first expenditure in your start-up be a lawyer to fight a breach of copyright claim would not look too intelligent.

The checking part was not nearly as hard as the thinking-up part. We went through about a hundred names and finally ended up with Sunshine Soldiers. No one else had the URL (sunshinesoldiers.com). This is determined by going to GoDaddy and asking them to sell it to you, and they surely will unless someone else owns it. No one did. Check. This is a good start. Next or even simultaneously you go to Google and look up "sunshine soldiers." There was a '60s rock song called "Sunshine Soldiers," but it was so obscure and so long ago that you couldn't even buy the song on iTunes. We decided to chance it and use that name.

Next of course you need a website, but first you really need a logo. The original AES logo was designed by a friend of Dennis Bakke's and cost three hundred dollars. It looked like this:

A little dated but it seemed to work fine. But time passed, and at AES eventually we decided that we needed a new logo. The arguments for why were a little unpersuasive but the CEO at the time was pretty convinced and besides for the first time ever we had a person in charge of PR, and what else was he (or maybe it was she, I don't remember) supposed to do if not change the logo? We hired a design firm and did a focus group and spent thirty grand and got a new logo that looked like this:

We never really asked anyone what they thought of the new one. And then we spent at least as much money—maybe more, as we never really tried to count this up—in throwing out all our old stationery and business cards, redoing our website, and repainting all the signs at our power plants, since they were all named "AES Something" with the something part being usually the name of the location—Deepwater, Beaver Valley, etc. And the logo was painted on the big sign in front of the power plant, or in one case in gigantic letters on the fuel storage building.

This inclination to change stuff that really doesn't need to be changed is not just a disease of the profit-making world. When I was at TVA we went through the same drill, spent actually more money, and had the following result:

Old logo:

New logo:

TVA TENNESSEE VALLEY AUTHORITY

In the case of Sunshine Soldiers, we decided to be more cost conscious. We found an image of the sun on a free site for graphic art. Then based on my extensive two-year's worth of knowledge of the army, we went to the Fort Benning website. There is a statue there at the head of the parade ground. It portrays an infantry platoon leader carrying a rifle and leading his men forward. The motto of the infantry school is "Follow Me," which is about as good as it gets for clarity and simplicity. We took the soldier image and stuck it on top of the sun image and here you have it:

Cost: nothing. And in color no less!

We then designed a website with all the usual stuff: who are we, what do we do, what we think, contact us—but short and uncomplicated. We needed a digital person for this, but we found a local and cheap one who did it all, and very well, for about six hundred dollars. You can spend more money, very much more money than that, believe me.

Lightning strikes. Much to the surprise of us and of our experienced lawyer, we received back our approval to become a charitable donation eligible, fully approved 501(c)(3) nonprofit, just over a month after it had been submitted. Pretty remarkable, and with no particular explanation; we had just followed the procedures correctly, hadn't tried to enlist political support—good thing, because we didn't have any—and had not wailed or complained or badgered the IRS. I don't really think there is a lesson here, but we were pleased.

We pressed what contacts we had locally and started with making presentations at the UCSD business school where we had been a modest donor, and with presentations to both the Yale Club of San Diego and the Cornell Club of San Diego. With Jared's help, we branched out locally and even got into Orange County.

The message was pretty simple. For starters we decided against using guilt on our audiences. Few people sign up to be told what bad human beings they are. I wouldn't. We also didn't stress the environmental benefits of renewables compared to burning fossil fuels to make electricity. Again, no guilt. We didn't even make suggestions as to what responsible, environmentally sensitive people should do. No preaching. What we emphasized were the economics and the costs. Our presentation was heavy on graphics and big on numbers. But that was natural because that was what we knew from all our energy career experience. You develop and build fifty-two solar plants in five years, you don't do it without understanding the numbers.

Here are copies of my two favorite charts:

#1 Solar prices

Solar Auction Prices—Last 2.5 Years

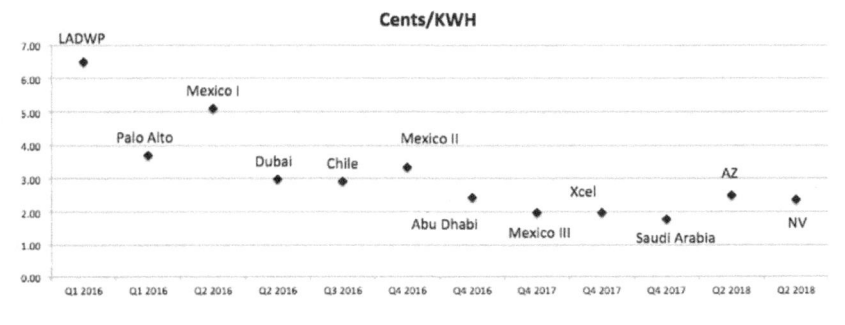

What's the cost baseline?

OPERATING COST

Hydro: 1-3 cents/Kwh

Coal: 3-6 cents/Kwh
Gas: 3-5 cents/Kwh
Wind: 4-6 cents

Nuclear: 5-9 cents/kwh
Oil: 16-20 cents/kwh  PLUS!

Solar/Saudi Arabia: 1.9 cents/Kwh
(Nov '17 auction—**Operating & capital**)

The short message was simple: coal and oil and nuclear are too costly to use to make electricity. Solar and wind are already cheaper than these alternatives and continuing to get cheaper. So that's what we should be doing.

Most people listened to the whole presentation; I cannot remember a case where anybody got up and left before we were finished. Nobody ever tried to argue with us, which was a little surprising. I expected at least an occasional nuclear advocate to make a pitch for this disappointing technology. Maybe anyone with those beliefs would not bother to attend such a meeting where beliefs might be challenged. Fight dirty, use the facts.

The fun part of making these presentations was that maybe we educated some people about the coming growth of renewals and the death of coal—good news for climate change and global warming that was entirely dependent on the technologies coming of age and continuing to decline in price. Everyone we presented to could understand this economic fact of life. In our presentations, we never mentioned "climate change" or "global warming" and we never suggested there was anything anyone in the audience needed to do—not write their congressman, not demonstrate at city hall, not put solar panels on their roofs (unless they wanted to). We tried to avoid the entire issue of rooftop solar unless pressed. Our numbers were all based on "utility scale" solar, not rooftop solar. Lots and lots of panels, all mounted on metal frames supported by posts in the ground. Ideally put on acres of land with lots of sun but otherwise rocky, salty, scrubby, unirrigated, low-quality land. The function of the land was to hold up the panels, that was it, and ideally it was the cheapest piece of land available. Not high-quality irrigated cropland, and certainly not vineyards.

The US has plenty of land that meets this test, most of it in the West. If you do the calculations using current panel efficiencies of converting sun to electricity, and other conservative assumptions, you find that you can supply the entire US electricity market with solar-generated electricity and only use up about ten million acres, which seems like a lot until you look it up and find that the US has 2.4 billion acres of land. Doing the math tells you that the solar use would be 0.4% of the total land in the US. We don't have a land shortage. And as panels continue to become more efficient, then the total amount of land needed decreases.

The good news about this effort was we liked doing it and audiences were polite and interested. The bad part wasn't really bad: we had to pay all our own costs. Or rather, our organization paid all our costs. Since we were the sole funders of the organization, we got the appropriate charitable deductions and were *very careful* to keep the organization's expenses rigorously separate from our personal expenses. Even though we didn't have donors to worry about, we had the IRS to worry about and there wasn't any good argument to fool around with the money. We didn't pay for anything with Sunshine Soldiers funds that was not clearly and unarguably business essential. I have been audited a couple of times, mostly for mistakes, and it was not a pleasant experience. It always costs more in accountant and lawyer fees than not making the mistake in the first place would have cost. It was an expensive lesson.

We started making presentations in the middle of 2016, at a local chamber of commerce meeting. No one booed or got up and left in the middle. Success! We did this for several years, averaging probably forty presentations a year, which might sound like a lot but is slightly more than one a week. We got paid an honorarium only once during this time period—a talk to the Solar Energy Association of Virginia and it only covered about one-third of the cost to fly to Arlington and back. We signed up with an agency that handled bookings for speakers, thinking, "Aha." But we never had one booking from them. Oh well, it was fun, and it kept us busy and connected with the industry and we hadn't really planned on it being an economic success.

We made about a hundred speeches over this two-and-a-half-year period, and we had audiences that varied in size from ten to sixty. We didn't repeat the book tour audience of one person who stayed for half the presentation. When we started making presentations in the fall of 2016, the most frequent question we got from the audiences was, "So does this solar stuff really work?" Two and a half years later, that question had become, "So how fast do we get rid of all the coal plants?" This progression in public understanding was hardly a result of our work, but we did play a very small part in it.

Here is an interesting indicator of progress. These are entries from several energy industry newsletters from the week of 30 August–6 September 2021. You could duplicate this for any time in 2022 or 2023 (as I write this):

- » Spanish wind developer plans 500 megawatts of new projects
- » Indonesia coal company plans solar projects on former mine sites
- » US installed record of land-based wind capacity set in 2020
- » Rooftop solar could meet 77% of total grid demand in Australia by 2026
- » Eskom considering $7.2 billion for wind and solar by 2030 (Eskom is the major utility in South Africa, largely coal-fired)
- » Masdar inaugurates 100-megawatt solar farm in Uzbekistan (Masdar is a Saudi government development company, formed to invest oil profits in non-fossil opportunities)
- » Work completed on first off-grid hybrid solar plant in Russian Arctic
- » PacifiCorp plans closure of all Wyoming coal plants by 2039
- » Colorado Springs shuts down one of last urban power plants in U.S.
- » World's largest solar and battery storage project to expand in Darwin, Australia; will export renewable electricity to Singapore
- » Duke explores shutting coal-fired plants by 2030 in South Carolina
- » India plans 600-megawatt network of storage around New Delhi
- » Global renewables leader Costa Rica mulls expansion of offshore wind
- » Philippines has OK'd 928 renewable contracts, 30 gigawatts of capacity
- » LA approves 100% clean energy by 2035 target, a decade ahead of prior goal
- » Colstrip operator Talen falls $4 billion into debt, bonds downgraded (Colstrip is a large coal mine/power plant in Montana)
- » Swedish investment platform plans financing for five African solar farms

I have left out all the ones that said "new coal-fired power plant planned" because there weren't any.

My only regret is that we never made up a Sunshine Soldiers T-shirt. Now it was time to start spending money on something else.

7

UCSD, the University of California for Silly Decisions

The Chancellor's Associates Saga, and We Give Money to the Faculty Awards—Once

My friend Tim Wollaeger, when I complained about not having any friends, said that he knew some people at UCSD in the business school, Rady School of Management, and he thought I might like to meet them. Never look a gift horse, etc., so I said sure. It was early days for me, so I was game for anything. Eventually through Tim I met a very good guy (not even a Yale graduate!) named Tim Sisk and he asked if I had heard of the Chancellor's Associates at UCSD.

A brief confession is in order. Not only had I never heard of the Chancellor's Associates, when I landed in San Diego I had no idea that there was a University of California campus or school or institution, part of the justly famous UC system, here in San Diego. This is a little hard to credit since I had gone to UCLA for graduate school, I had much earlier fallen for a woman attending UC Santa Barbara and even visited her there, and my brother was a Berkeley graduate. I was also confused for a time by the fact that there is a University of San Diego here, a modest-sized Catholic institution that has a distinguished law school, something that UCSD does not have. Eventually this got sorted out by people patiently explaining the difference to me between UCSD and USD. Should we add that there is also a San Diego State University in town, with a very good basketball team, which has no bearing on the story?

The Chancellor's Associates, as Tim explained, was a program started by the chancellor, a designation in academia and Germany meaning the head of the institution. They asked you to give them $2,500 a year and then you became a member. I guess you became an "associate" actually. In return you got something, which is rare in charitable/academic circles. Here is what you were entitled to:

1. They put on three or four academic programs a year, each one a lecture/presentation by one of the better scholars at the school. The sessions lasted for about an hour and were technical enough that you had to pay attention or you'd get lost. There was time for questions. They cost you nothing. They were held in the Faculty Club, and they included a couple of tables of hors d'oeuvres—not lobster claws—but okay. There were two bars available, although you had to pay for your own drinks. There was a thirty-minute happy hour/networking period before the presentation, and you could stick around afterward if you wished, corner the speaker, and generally flatter yourself with how nice and academic this all was except there wasn't a test afterward. And there was alcohol. And the people were friendly and happy to meet new folks. And they used name tags, one of my lifelong pet suggestions for networking gatherings. The print was large enough to read without sticking your noses into someone's breast or chest, my name tag sub-peeve. All very good. But there's more.

2. You got a university parking pass that allowed you to park virtually anywhere on the campus, except I think in the chancellor's reserved space, although if he was on vacation, you could probably park there as well. Add this to the fact that the Faculty Club already had decent parking, reserved of course for people going to the club. I have

checked with many academic friends, and all agree that parking at any university worth the name is always a horrible problem. Spaces are allocated by a mystic and undisclosed system not subject to discovery even in a lawsuit. No one ever thinks that their department or lab or office has enough, and that the idiots in medieval Russian literature and their 1.5 grad students always have too many. By the way, the availability of grants from outside institutions to students of medieval Russian literature are only slightly more than those for Icelandic studies, which means miniscule. I have checked. The parking pass was golden.

3. You were allowed to join the Faculty Club, but you had to pay what the faculty members paid. This wasn't much and the food wasn't great, but it was a nice place to meet people and had a certain cachet.
4. You were given unlimited access to all the university's athletic facilities. You could run on the track and work out at the gym. You could use your magic parking pass to park near enough so that walking from your car to the gym didn't count as part of, or possibly the whole of, your workout.
5. You had unlimited access to the libraries on campus. I am not sure if you could check out books, since I never went to one. But it was nice to know that you could.
6. You were invited once a year to the chancellor's large and nice house on the edge of the La Jolla bluffs, where a cocktail party was held to celebrate what the chancellor was doing with the money you had paid the university. The marketing deal here was that the funds all went into a special fund that only he could spend. Universities do not have unlimited amounts of money except to pay professors way too much and build huge buildings. All professors complain about this. What money they get outside of their salaries they have to raise by getting outsiders with money to give them grants. For which they have to prepare grant applications, and write reports, and keep track of the money, spending it on the things that the grant application said they were going to spend it on, and other insulting requirements like that. This was quite a good deal for the chancellor; it

was "free" money and not carefully monitored, and he didn't have to send anyone any reports. I doubt that he was allowed to spend it on trips to Baja or high-quality booze for himself or bonuses to special faculty members, but still anything even remotely academic was okay.

There were about six hundred members of the Chancellor's Associates, so every year these fine people contributed to the chancellor (after modest expenses for cheese and crackers four times a year) about two million dollars. This is not a small chunk of cheese in Academic Land. No wonder he gave us an annual cocktail party—which we of course paid for. When all this was explained to me, I was pretty dazzled for a while. Then I sat down and thought about the real world.

Having four academic lectures once a year was nice, but the faculty was already there and already being paid, so the incremental cost was zero. Ditto the Faculty Club, the venue, which was also already there and no doubt cost nothing, except for the meatballs in sweet and sour sauce.

The parking place seemed valuable, until you asked yourself, "Self, why exactly would I be coming to the university and thus need a space?" Every faculty member I ever met with was happy to meet me at the Faculty Club, where there were already parking places. The access to the spaces was not reserved, you had to be able to find an empty one, and they did seem basically over allocated.

But you could go to the gym! First, it's San Diego, where the weather is always seventy-two degrees and sunny, so you can always walk or run or bike outside. Or even lift weights outside, although they might get rusty in the occasional rain. We live forty-five to sixty minutes away from the university. We bought for three hundred dollars a used treadmill that works great, and a new rowing machine (seven hundred) that is wonderful, and a run-of-the-mill exercise bike on which you can hang clothes to dry. Why spend two hours in traffic for a thirty-minute gym workout? Oh, and we have already showers and towels in the several bathrooms the house came with, and don't have to wait behind anyone to use them.

But you could go to the library! Even when I was evaluating all this, years ago, the internet had already been invented. If I really wanted a book, I could just buy it on Amazon. Besides, we were not doing any special academic research that needed something that for some unexplained reason could only be found in a small library of a somewhat obscure California university? Really.

But we liked the sound of the program, and we liked going to the lectures a lot, and we enjoyed meeting new people at the programs. We liked getting to see the chancellor's house for two hours once a year, which even included gratuitous valet parking.

The university development people we dealt with initially were pretty smart. They created levels of Chancellor's Associates, and giving the program more money got you invited to a couple of more things. But no guaranteed parking place.

Pretty soon we got to the top level. This required that we contribute about ten times what we had originally contributed but we got separate dinners with the faculty, and we became members of the Chancellor's Associates Advisory Committee, a group of about six of us outsiders who were similarly easy marks. The development mechanism of the university had high hopes for taking us even further.

And then they couldn't help themselves. You will see some similarities in what follows to widely known fairy tales. Look up "goose" and "golden eggs." The university brought in one of their newly hired development vice presidents and assigned her to monitor and one presumes push on the Chancellor's Associates. Her initial smart idea was to call a meeting of the Advisory Committee wherein she didn't even buy us lunch. Nor did she tell us the subject of the meeting. So, fat, dumb, and happy, we all showed up, secure in the feeling of modest superiority to the other Chancellor's Associates who had not been asked to be on the Advisory Committee. Nor asked to come to the meeting to meet the new Chancellor's Associates supervisor. Who by the way had only been at the university for a couple of months and had not been to a meeting of the big Chancellor's Associates group.

She began the meeting by saying that she and the chancellor had decided to make some changes to the program. First, they were eliminating the free parking pass, as it was too expensive. We asked with some surprise to whom it was expensive since the university owned all the spaces. Well, she explained unclearly, the parking administration charges the program for these spaces, and we have to transfer to their account the appropriate amount of money from the Chancellor's Associates budget. We pondered this for several minutes. But doesn't all that money still stay in the university, asked one of our members? Or couldn't the chancellor tell the parking king to stop this policy for this particular program? We presume that he or she works ultimately for the chancellor.

No, she explained, the chancellor agrees with this concern.

She continued with the other changes: no more use of the gym for free, no more use of the libraries for free, and no more discounted beverages at the bar during the seminars. I had not noticed that there was any discount there—the beer was seven dollars, and the not-very-good wine was nine dollars a glass.

Additional questions followed as we all tried to figure out what was really going on here. Why do this? If you really hated the program, just shut it down—it was the university's program after all. The "it's too expensive" explanation made no sense. And if it was "too expensive" then just charge more. Making it three thousand dollars per year probably wouldn't do much harm. Besides, was there any data on how many of these "free" parking spaces were actually used, or how often CA members overwhelmed the libraries or the gyms? No, there was no such data.

Finally, I got annoyed. "So," I said politely, "I assume that you have convened this meeting of the Advisory Committee to ask our advice on these proposals."

"Not really," she said, "these decisions have already been made."

"Golly, can I ask you why we are having this meeting? And more important, what advice you would like to receive from the committee? If you want my advice, I advise you not to do this, it's a bad idea and not backed up by any data or analysis that you have showed us."

"The purpose of this meeting is to inform you of these changes," she responded, "not to ask you your advice."

And so, throwing caution to the winds, I said, "Okay, at least that's clear. So now, with all due respect, I hereby resign from this committee." Another member, also a Yale grad, also stood up and said, simply, "I resign as well."

So much for that good and cheap program. I checked at the beginning of this April, and the number of participants was down to 250. Might be a correlation here, who knows.

But we are slow learners. We continued to look ineffectively around for things or causes or charitable opportunities where we knew the organization and the activity and could have an impact financially and could also contribute our energy and intelligence. Our approach was not yet carefully formulated, but it was more than just the odd hundred dollars to worthy causes.

Up to that point, about the end of 2016, I checked on our tax records and we had made deductible contributions for the five years of 2012 through 2016 that looked like this:

> 2012: $1,405
> 2013: $13,800
> 2014: $13,072
> 2015: $32,775
> 2016: $58,633

Even without much thought, this struck us as not so impressive compared to our annual income and assets. That's the background. Here's the next act.

Because despite our crankiness with the Chancellor's Associates program, we were still well known to the development department as we had made several multi-thousand-dollar contributions to the Rady School's diversity efforts, and to specific individual professors who we had met and who impressed us with their fields of study and capabilities. They figured out that we were interested in professors. Well not exactly but what the heck. In any event we found in our mailbox one fine afternoon an invitation to the annual ceremony for the top professors awards. It was a typical four-in-the-afternoon academic get-together of cheap wine and saltines and networking, and then speeches by the top officials and presentation of the awards.

I called one of the development people and asked politely, "What's this?" I won't replay the entire conversation but it boiled down to a university-wide solicitation open to all staff and faculty members, for nominations. There was a selection panel, and then five professors were chosen. They each received, hold on to your hats, two thousand dollars. These are the five most valuable professors according to their colleagues, and they get a measly two grand. Not exactly winning the lottery. Well, there are the several glasses of cheap wine.

I said, "This seems cheap to me," to which there was legitimately no response from my development officer friend.

"What if we gave you some money and you made the award five thousand dollars?"

"Oh, that would be great, but I would have to check with the administration to make sure that it's all right."

"Fine," said Mr. Big Spender, boring in for the kill, "and I will commit to the same amount for this program [ten thousand a year if you haven't already done the numbers] for two more years. A total of forty-five thousand dollars over three years."

"Oh, that would be very generous, I will walk that through and get right back to you." We had at that time less than two weeks before the award ceremony.

"I have one more request." I was honestly winging it but what the heck. "I want to have lunch with each of the winners. My treat, and we can do it at the Faculty Club on a schedule that works for each of them."

The development officer hustled off to secure approval for the university to take money and spend it on its professors, with essentially no quid pro quo.

Here's a surprise, it was approved. The ceremony was nice, the award winners were diverse but impressive, and we were given credit publicly at the ceremony for supporting it. That was all fine, and the wine wasn't even that bad.

Before the award ceremony, I was informed that the vice chancellor needed to have me sign an agreement on my contribution. I said fine, expecting a one-paragraph acknowledgment that I could use if ever audited by the IRS.

I received instead a three-page contract with language that obligated me to make the annual $15,000 contribution to the university for this program. But it was written as a hell or high water commitment, and not conditioned on anything—on the university still being a university, on there being enough professors to have the award, etc. Because of the previous advice already mentioned, I did read the document. Then I read it again, muttering literate comments like, "Whisky tango foxtrot," and "What stupidity," and "Why would anyone sign such a document?" This "anyone" had no intention of doing so, and fortunately had not yet sent them the money. I should have made a note of this worthwhile policy at the time.

I called the development person, but she deferred and said that this was "administration policy." I replied that "Hemphill policy" was not to agree to such conditions, and besides they'd left out the faculty lunch dates. She said she would check and I would probably have to talk to the vice chancellor.

The vice chancellor and I had a short and not entirely cordial conversation, during the course of which it became clear that they had already told the five awardees that the stipend was now five grand, not two grand. Bad negotiating mistake. I stuck to my guns and she agreed to change the agreement as I requested. Which in essence made it a non-agreement as I put in a clause allowing either party to terminate it for any reason at any time with one week's notice. You will note if you have the slightest experience with contracts that this clause makes the agreement essentially worthless. I could in theory sign it, then call the university the next day and give the one week's notice of cancellation.

Given the situation, the vice chancellor grudgingly agreed, but on one condition. I had to have my signature on the agreement notarized. I am not making this up. I asked if her signature would also be notarized, but she said a bit frostily, "Certainly not, I represent the university." That of course does not logically follow, but never mind. Deal done, I sent them the money for the first year, and the ceremony was just fine.

Coda number one: During our discussions I had also asked to sit on the committee that made the award selections. Much angst, and many responses along the lines of "We never allow outsiders to sit on our award committees, it would be a violation of intellectual integrity." Note that I had not asked to chair the committee, or to have a veto on award selectees. But I decided that this was okay, and stopped objecting.

About a month later I was talking to a new friend of mine, who coincidentally I had met at a Chancellor's Associates session. I recounted to him the drama and relatively modest success of my effort to give the university money. "Oh, I know that award," he said, "I was asked to sit on the committee that made the selections. It was a whole lot of work, reading all the nominations, even after they had been screened a couple of times. Good choices in the end, I think."

Coda number two: Six months later, the university cancelled the whole faculty award. Nobody called me, of course, and I didn't find out until several months later when I asked about the next round. No next round, we're too busy building big new buildings. I thought it was a silly decision, but at least I wasn't on the hook for another thirty grand to go to them to do with as they wished. I sent the vice chancellor a letter cancelling the agreement but never got a response. Classy.

8

Just When You Thought They Couldn't Get Any Stupider, It Turns Out They Had Stupid Friends to Help

We Try to Pay Off Student Debt

We were sitting at breakfast one morning in early 2016, working on proving how old and old-fashioned we were by reading newspapers made out of newspaper rather than reading them on our tablets, in which case I guess they would have been made out of electrons.

The *Wall Street Journal*, one of our subscriptions that lets us pretend that we were still deeply enmeshed in the business universe rather than sitting on the sidelines and hoping that the government didn't destroy our portfolio anytime soon, had a very good graph on the student loan problem. Here is the accompanying graph:

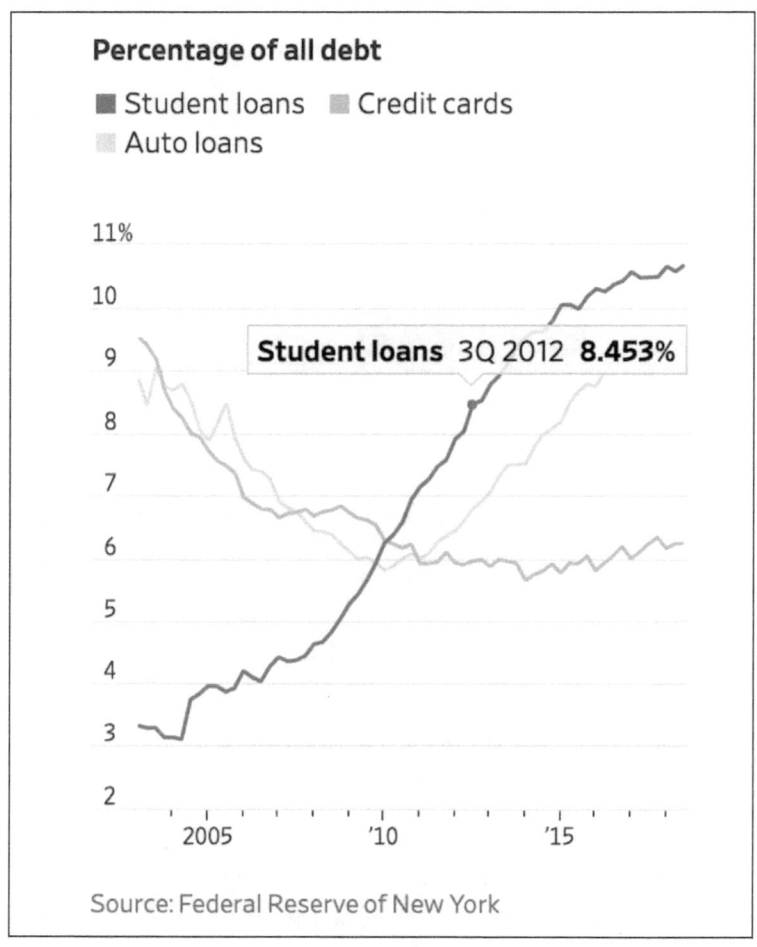

The "problem" has been with us for some time, and like so many problems, originated in a good idea and good intentions. The idea was to give poor kids money so they could go to college, which as all the data shows, leads to better careers, more income, and nicer cars. This laudable goal has been attacked in a number of ways. One was to create more colleges, then more junior colleges, land grant colleges, black colleges, etc. And more grants to professors at colleges hoping that somehow this would result in more students, etc. And some programs of direct aid—Veterans Administration support, Pell Grants, and all manner of private scholarships of various sizes and persuasions. Many, perhaps most, are administered through the colleges and universities themselves, with the ultimate sources of the money as varied as the United States.

While at Yale, I received a scholarship "package" that ultimately included $3,000 of loans. It was a while ago and I do not remember where the loans came from, if I ever knew. I do know that they had some magical qualities—they did not accrue interest during my education, nor did they accrue interest if I went into the military, which I did. They also were accrue-less if I went to graduate school, which I also did. It was only when I finally quit screwing around and got a real job that I started to have to pay them back, but it was still the same $3,000 it had been when I left Yale three years previously. I was not smart enough to understand what a good deal this was, as debt instruments go. Just for fun I looked up what $3,000 in 1966 would be worth today; the answer is $27,855.56. I do know that without that level of financial support I would not have been able to attend Yale.

Somehow, somewhere, all this changed. Sources are not clear exactly what happened although I suspect it was the frog in the boiling water problem. It was coupled with the very reasonable expectation of nineteen-year-olds that they will live forever, and have perfect spouses and children, have great careers, and naturally make lots of money. But all this is based on the acquisition of a college degree. Who cares about a few loans. But two things must have happened while no one, especially the nineteen-year-old, was looking: (1) grant money was replaced increasingly by loans, and (2) colleges and universities got more expensive. We could spend a lot of time researching to see if these theses are true, but it doesn't matter. More and more kids graduate with large loans, the outstanding debt is getting larger per graduate, and the total indebtedness is getting larger absolutely. This is the message of the graph.

Looking up from the *Wall Street Journal* and its compelling graph, I realized that we should do something about this. I was pretty eager, echoing those dangerous words, "We have money, they need money, we want to give it to them, how hard can it be?" This is the intellectual equivalent of the famous YouTube introduction to numerous videos of calamity that goes more or less like this: "Here, hold my beer and watch this!"

There were questions that arose when the initial euphoria subsided. After some modest discussion, we debated what format to use. Answer: money.

How much: We decided that $10,000 per kid was a reasonable number, and kept us from having to assess individual debt levels and ability to pay and parents' economic status, etc.

We thought about what size program we were comfortable with. It needed to be large enough to be interesting—no more Kiwanis $500 grants to local outstanding student of the year who best lives up to the ideals of the Kiwanis, whoever or whatever that is. Or they are.

We debated some limitations: geographic, institutional, based on where the student went to school, etc. It's a big universe and we needed to limit it so we could deal with it administratively.

Should it be open to all graduates? Yes, but only for the year immediately following their graduation from a four-year accredited institution.

All US institutions? Yes, but only for students who were residents of San Diego. And how is "resident" defined exactly? Driver's license? Mailing address? Passport? The questions were not trivial, and frequently required at least a little bit of research.

We were adamant about a couple of things: First, this was to be merit based. If you were smart and got good grades, you had a good chance. It mattered not what the economic status of your parents was—we didn't care. Parenthetically when some people objected to this, we replied that if your parents were millionaires, it was highly unlikely that you the graduate would have any debt at all, so this didn't really apply to you.

Second, it had to be local. We finally narrowed it down to residents of Encinitas, where we live. You could go to school anywhere, but you had to start out here.

Third, no long, troublesome application requirements. No three-page essay on people you had met who were the biggest influences in your life or the three people you would most like to have dinner with or your views on the largest social problems in the third world. Just your name and your address and your transcript, thank you very much.

After some initial program drafts, and some very helpful consultations with a friend of ours who had only the year before retired as principal of the biggest Encinitas high school, we wrote up a program draft. Here it is:

Encinitas Student Debt Project ("ESDP")
General Description, 21 April 2019

Summary: A program to award up to ten $10,000 grants, for a total of up to $100,000 per year, to recent college graduates, to be used exclusively to repay loans incurred by the awardees to finance their college education.

Eligibility: Any student who has graduated from San Dieguito High School Academy or Sunset High School, successfully completed a continuous four- or five-year academic program, and is receiving a bachelor's degree this spring at an accredited college or university in the United States is eligible to apply. The student must have college-related debt of $10,000 or more and have no incidences of arrests or incarceration.

Selection criteria: Graduates who meet the above qualifications should apply. The sponsors will select awardees based upon their academic performance. Demonstrations of academic merit may include:

- Academic excellence, based on student's college academic transcript
- Student's ranking in his or her college graduating class
- Academic honors at graduation—dean's list, graduating cum laude, etc.
- Membership in a merit-based organization, such as Phi Beta Kappa
- A rigorous academic program, with STEM curricula favored
- Post-graduate awards of merit—Rhodes, Fulbright, or Marshall scholarship, etc.

Not to be considered:

- Financial need, income or assets of parents or student, other than that the student must have college-related debt of $10,000 or more
- Extracurricular activities such as athletics or public service
- Race, sex, gender, age, religion, national origin

Administrative mechanics:

- Awards to be made once a year on or about June 30, with 2019 a pilot year for the project and will determine whether the project is repeated in future years.
- An advisory board will assist in determining winners of the awards Members of the advisory board include the donors Tricia Smith, Steve Levy, and Evelyn Luecker.
- All decisions will be strictly at the discretion of the donors. If there are not sufficient qualified applicants, the project is not required to award all or any awards.
- Awardees agree that the awards may only be used to repay legitimately incurred student debt. Awards will be made to the student directly.
- Program may be publicized through the website and other social media, local newspapers, and by Encinitas City government. Awardees when selected agree to be named in project announcements.

Website: encinitasstudentdebtproject.com

Project address: Encinitas Student Debt Project
PO Box 232262
Encinitas, CA 92023-2262

We also, because we are organized and because sometimes you don't really know what you think until you have to write it down, put together an FAQ document ("Frequently Asked Questions") although though no one had actually asked us any questions since we hadn't really launched the program yet. Here's what we said:

Frequently Asked Questions, ESDP
19 April 2019

1. What are the Encinitas high schools whose graduates are eligible for financial awards?

San Dieguito High School Academy
800 Santa Fe Dr, Encinitas

Sunset High School
684 Requeza St, Encinitas

2. Why is the project limited to Encinitas students?
Encinitas is where we live, and we love the city. It was natural for us to start the program here and focus it on this city.

3. Why is there no income test for the grant recipients or their parents? Why isn't financial need considered in this program?
Any young person who graduates from college with a large amount of debt clearly has a financial need. We do not expect that we will have applications from the children of wealthy parents, as they will, by and large, have been supported without the necessity of taking out loans. But many middle- and lower-income families will have had no choice, and these are the students who will benefit from this.

4. Who are the members of the advisory council?
Robert Hemphill, Leah Bissonette, Tricia Smith, Steve Levy, and Evelyn Luecker.

5. How will you ensure that the grant that goes to the student as a gift will in fact be used to pay down debt, and not for some other purpose?

We will require a commitment from the student to use the funds in this manner. We will also notify the institution that holds the recipient's debt about this grant. But ultimately we will rely on the integrity of the recipients.

6. Why didn't you just create a scholarship program for Encinitas HS graduates?
There are lots of those programs, but nothing that we could identify that attacked the problem of debt of college graduates. We decided that we could have the biggest impact there.

7. You require that the recipient graduate from an accredited college or university. Where can someone find out if the school he or she attended is accredited?
Go to the US Department of Education site: www.ed.gov/accreditation.

8. Where can a student find out more about this program?
The student can go to our website, www.encinitasstudentdebt-project.com. Program guidelines and an application form are available there.

Okay, we were rolling! And it was a good thing since we wanted to hit the coming graduates in June, and by this time it was late April. We did get what seemed a useful piece of advice during the April program formulation period. One of our friends with whom we discussed this said, in summary, that once we launched, it would not be long before we started drowning in applications. So how were we going to process them all? And check against fraud, for example? And write all the checks? And on and on. Also, we wanted to be credible to the applicants. It couldn't just be "Good Old Bob's Loan Repayment Program."

It was suggested that we see if we could work with, one way or another, an existing nonprofit who did this sort of thing for a living. The San Diego Foundation, a "community foundation," was suggested. This turns out to be a somewhat specialized nonprofit that is an intermediary for handling charitable donations from such people and then establishes "programs" to carry out their wishes.

We thought this was an idea worth exploring, so after some back and forth we met in their offices in the Liberty Station area. Our trusty lawyer was with us, Mitch Dubick, and there were two executives of the foundation, the head of development and the head of operations. We sent them our program description ahead of time.

We introduced ourselves and suggested that they could help us, and they spent some time telling us what they did. Which was good since I didn't really know. We then mentioned that we would be happy to make a direct donation to them if necessary so they could cover overhead costs and the work they would do processing applications, making recommendations, and sending out grants on our behalf.

They could not have been more excited. Comments included: "This is *so generous* of you!" "This is so badly needed by these graduates!" "We don't know of anyone else who is doing this, you'll have a groundbreaking program." "This is something I am sure we could support, and we would be eager to join with you on this."

We interpreted this to be a positive reaction.

They asked for a couple of days to discuss it internally, check with "legal" and other departments, and then they would get back to us. They did understand that time was of the essence here, so they promised to move quickly.

Three days later we met again in their quietly elegant offices in Liberty Station. I said to Mitch walking in, "Nice offices for a nonprofit." Sometimes you should keep such thoughts to yourself.

We met with the same two people as before. They were not as cheery.

We have bad news, they said, the IRS won't let us do this. It seemed unlikely that, even as evil and vindictive as the IRS is, they would have reached down into the inner workings of a modest-sized charitable organization and forbidden them to do what we were proposing. How did they even know?

They further outlined the problem. As we understood it, and corroborated later, the most important thing in the world for a charitable nonprofit is to keep its 501(c)(3) designation. Without this, they are unlikely to raise any money as contributions no longer can be deducted from the donor's gross income. That is an understandable concern. But why would our program be a problem, we asked?

As best they explained, if a charitable nonprofit engages in activities that in themselves are not "charitable" by the definition of the IRS, then this can or perhaps is likely to disqualify their status and they sink back into the nonprofit world but without the charitable deduction banner heralding all their fundraising activities. There is, for example, a nonprofit designation called 501(c)(4) that can be sought by lobbying and policy entities. Many of the groups that put forth requests, complaints, and suggestions to Congress or other political bodies have this designation.

"Giving money to kids to pay off the debts incurred in completing their college educations is not okay, but giving them scholarships while they are in college, with the purpose of completing their college educations, is okay?" we asked in some disbelief.

That's our reading of the IRS code they replied, and we are careful in all our activities only to engage in those that are "charitable."

I found this so hard to believe that I asked the same question in several different ways, sometimes with a conditional clause first, sometimes as a negative as in "Surely you don't mean ..." even though neither of them was named Shirley. The answer remained the same. I considered asking it in French but I was too rusty. Besides, if they had answered me in French, I might not have understood the answer.

Then we got creative. Not for nothing that I used to structure finance deals for a living, and always there was some regulation or condition that had to be creatively dealt with. We suggested some: Why not set up a wholly owned subsidiary of the foundation, but make it a nonprofit but not charitable organization? This is not desirable from our standpoint as we lose the tax value of our contribution, but we can still have your assistance in sorting through the grant applications. We will get the benefit of your reputation and of your experience in doing this, so that's good. You'll keep the parent charitable deduction designation, which you need. We will pay the costs of the new entity plus an overheld contribution. The parent foundation can contract with the subsidiary to do the actual work. How about that?

No, too risky.

Okay, how about this: You guys set up a wholly separate entity called "San Diego Foundation II" that has no ownership or organizational ties with the main foundation. But it does the work, and contracts back with the main foundation for all its assistance. As before we pay the costs of SDF II plus overhead. Again, we lose the charitable deduction, but we're willing to do that.

No, too risky.

What if we drive to Nevada and set up our organization there and you do the same and then we go forward on the same program, we just have a Nevada mailing list—that should confuse everyone enough that the IRS never challenges the parent foundation. And while we're at it we could all become card counters and raise some money in Las Vegas until they find out about us and kick us out of all the casinos.

No, too risky.

We began to suspect that their interest in helping kids pay for the debt of their college educations was eroding, if it ever existed. As we were walking out of this most unsatisfactory meeting, Mitch said, "Screw these guys, I know the people at the Jewish Community Foundation, and they are much more flexible and responsive. I can set something up with them. You interested?"

I was at that moment somewhere between pissed off and depressed, so I said sure, contemplating how much fun it would be to send our press release, once we were successful, back to every board member of the San Diego Foundation. Not that we are vindictive or anything.

Several days later we were in the Jewish Community Foundation conference room, meeting with the executive vice president, which was higher up the chain than we had ever gotten with the San Diego Foundation. We went through the same drill, using the same program description, but saying nothing about our recent unsuccessful experience. We didn't want them to get any ideas.

Once they had digested the proposal, we got very close to an identical initial reaction: "So generous!" "Badly needed!" "No one else is doing this." We were encouraged, surely this time would be different. Besides their conference room was functional but not as lavish as that of San Diego Foundation.

Three days later: So sorry, IRS problem. We cannot do this. I didn't go through the alternatives as I was beginning to get the message. Hit me over the head enough times, and even someone as slow and bullheaded as I sometimes am figures out the message.

Again, Mitch said, "Here's a better idea. You know that there is a foundation in Leucadia with a good reputation, called the Leichtag Foundation after its founders. They focus on stuff in Encinitas. Since this program would especially benefit Encinitas kids and their parents, this would be right up their alley. Besides, I know the woman who runs the foundation, and I am sure they'll meet with us."

"Okay by me," I said, although I was losing my faith in the helpfulness of foundations or their willingness to help kids.

Several days later we met with them in Encinitas. Furnishings only average. We made our pitch. And, surprise, they had almost exactly the same initial response, plus they liked that it was especially for Encinitas. They were straightforward about needing to get paid to assist us with the sorting and evaluating part of the task. My hopes were high, and it would sure be a double win to do this with an Encinitas organization.

Three days later, same story. We can't do this, the IRS won't let us, and besides we're too busy. So where did that busy part come from? At our first meeting they were quite bullish on their ability to take this on. Did they suddenly get lots more money to administer in the intervening two days? I didn't read anything about it in the paper. They were almost brusque in brushing us off.

"Can you think of anyone else who might be interested in helping on this?"

"Nope, don't know of anyone."

I didn't bother going through the structuring alternatives. We didn't even get offered a cup of coffee we were so quickly in and out of there.

It was clearly time to rethink our approach. Plus, time kept passing and I was worried that if we didn't get this finalized, we would not have time to publicize the program before the target kids graduated and dispersed to the four winds.

We asked ourselves more carefully than before just how hard this whole process could be. The people we had been dealing with to provide us help did not seem like Rhodes Scholars.

We speculated on the numbers. The reasoning went like this. Assume a graduating class of 400 seniors from the Encinitas High School, four years ago. Maybe half went to college. Of that, perhaps 75% actually graduated, and that's generous. You're now down to 150 kids with new degrees. Assume only 75% took out loans. That takes you to 112 students. Yes, I know, it's actually 112.5 but we didn't plan on dealing with any half kids. Or were-wolves either. Only half of them will have grades good enough to make the cut. That's 56 kids. If we received 56 grant application forms, and if we held to our commitment to make it a short, no-essay type form of no more than two pages, the two of us could handle that. That's not assuming that some additional percentage never heard about the program, some of them wrote our address down wrong, the dog ate some of their homework, they had to try out for the baseball team that day, etc. WE COULD DO THIS. To heck with trying to find big-name helpers, this was a test program. If it was well received, we could figure out what to do next year when next year showed its ugly head.

If you have been reading carefully, you will note that this did not solve all the problems, only the problem of processing and grading the applications. How about the problem of getting the word out in the first place? That should be easy enough … Write a flyer about the program and send it to all the eligible kids.

Okay, good plan. How do we find the list of the graduates and their addresses or email addresses? So we can send them our flyer and invite them to apply? Easy, we know people at UCSD, let's start there and have them give us a list of graduates who came there from the Encinitas high schools. Then we can go to the other San Diego universities. The ones who went out of state will be more challenging, but let's start here. Or if they don't have that information then the list of kids who have addresses in Encinitas. And so began the even more frustrating part of this exercise.

We knew a smart woman who worked as special assistant to the chancellor, and this seemed like a good place to begin. We met with her and explained the program and the benefits and what we needed. It may be hard to believe but the initial reaction to our efforts was the same as from the three foundations—"Generous!" "So needed!" "No one is doing this!"

She then connected us to the College Dean of Student Affairs' Offices, the admin center of the university. We met with a mid-level functionary, got the same reaction of how wonderful we were, and were asked to come back in three days after they had checked out our request. We wondered why this would take three days, either you had the data and could sort it, or you didn't. That should be the work of thirty minutes, maybe an hour. Okay, never mind the lecture on academic efficiency.

Three days passed, we drove down to the UCSD offices, found the parking place that they had graciously reserved for us—a good sign. We met with several administrators this time and waited for them to give us the data stick or the printout or whatever they had the data on. We did not expect to be given unfettered access to the whole data system of the university.

And we were not. We were given nothing. They couldn't do it, they all said, everyone nodding at once, because of federal privacy rules. We discussed this for a while, trying to understand the rules, and suggesting alternatives. What if they asked each student and those who were interested could contact us directly? What if we gave them the flyers and they mailed them out for us, with us never seeing the all-important addresses? What if we hired a helicopter and flew over the campus, dropping out flyers? Which would be interesting as the flyers would then actually be flying. Finally, we came to what seemed to us a perfect if stupid solution: What if we just sat at a desk they provided in one of their conference rooms and addressed all the envelopes by hand? They could even have a campus policeman watch us while we addressed the envelopes to make sure we weren't secretly stealing addresses. And after we were done, we would GIVE THEM BACK THE DATA. They could take it away and put it back in the safe or the dungeon guarded by Cerberus, or wherever they kept it.

Nope, they kept repeating over and over, "Privacy, privacy, privacy."

I even suggested that they ask for a privacy waiver from the Department of Education. Nope.

Then I suggested that they just disregard the rules, give us the data, and see if they got caught. If they did, we offered to indemnify the university if they got fined by the government. They did not seem to know what the word "indemnify" meant.

We tried everything we could think of but the idea of helping their immediate graduates get out, at least partially, from the very big burdens of debt did not seem especially interesting to anyone to whom we spoke. What they suggested way more than once was that instead we take all this nice money that we clearly didn't care about and give it to them, and they would use it for scholarships for needy kids or whomever they pleased. The problem with this, of course, is that it would only be displacing other money from scholarship funds, not displacing debt. Besides it wouldn't just impact Encinitas kids.

You might think that by this time we were getting tired of the whole thing, since so far we were getting zero for all our efforts. But no—stubbornness, thy name is us.

We played our ace in the hole. As mentioned above, we had tried the idea out earlier on the former, just-retired principal of the local high school, and he really liked it and had some good suggestions. I don't think it was just because I bought him lunch. So now we asked him to get us an introduction to the current principal and maybe he would be able to give as the list of graduates from four years ago.

He did so. We called the guy, leaving a message explaining who we were and what we wanted, and that we knew his predecessor who was sure he could be helpful. And then we called the guy again. And then we called him a third time. He finally decided to return our call. Here is the gist of the conversation: Privacy, privacy, privacy, no.

By now we were pretty much out of time and running short of energy. To make matters even better, we got a message from the actual dean of students at UCSD, who had never bothered to meet with us. Perhaps a classic of genre of "We superior beings need to explain to you peasants things that you are clearly too stupid to understand." I quote:

Dear Mr. Hemphill and Ms. Bissonette:

Thank you so much for your generous support of UC San Diego, and in particular your most recent gift to support the Chancellor's Associates Faculty Excellence Awards. We are all so enormously grateful.

Vonda and I have been alerted by Ann Spira to your generous intent and your unhappiness with the policies which prevent us from assisting you with your offer relating to graduating seniors who came to UC San Diego from Encinitas high schools. We write in the spirit of sharing information with you and with the hope of your understanding.

As officers of this esteemed public university, we are pleased and honored to carry out our fiduciary and legal obligations to UC San Diego. That is a primary responsibility, and a role we cannot apologize for. We must adhere to federal and state laws such as FERPA related to our students, IRS regulations, and UC policy related to charitable gifts, and all manner of many other requirements and policies that pertain to our positions. As such, we cannot violate them even if the intended outcome may be for good. That includes the access and use of our data pertaining to our students.

While we understand your frustration, we hope that you might better understand what is required of us. We thank you again for your support. We agree with your view; it is the best university in San Diego, and well beyond! If at some point you in the future are able to reconsider the terms of the awards, we are sure the team would be pleased to present some options to you in compliance with our university requirements.

Best, Dean of Students

It was all I could do not to fashion a suitably snippy response. But I didn't. Instead, we figured that by this point, early June, we were out of time so we were done for this school year. Warren Buffet is said to have a simple

ABC structure for explaining why institutions decline and eventually fail: A—arrogance; B—bureaucracy; and C—complacency. This simple construct surely fits our experience with UCSD.

9

It's Not Just the University, There's Dumbness Everywhere

The Canary Project

I was sitting around in my office, which is a small corner of our larger study and TV room but has a small desk overlooking the ocean. It is hardly a hardship to sit there and watch the palm trees and the ocean and the flights of pelicans going by. It's nice that we didn't kill them all thirty years ago before we prohibited DDT's use as a pesticide. It was close.

A very smart and interesting guy called me. His name was Mark Thiemens and I had met him at the request of one of the UCSD development people, not for any specific reason but because she thought we would like each other. We did and so had begun a casual friendship. But this time he had a serious mission.

The background is interesting but requires some long and semitechnical explanation.

The state of California is blessed (I use the term loosely) with two nuclear power plants. One is called San Onofre and is technically a three-unit plant—three reactors on the same site at the northwest end of the Camp

Pendleton marine base, sitting on the ocean between I-5 and the sea. You drive right past the plant when you come from Los Angeles to San Diego. You don't have a choice; there is almost no other way to get from LA to San Diego unless you want to drive off into the mountains to the east, then south through California's biggest state park, Anza-Borrego, then come back west into San Diego proper. Camp Pendleton is very big. The marines do not think it is a good idea to have highways running through the middle of their training areas and they are right. Everyone takes I-5.

The plant started construction on its first unit in August of 1964. It went online four years later, remarkable for nuclear construction. The history of the site is a little confusing because Unit 1 was small—395 megawatts—and to some extent experimental, kind of a baby reactor. It has been closed since 1992 and its spent fuel rods cocooned in "dry storage" since several years after closure to now, twenty-plus years later. The other two units, imaginatively named "#2" and "#3," are bigger, more the "standard" industry size of approximately 1,127 Mw each. They came online in August of 1983 and April 1984, respectively.

After about twenty-plus years of operation, someone in SCE convinced someone else to upgrade a critical part of each reactor, the heat exchangers, to allow more efficiency and a higher output. They were doing an outage every eighteen months for fuel replacement and decided that this should be a part of it.

There is a whole cottage industry explaining why this resulted not in more power out, but in something like three thousand tube leaks. A "tube leak" is close to the worst thing that can happen in any steam-based power system—gas, coal, wood, or nuclear. They are hard to find and hard to fix and one presages more. In 2012 both reactors were permanently shut down when it became clear that they were not fixable.

The units are pressurized water reactors designed and fabricated by Westinghouse before it went bankrupt over problems with the construction of the two newest US reactors, Vogtle Units 3 and 4, in Georgia. These Georgia units are the only new nukes being built in the US, and given their history of cost overruns and schedule misses, are surely the last ones that will be built here for a very, very long time. The eleven remaining nuclear advocates in the country will not agree with the last prediction.

Diablo Canyon is the other plant, located just north of Morro Bay in San Luis Obispo County. It, too, has two reactors—pressurized water reactors made by Westinghouse. Diablo Canyon is also located on the ocean. The ocean part is not because the designers wanted the operators to have a lovely sea view, it's because the nuclear reaction works like this: The fuel rods—long, round, pole-looking pieces of hardware, filled with a mix of U-235 and U-238—when left to their own devices do not explode and kill seven gazillion people not to mention a couple of sea lions. For that you would need really highly "enriched" uranium, which means a blend with more U-235 and not so much U-238. Or you could just use plutonium, but that's a longer story.

The reactor vessel houses a "bundle" of these fuel rods—like a huge barrel of graphite, with individual channels for the fuel rods. The barrel is also interspersed with other long metal poles, this time made of boron or other neutron-absorbing material. Generally, these are called control rods and they can be raised and lowered, individually or serially, to catch the neutrons that are naturally occurring as the uranium-blend fuel rods sit there and decay. But in addition to emitting neutrons, the decay process releases heat, which is way more useful than a bunch of unprogrammable neutrons bouncing around. The fuel rods and the control rods sit in a carefully controlled matrix with spaces between all these metal poles. Water is circulated through these spaces and picks up the heat. It circulates back out of the reactor, is allowed to become steam, and this steam runs through a traditional steam turbine, turns the rotor in the generator, and voila—electricity shoots out. The ocean part is used as a heat sink to cool the spent steam back into water so it can again circulate through the reactor.

Okay, hang in there, there's not much more of this basic stuff, but it's important.

Once the fuel rods have grown weary of emitting heat and neutrons, they are declared "spent" and removed from the reactor and new ones inserted. However, there are a couple of problems with this next step, the step of putting them someplace. It turns out that the process from the standpoint of humankind is not perfect. Yes, you get electricity without creating any CO_2 or other pesky greenhouse gasses. But what also happens is that a portion of the U-235 in each fuel rod has, in the process of emitting neutrons, become a different element entirely. It would be nice if it turned into gold or maybe something useful like copper or even a ham sandwich, but instead it chooses to become plutonium. Unfortunately, plutonium is (1) highly radioactive and so very difficult to deal with, and (2) fissile, that is, you can use it to make atom bombs. By the way, this might have been a secret in 1945 but it has long since ceased to be a secret. What it has become instead is a nightmare.

And that is not simply because of the radioactive and fissile characteristics. It is now an entirely different element with the atomic number of 94.

Why is that important? One of the bugaboos of the U-235/U-238 mash-up is that each of these isotopes, though slightly different, is still uranium and has the same number of protons in each atom's nucleus. This means that you cannot chemically separate the two elements. You can't just grind them up and add sulfuric acid and have one precipitate out and the other stay in solution like you did in high school chemistry with something or other. To get enough pure U-235 you must *physically* separate the atoms of the two types of uranium from each other. And since the 235 and 238 numbers designate atomic weight (neutrons and protons together) you can do the math. You will notice that the weights differ by about one-third of one percent, 0.127% to be exact. The other problem is that "natural" uranium contains only about 0.7% of U-235.

The final fact to know is that the fuel rods for a nuke plant only needed to be "enriched" to about 3%–7% of U-235. To make a bomb you had to get pretty close to 100%, which was obviously more complicated. This is why there is all the talk about Iran going from 20% to higher for their enrichment process and why we should be worried.

Separating two isotopes of the same element based on atomic weight is not at all easy. But it is the critical step to making a bomb, the rest is just engineering and metal fabrication. The Manhattan Project opted for creating miles and miles of the equivalent of heating ducts only more substantial, making the uranium into a gas (uranium hexafluoride or UF6 if you're interested) and then forcing this gas through this tubing, except every few feet there were large filters. Eventually the heavier atoms sank to the bottom of the gas flow and the lighter ones were on top. You siphoned them off and you had better quality uranium, better as in closer to being able to explode. Two of these facilities were built in the south, in part because it was recognized that pushing this gas through filters would require pumps and thus a great deal of electricity. TVA was ready to provide it. The facilities in Oak Ridge, Tennessee, and Paducah, Kentucky, were great customers, we loved them at TVA, they worked around the clock and always paid their bills. They were also, needless to say, a good deal more complex in terms of instruments and measurements and sensors and so forth than this simple explanation may have implied. As more evidence of the distress of the nuclear industry, both enrichment plants are now shut down.

Eventually scientists and engineers figured out that this was an awful process, and it was. Gradually, the idea of using centrifuges to replaces miles of tubing gained popularity and new plants began to get built with centrifuges. Lower cost, smaller footprint, still a lot of electricity use since something had to power these spinning machines. But as they spun, the same UF6 gas was used and the lighter U-235 gradually migrated to the outer shell of the centrifuge where it was extracted. Hence all the discussion about Iran's centrifuges and how Israel apparently screwed them up with some kind of computer virus.

But back to our story. The spent fuel rods have to get put somewhere once they are removed from the reactor and new ones put in. This is a complicated and expensive process that usually takes twelve to eighteen months, but once refueled a traditional nuclear power plant is good for another twelve to eighteen months before it needs more fuel, and the process starts all over again.

But where to put the spent fuel? This turns out to be a very big deal for a number of reasons, some obvious and some not so. There are good objections to having nuclear waste for your neighbor, and some not so good ones. Let's deal with the latter first.

Do Not Worry #1: The fuel rods cannot cause a "nuclear" explosion, as in Hiroshima. A nuclear weapon needs to be made with fissile material, such as U-235 or plutonium. It needs to be pure so that the neutrons naturally released can cascade quickly enough to blow the world to smithereens.

Something called "critical mass" is involved here. This is a calculated total, and it is generally thought to be 22.5 pounds for pure plutonium, about four times this for pure U-235. There were several engineering solutions in the bomb world to this problem—the need to keep the bomb pieces each below the 22.5 number, and then suddenly put them together when it's time for the explosion. One solution called for machining the metal—since that's what uranium is at the end of the day—into two large bricks, with the very smoothest sides of each block carefully facing each other. Then when the time comes, two conventional charges on the outside of each block are simultaneously set off, slamming them together and watching the world end. As noted, this is usually done with traditional explosive charges. In theory you could take a suicide bomber and have him just slap the two bricks together.

The alternative, and I believe current design of choice, is to use a "slice of pie" design, but in three dimensions. You put most of the uranium into a spherical shape, being careful to keep it under critical mass. You leave a cone-shaped hole in the sphere. With the remaining uranium you create a cone that will fit exactly and beautifully into the cavity in the sphere. Again, conventional explosives are used to propel the cone into the sphere and hold it there long enough for the explosion to happen. This is not very long, but if you blow the bomb up before all the uranium has had a chance to react, your yield will be lower and you'll blow up less real estate, buildings, people, etc. This is not a result that most bomb makers aspire to. Please note that this is not a treatise on how to make a bomb, as I have never made one nor been employed by anyone who does. All this information is by now public knowledge, although it also was when I was in high school, so these are not big secrets.

What makes this risk something not to worry about is the mixture and purity question. The fuel rods can't cause a nuclear explosion because the mixture of elements in the fuel rod does not have enough U-235 and they are not pure enough, as mentioned above. Their geometry also doesn't work. They can be stored somewhere (ah, that's the question) without worrying about a giant explosion.

Do Not Worry #2: The fuel rods will kill all their neighbors with their poisonous radiation. This is a little bit more likely than Do Not Worry #1 because this is at least physically possible. If your local nuclear plant sponsors an Adopt-a-Spent-Fuel-Rod Fair and urges everyone to take one home and "foster" it until a better storage location can be found, do not attend. If they offer to drop by and leave one for you since you weren't able to attend the fair, arrange to be not at home that day and don't let them leave it on the doorstep.

Fortunately, the utility has not employed morons to work at its nuclear plants, and doubly fortunately the Nuclear Regulatory Commission does not permit them to even if they wanted to. Everyone knows that spent fuel rods are still radioactive, they are just not "hot" enough to be used to make steam anymore. Given that, they must be put in containers with shielding, and then these containers must be put inside thick-walled concrete sarcophaguses with big, heavy lids. That is what has happened at San Onofre and what will happen at Diablo Canyon.

It should be noted that when these plants were permitted by the state and the NRC and by the Coastal Commission and anyone else who thought he or she should exercise permitting authority, it was generally assumed that these large, heavy, steel containers filled with spent fuel rods would be taken away by the federal government and put somewhere else. A federal law had been passed that explicitly required the federal government to do just that. Problem solved.

Well not quite. It turns out that there are so far no neighborhoods holding up their hands and volunteering to be the final resting place of hundreds, perhaps thousands of pounds of elderly spent fuel from all ninety-two of the nuclear power plant reactors in the US. This is a potentially worse neighbor than even a coal-fired power plant or a high-voltage transmission line.

There have been some heroic and expensive efforts by the government to perform its responsibility for providing a centralized site for all the power plants' spent fuel. The biggest was the designation of Yucca Mountain in Nevada as the location. What followed was an enormous amount of civil engineering to dig out the mountain, carve the insides up into storage rooms, pave the roads in, do whatever reinforcing was necessary, and so on. At the same time a lot of geotechnical studies were done, since the mountain didn't come with its own nice handbook about its geology and water table and so on. This work was a great boon for the University of Nevada and other local institutions as the feds literally rained money down on the site and all the necessary studies that everyone agreed had to be done. But Senator Harry Reid, at the time the majority leader of the Senate, had no intention of doing anything other than funneling pork to his state. It has been widely reported that during the first Obama campaign when the contest was in doubt, Reid went to Obama and said, you need to declare that Yucca Mountain is dead, that you will cancel the work there and the plans to move waste there, or you will lose Nevada. And if you lose Nevada, there is a good chance that you will lose the election. Obama made such a commitment, won Nevada, won the presidency, and the rest is history, so far as a federally managed central waste repository is concerned. As in, there isn't one and there are no credible plans to have one somewhere. The "somewhere" is naturally the key.

That leaves us nine million people within fifty miles of SONGS (San Onofre Nuclear Generating Station) to worry about the hazardous waste just up the highway, which is unlikely to go anywhere but stay right where it is for at least another twenty or more years. What are the circumstances exactly that we should worry about?

Do Worry #1: Ideally, the spent fuel rods should sit in the containers and quietly decay, emitting heat and radiation that never goes anywhere due to the heavy shielding. And now we come to the concept of "half-life." Scientists calculate how long radioactive decay takes for various radioactive elements and express it in a tricky form—the amount of time it takes for half of the amount of material to have decayed and turned into something harmless. If they say ten years, you would then assume that in twenty years the nasty stuff, whatever it is, will all be gone.

Unfortunately, no. Decay functions are not linear, they are almost but not quite as bad as Zeno's paradox, the fable where that arrow never hits its target as first it must go half the way to the target, and then half of the remaining way, etc. A simple rule of thumb to use instead of mastering the appropriate quadratic equation is simply to multiply half-life by seven. At that point the amount of troublesome material will be so small that it won't be troublesome anymore.

Unfortunately (again) the half-lives themselves are not short. Plutonium has a half-life of 25,000 years. And plutonium is really unpleasant. To get to the real end of its life, using the seven-times shorthand, will require 175,000 years. Humans on this planet have only been practicing sedentary agriculture for 10,000 years, since the first nomads figured out that they could stop wandering around and just grow stuff. All this first occurred in the fertile crescent in the Middle East, and rapidly the technology disseminated, and now we have the pyramids, the Eiffel Tower, and Facebook.

But are we responsible enough to keep track of a lot of radioactive waste (which because of the plutonium has the possibility of being turned into atomic bombs in the hands of the Taliban) for seventeen and a half times as long was we've been raising millet? Fill in your own answer.

Perhaps the "diversion" risk isn't so likely. It would require massive amounts of capital to separate the plutonium from the other elements in the fuel rods, and then to process and machine it and get it into a usable bomb. It would also take quite a lot of fuel rods. It would be very difficult to keep this a secret, and besides first one would have to steal (or buy?) a lot of fuel rods out of whatever storage site they are sitting in. They are not really for sale, even on Amazon.

Which takes us to Do Worry #2: Forget the thousands of years, what about the next twenty years? What if one of these large steel containers springs a leak? Remember that both of California's plants are sitting on the ocean. If you've ever had a boat or even been on a boat, you will know that all water is corrosive and salt water is especially corrosive. The canisters are also hot, somewhere around five hundred degrees centigrade when deposited in the concrete chambers. This diminishes after time as the contained fuel continues to decay, but it takes some time. See discussion of half-life above. The concrete silos are ventilated so that the heat can escape, which means that air carrying salt molecules gets into the silo chambers. If the canisters never rust or corrode, then all will be well, but several laws of chemistry and physics would have to be repealed.

So it leaks a little, so what? Well, first of all more radiation gets out, making it more dangerous to hang around the containers and try to do things like measuring the radiation level. Leaks tend to enlarge over time as the corrosion eats at the steel. Remember the 1979 Neil Young album *Rust Never Sleeps*? Also, the steel containers are hermetically sealed and pressurized before being deposited into their concrete silos. But rust and corrosion will eventually penetrate the steel and let out the pressurized radioactive gas. At some point the pressure inside the canister and outside the canister will be equal, and gaseous equilibrium flows will take place, allowing seawater as vapor to get inside the container.

Again, a big so what? Eventually someone will notice that radiation levels around one particular silo seem to be elevated, and even more eventually it will be decided that the canister needs to be inspected. This is no simple process, as you have to cut off the bolts holding the silo top down and lift it off. With a special crane, as the "lid" itself weighs several multiples of tons. You may wonder, as I do, why something that heavy needs also to be bolted down, but some questions cannot be answered. Once exposed there are fancy cameras that will fit down between the canister and the silo wall, a space of only a few inches. They can scan for the leak, and probably even find it. Being the camera operator is not a job I intend to apply for.

Then a really special crane will have to lift up the canister and put it—somewhere—so it can be fixed, the corrosion routed out, and the thing sealed shut again. There is no "canister repair dock" on the site so this will all have to be improvised. The designers did believe that someday the canisters would be moved, so they are made to be lifted out and put on specially designed railcars and taken by train to—somewhere.

Here is the real problem: it's a chemical process called electrolysis. But it is not the simple one where you run an electric current through a beaker of water and get oxygen and hydrogen. Electrolysis also occurs when water is exposed to enough nuclear radiation. As in a spent fuel canister where water has leaked in. Then if enough hydrogen is generated and collects in one place you can have an explosion. Not a nuclear explosion but a big enough explosion to blow apart the canister and its spent fuel rods and scatter miscellaneous radioactive matter about the countryside. There are 123 canisters at San Onofre, and they cumulatively contain about sixteen hundred tons of spent fuel. That is worth worrying about.

Here is where we are. The San Onofre Nuclear Generating Station closed in March of 2013. As part of the closure, all 3.55 million pounds of spent nuclear fuel is being moved to dry cask storage on-site. Fuel rods are placed into the steel containers, the containers are placed in the circular "vaults," and the lids bolted down. Managing the SONGS facility has changed from emphasizing safety for an operating nuclear plant to emphasizing safely managing the extended storage of the spent fuel at the site. The facility is not ideal for storage as it is only 108 feet from the ocean and, as is all Southern California, in a relatively active fault zone. However, given the present regulatory situation, it is unlikely that the fuel will be moved anytime soon, if ever.

The spent fuel storage will consist of 3,968 individual fuel assemblies housed in 123 steel canisters inserted into the concrete silo configuration on-site. The canisters have been extensively studied and tested. However, the salt air environment is hostile, and a number of scenarios have been postulated that could create an even more difficult environment. No one has ever used this storage system for the kind of extended storage that is necessary. Even a tiny leak could cause a devastating outcome. Under such difficult circumstances prudent management calls for best practices in monitoring. Luckily, as a result of the recent Fukushima tragedy, we now know that a superior early monitoring technique is available. Even better, it is relatively low cost and nonintrusive. Let me explain.

The Fukushima Daiichi Nuclear Power Plant in northeastern Japan was one of the largest nuclear plants in the world. It had six reactors in a large building located immediately next to the ocean. No US power plant has more than three. In March of 2011, a 9.0 magnitude earthquake offshore created a massive tsunami that disabled the plant's reactor cooling system and created system failures leading to nuclear radiation leakage. Three weeks after the damage it was evident that there had been a partial core meltdown in Units 1 and 3 and possible uncovering of the spent fuel pools.

At the beginning of the emergency, the control rods of the units had been automatically inserted into the fuel assemblies to terminate the fission reaction. The reactor design required that these fuel assemblies be continuously cooled to mediate the massive heat from the fission reaction and prevent a core meltdown. With the lack of both outside and emergency power to the reactor following the tsunami, pumps for the circulation of the cooling water shut down and the water could not be pumped and the fuel cooled. The site managers elected to admit seawater to the core to prevent a meltdown. This addition of seawater to the damaged reactor cores between March 17 and 26 created substantial volumes of steam, which had to be vented to the atmosphere. A few hundred tons of seawater were admitted to the two damaged reactor cores before some power was restored and the operators were able to switch back to freshwater coolant. The team at the UCSD isotope lab knew that Tokyo Electric had used seawater as a coolant weeks before it was publicly announced, because they had been monitoring for S-35 in the atmosphere on Scripps Pier and detected a significant spike in this element.

What is S-35, you may ask?

The major element in seawater, aside from water itself, is sodium, one of the constituents of salt (sodium chloride, or NaCl.) Sodium in the presence of radiation has a very high probability of reacting with a neutron and emitting a proton to create radioactive S-35 ($^{35}Cl_{17}$ + (n,p)$\rightarrow$ ^{35}S), a radioactive sulfur isotope with a half-life of eighty-seven days. Chloride's atomic number is 17, but when it loses a proton it transforms into sulfur whose atomic number is 16. However, the particle keeps its same number of electrons (35) and thus becomes a new beast. But one that you can keep track of until it decays into normal sulfur (S-32).

My friend Dr. Thiemens is an isotopes expert, and a very good one. He is a member of the National Academy of Sciences. He is a tenured professor and has written books and articles without number about isotopes. He is especially good at measuring elapsed time by examining isotopes in a particular sample—ice cores from the Himalayas, for example—and determining their age based on the decay rates of the isotopes found therein. He also measures isotopes in the atmosphere, for both timing and pollution determinations. He runs a sophisticated lab for the gas analysis, where the samples are collected on the Scripps Pier. The UCSD lab was already routinely measuring S-35 in March of 2011 to determine atmospheric transport rates around the world. But now there were much higher levels of S-35 being measured. Once they surmised what was going on, subsequent measurements of S-35 were made from air samples taken from the pier to track the fallout/pollution plume from Fukushima. The laboratory, although five thousand miles away, was able to capture the S-35 data that were the result of the chlorine reaction from the seawater addition to the failed reactors *some five days* after the ocean water was admitted. This was before any public admission by plant operators that seawater had been used as an emergency coolant. And the lab documented this conclusion before Tokyo Electric came clean on what they had done.

The measurement technique is so sensitive that Thiemens' lab was able to apply fundamental nuclear reaction theory and atmospheric chemical transport models to precisely calculate the neutron leakage at the reactor itself. This work was published in the *Proceedings of the National Academy of Sciences*. This was the first scientific article to define and quantify the reactor damage long before any other observations were made. This S-35 measurement technique is extraordinarily sensitive, fast, and accurate; moreover, the isotope specifically only occurs when sodium reacts with a neutron. The most likely place for this to occur is in and around the radioactive fuel. It does occur in small but measurable amounts in nature and its relatively short half-life makes it even less likely that any observed concentrations can come from any other source than a nuclear problem in the last eighty-seven days. Measurements of the natural background S-35 levels are known and used to study atmospheric mixing. Thus, a solid baseline measurement is documented and available.

Cooling the cores at Fukushima with vast amounts of seawater emitted a large amount of S-35. However, it is not necessary to have large amounts of S-35 in order to determine its presence. The Thiemens lab routinely measures S-35 in very small amounts—as low as 100 atoms/second. As noted from Fukushima, it is not necessary to be near the emitting site to measure S-35; this allows for measurement off-site from the generating facility. Atmospheric mixing and transport are pretty powerful things. A molecule of oxygen that you breathe in today can be anywhere in the world in about four months.

Once we had spent enough time on the science, we were convinced that S-35 monitoring for SONGS was a good idea. The reason that Mark Thiemens had called me was that he knew we were old energy geeks and perhaps could help him get his technology/system recognized and adopted as an additional layer of safety in monitoring the integrity of the canisters. It would give you the earliest possible notice that something was amiss and allow preventive actions before the situation became worse. We decided to call this effort the Canary Project, an obvious reference to the early days of underground mining when canaries were carried to monitor for methane in coal mines. It is true that the canaries announced the presence of this gas by dying, but it alerted the miners who could get out before they joined the canaries or, worse luck, got blown up in a methane explosion. We thought this was a pretty good name for the effort, and even enlisted our next-door artist neighbor to draw up a logo for us. This is what she came up with.

Then we wrote up a fact sheet for the proposal, part of which is reproduced here:

> The spent fuel storage at SONGS is presently monitored by SCE following existing NRC protocols that do not include S-35 monitoring. The Canary Project has been initiated to use the new practice of monitoring S-35 in order to provide an early detection system for a possible leak at the SONGS spent fuel storage site.
>
> The project will measure S-35 at several locations on accessible private property surrounding San Onofre. There is

a control site on the pier at UCSD, and also one in El Centro. These are both areas that are in the normal wind patterns from SONGS. All sites are outside the restricted access area of SONGS.

The Canary Project organization will be administered as a nonprofit university project.

The program has been conducted as a pilot project and is only funded through the end of 2019. Annual expenditures for staff, equipment, and overhead support for the full-scale project are approximately $500,000. At present the project is privately/university funded but it is anticipated that the project would work with the utilities to secure funding through CPUC approved rates.

As expected, there has been no indication of a canister leak to date. If no problems arise with the canisters, they will remain intact, no unusual S-35 will be detected, and the public can rest easy that the systems are secure. However, if a leak were to be detected, that information would come sufficiently early in the leakage process that remedies could be applied. The project anticipates working with SCE, Holtec [the canister supplier and soon-to-be-site manager], and the appropriate regulatory agencies to establish protocols that would be followed in case of a measurement signaling a leak from a canister.

This proposal for continuous monitoring would provide a sensitive early warning system for any leakage from a canister and could provide valuable time for correction of a problem before it reaches a dangerous state.

Once we had a structure and a reasonable proposal, we went about the process of trying to convince the utility business—regulatory and nuclear establishment—that what we were proposing, and already carrying out in a limited fashion, was a good idea and should be adopted. We had been funding it ourselves for six months or so, and Mark had been chipping in some research grant money, but we were getting close to the point where we were no longer comfortable being the only players with money in the game.

We decided that we were ready to start enlisting support, but first it might be a good idea to actually see the site up close. Fortunately, the Southern California Edison people had set up a monthly "Meet Your Friendly Local Nuclear Plant" session on-site at SONGS. You had to apply to attend and send a copy of your driver's license for a security check. We were accepted, and drove up to the plant, got through security, and then had a quite professional session on what the plant used to do, and how, and what it was doing now—sitting there quietly except for the radiation.

Our interest in all this had been piqued by an "incident." There had been a big problem about six months prior to our visit when one of the operators whose job was to lower the very heavy canister into its assigned concrete-lined hole in the ground had a problem. The operator managed to get one edge of the cylinder stuck on one of the internal rings that had been installed to guide the canister into place. This threw off the procedure and besides there was no procedure guiding what to do at that point. The one thing that you really, really don't want to have in a nuclear plant is to find yourself in a situation for which there is no procedure. Having a canister stuck partially in its silo, tilted at a slight angle instead of going straight down, caused confusion, calls for help, and cover-up. The fear was either that somehow in trying to dislodge the stuck canister it would either fall on the edge of the silo and get cracked, or it would not be anchored correctly and would somehow get loose from the crane and plunge downward into the silo, and rupture when it hit the bottom. The standard called for it to be lowered at no faster than a few inches per second, and certainly not to just to let it go while gravity did what gravity does to heavy objects.

After the requisite amount of standing around and chin rubbing and walking around the canister to look at it from all sides (it pretty much looked the same being cylindrical), eventually everyone decided to reengage, lift it up slightly so it disengaged with the guide ring where it was caught, and then let it down very slowly and very straightly. Slowly so it wouldn't swing and straightly so that it wouldn't hang up again. There was one school of thought that said do nothing until an Edison vice president arrived so there would be someone else to blame, and another school argued that the plant should request a ruling from the NRC. There was no one arguing to make a public announcement that there was a problem and perhaps the nearest seven million people in the neighborhood should consider a quick visit to their respective aunts in Toledo until this was resolved.

The "lift and reinsert" strategy won the day and was cautiously carried out. It worked, which was a good thing as there really was no plan B. Moreover, some of the outcomes would have been even more unpleasant. For example, in attempting to swing the canister free, what if the crane operator swung it too far and tipped over both the canister and his specialized crane? The crane was a combination crane and tractor since it needed to lift the filled canister out of the storage pool where it had been loaded, then carry it slowly to its designated spot in the silo arrangement, and then lower it into said silo. It was never designed to lift and swing 150-ton weights about.

When this was all explained to us at the briefing, I couldn't help but think of the story that they tell at Vandenberg Air Force Base. I worked there one summer as a draftsman, a long time ago, when the Atlas missile was just being developed and tested and the whole concept of shooting one out of a silo and over the pole to cream the Russians was being developed.

The Atlas was a liquid-fueled rocket, unlike later missiles that were sold fueled and much more storable, reliable, and transportable. The Atlas had two fuel tanks, one on top of the other, one holding liquid oxygen and the other hydrazine, N_2H_4, which is a colorless, liquid kind of high-energy fuel. Neither one of these is very storable. The plan was to put the fueling capabilities underground as well, next to the rocket's silo, then fill it up just before it was launched. Since we were judged strategically to need a "second strike" capability for real deterrence, the silo itself was closed with a 350-ton concrete and steel cap that had to be moved out of the way when it was time to launch the missile. The cap ran on rails and moved back just far enough to let the rocket out. The missile rode up to the top of the silo on an elevator, and when it reached the top, ignition occurred and away it went.

At one point a visiting USAF general, probably a pilot and not a missile guy, was observing a launch. When the test missile was fully loaded with fuel, and about halfway up the silo on its elevator, the general said, "Move it back down to the bottom."

The launch officer objected in polite, "But, sir . . ." sort of language.

The general said, "You heard me, Captain."

Perhaps he thought that we would need to hold our fire if it turned out that the Russians had not attacked us. The launch officer stopped the elevator and then hit the "down" button or whatever control he needed. But of course, the elevator had never been designed to work backwards under this amount of weight. The brakes and the motor failed, and the rocket picked up speed as it headed to the bottom of the silo where it hugely exploded.

No one was hurt, which was amazing. The explosion blew the 350-ton blast door approximately 1.5 miles toward the ocean but it landed inside the base and not on anyone.

The silo, when it was cleaned up, looked like half of it had been pushed about twenty-five degrees off center, and now was leaning a bit. The silo was never used again, and the general was quickly retired.

When I told this story to the SCE people during our tour of the SONGS plant, no one seemed to think that it was very funny. The tour was excellently done, questions were carefully answered, and the things that should have been covered were covered. There was a certain tristesse, though, among the briefers from the plant. Many of them had worked there a long time, in some cases their entire careers, and they were understandably sad to see something they had put so much time and effort into now being shut down before its useful life was really over.

Visit over, we left and started the sales effort, since that's what it was, by going back through our contact lists and our memories to see who we knew well enough to call, and to speculate on whether they were still in the business, or moved away, or retired, or—perish forbid—had expired. We called and had useful and helpful conversations with the former head of the NRC; with the former chairman of the California Public Utilities Commission; a former VP for SDGE now living a life of right-wing freedom in Wyoming; and our congressman, Mike Levin. Levin had organized his own task force on SONGS headed by a very unpleasant and disappointing admiral who L had helped get fired from his former job. Neither of us was invited to Levin's task force, and no one on the committee ever really talked with us about our idea. Nor was Levin very helpful. Not invited here?

Our most useful conversation was with a woman in SCE, now a VP of customer relations, whom we had met through our serving together on the Boston University Energy Advisory Board. The hardest part of all this was convincing any nuclear people to meet with us. Understandably—they were all sick to death of getting harangued by private citizens about questions or concerns that they were pretty sure they had already fixed and dealt with and explained a hundred times. Those proponents, when their views and recommendations were not accepted, reacted not by better analysis or more convincing science, but by talking louder, making ad hominem attacks, and writing op ed pieces calling all the SONGS people clowns or worse. I had several conversations with one of these people, a woman named Mandy Sackett, and while it started out sensibly, it rapidly drifted off into a conspiracy whose purpose was hard to assess. A conspiracy by the plant operators to kill themselves, their families, and all of us? Why? Maybe the opponents had been at it so long with so little to show for their efforts that it had made them a little bit crazy.

This is the background against which our project was measured. High levels of skepticism were not surprising given the quality of the debate at this point, i.e., quite low. This meant that we had to assure the mid- and senior-level plant people that we really were on their side, while at the same time telling them that they had to do something new, something other than that which they believed they were already doing pretty damn well, thank you very much, and with no appreciation and little career path future.

We eventually got a serious meeting with the VP for nuclear stuff and two senior nuclear engineers, one of whom was the plant manager, thanks to the reassurances of our friend Jill Anderson that we were not in fact nutcases. Even she was probably not entirely convinced since it was hard to determine what we were getting out of all this. Every time we had to send UCSD the money for another month's monitoring work by Mark's lab, we asked ourselves the same question.

The meeting was courteous, and the SCE engineers were attentive although skeptical. Mark was our ace in the whole as he was the science maven who could address if not entirely answer their questions. As so frequently happens in the government, our goal for the first meeting was to get a second meeting. After an hour and a half, we did not get a "Oh my God, you're right, we have to start doing what you recommend right away!" But we also didn't get a "No, you're crackers, we're never going to do what you're talking about" response either. What we got was a very cautious "Send us some more data and we'll think about this some more." This is a big win in the Land of Nuclear Power. We left the meeting feeling pretty clever having gotten a meeting of this quality without using any political power or screaming to the press. Of course, this was a good thing since we didn't really have any political power.

We were ready to go, find the data, dress it up in pretty PowerPoint format, and get back to the SONGS guys for the next meeting. But then it all came apart. Mark had a fellowship to Harvard as a visiting scholar that started immediately after our meeting and lasted several months. This was a big deal, a quality honor and hard to get. He had already committed to accept it, and he really felt unable to postpone it or back out. Besides he thought he could do some of the work from Boston, and he had several guys at his lab that he believed could do the rest of the work. And that he'd be back in three months (Christmas was in there somewhere) and then we could go back for a second meeting.

We suggested that "strike while the iron is hot" was a rather important description of this opportunity and tried to convince Mark to come back so we could have our second meeting. We emphasized that we had gotten further in six months with the SONGS management than any of the other many complainers had ever done. But we couldn't do it alone, we weren't technical enough to answer any second-level questions; he was the only person on the team who could do this. In retrospect, we really needed more than one expert at the lab to continue the effort, but even getting one National Academy of Sciences-level academic was a challenge.

Probably we don't understand universities and academia. We do understand utilities and regulations and how hard they are to change. We had a real shot to do something important here for spent fuel storage safety and we couldn't muster the resources or convince our key player of how unique the situation was.

We couldn't get back to the SONGS guys immediately to push for a second meeting, as we could not predict when Mark would come back from Harvard, and Christmas was coming.

By January when we called them again, they were much less receptive and said, in essence, thanks for the interesting idea, but we're sure we're doing fine. The canisters are fine (even though we almost dropped one) and they'll never corrode, and everything will be fine forever (175,000 years?) so we don't see the need for any more meetings.

We gave up and stopped funding Mark's lab, as we had told him we would do if we could not make progress with SCE. It was an expensive effort.

I guess we learned that when institutions and people in these institutions act in the same fashion when addressing a new challenge or issue that they have been trained to act in the past, and been successful with such actions, then it is very much more difficult than one would think to convince them to adopt different activities, even ones as simple as monitoring an additional pollutant. It also planted the seed that maybe we should work on things where we had more control so that when things went south at least we wouldn't be blaming our friends.

10

Finally, a Small Success!

We Give Money to the Employees at Peachy's and Seaside

Perhaps you have been incarcerated at the bottom of an underground coal mine and kept in the dark with no light, no reading materials, and no electronic media of any kind, being served your food by deaf mutes and never being allowed out for exercise. In which case it wasn't such a good idea to go to North Korea, was it? And in that special case you will not know that the world—for about thirty-six months starting in 2019—was blundering around in the grip of an ugly virus that infected more than four hundred million people, killing almost seven million of them around the world. Maybe more, since lots of serious public health authorities think this number is underreported.

We did notice what was going on. We try to stay current, although we do admit to having some misdemeanors to account for. Since coal mine incarceration is not the approved penalty for the trivial sins we have committed from time to time—such as coasting though a stop sign, failing to signal sixty feet before turning at an intersection, and occasionally putting plastic bags in the recycling bin even though EVERYONE KNOWS that most plastic cannot be successfully recycled—we weren't worried about the sheriff coming after us in particular. Especially in the middle of a dangerous epidemic. But like everyone else for a time we were baffled as to what to *do* about Covid. In fact, was there anything to do except get vaccinated and wear a mask and wonder when oh when it would all be over and who by the way were these people refusing to get vaccinated? Could there really be that many stupid people in the US? Well, yes, but so long as they refuse to get vaccinated, their numbers will decrease daily.

Eventually we came out of our lack of good information funk and found that our new and clever strategy for portfolio management was really working great! I suppose we can now reveal the complex methodologies of data management and market timing that we adopted to see our net worth increase 1% to 2% per month. Yes, probably 12% to 20% on an annual basis and that's after we used some of the money to buy cheap wine and expensive chocolates.

Our strategy: doing nothing. Alternately expressed, do not do anything, just leave the portfolio alone and let it grow quietly.

It's not that we were doing much "management" before this, for two very good reasons:

1. I was clearly no good at it. The few times I tried to inject myself into the asset management business, even thought it was just management of my own assets, the results were always the same: I lost money. I have had advisers who were also able to lose my money, but at least they occasionally made money. Not me.
2. I had finally, painfully, late in life, recognized that it was better to avoid doing things I was not good at. This was not easy, for example: baseball.

I confess that there is a bit of a stubborn streak in my makeup. When I was a kid, I loved, positively loved, baseball. Not that wimpy softball where the ball is big and the pitches are slow, but hardball. I played it after school every day with my friends. We lived in the deep suburbs of Albuquerque, so the weather was fine for this probably ten months a year. Since we were in a bit of a ratty development there was no shortage of dirt-paved vacant lots on which to play.

When I wasn't out playing in the summer, I listened to the baseball games on the radio. I would sit in my bedroom and act out every pitch and every swing of the bat. My favorite team was the Brooklyn Dodgers, which was odd since our family had never lived anywhere close to Brooklyn, nor had we even visited Brooklyn. Although who would want to? I had never seen a major league game, and my dad was about as unenthusiastic about baseball, or any sport except golf, as I was enthusiastic. He did take me to one or two minor league games in Albuquerque featuring the hapless Albuquerque Dukes.

And then we moved from Albuquerque to Roswell and got a house on the air base itself. There we had fewer vacant lots, but much more organized athletics. We had LITTLE LEAGUE uniforms! There was a whole league on the base, each team supported by one of the base units. We were the 509th Air Base Group Pirates. There was also the 6th Bomb Wing Giants and two more similarly named teams whose names I don't remember. Okay, four teams aren't much of a league, but it was what we had.

A small post-Korean War air base was really not a huge base of kids to draw from for your teams. This could be good, could be bad. The good part is that it let pretty much anyone who wanted to play, play. The bad part is that as a general rule, we were terrible. There were one or two big kids who were right on the cusp of having to step up to the PONY League because they were eleven and seven-eighths years old. PONY League took you at eleven and you could keep playing until you were fifteen, at which point you were supposed to be on your high school team or chasing girls or possibly both.

Because of the dearth of not only talent but just plain players, I got to start at short stop. I was no better than average okay at catching and throwing, which is a useful baseball skill but not the critical one. That's hitting. We were playing hardball, so it was overhead pitching and all that stuff. I was, in plain terms, afraid of the ball. My strategy was to stand close to the plate, to "crowd" the pitcher and make him throw me a ball so that I could stand there and after four balls, get a walk and go off to first base. The careful observer might note that the ten- and eleven-year-old pitchers were hardly the masters of control of where they threw the ball. So "crowding the plate" analytically simply made it more likely that you'd be hit by the ball.

This was way before the era of batting helmets. Getting hit with the ball hurt and was worth avoiding. But confronted with this approach/avoidance conflict, I hung in there. In the end I either walked or got called out on strikes. What I didn't do was hit the ball. Oh, maybe once every six or seven times at bat, but I was not good at this. But I was determined. Besides we didn't have anyone else to play short stop.

While we're on the subject of blind determination, I should point out that my mom in this case was a real trooper. She was hardly a sports fan except golf; when younger she had won several tournaments and even a trophy putter. She came to every single game that we played in the two seasons I was in the Little League, bless her heart. She never said anything other than "Good game!" to me, which it generally really was not. I think we ended the first season with two wins and eighteen losses. The next year we dramatically improved to 3 and 17. I never calculated my batting average, probably because I wasn't sure how to do that and partly because no one kept a box score of the players.

And then came the PONY League. By this time, we had moved to Japan and lived in a US military housing area called "Washington Heights." A little slice of America right there in southeast Tokyo. However, there was still a bit of a shortage of players. The housing area in this case only fielded one team, and we had to get on a bus and drive all over Tokyo to find games.

Our season was thirteen games. Our coach was born well before the era of "everyone gets a prize for showing up" ruined kids' sports. He put the best of his group of players on the field for every game. That did not include me. Although of course I showed up for every practice, on time, and I showed up for every game, dressed exactly as required in my uniform with the short-sleeved, gray flannel trousers and collarless top. This was way before the tradition degraded to uniforms that could include knit shirts and T-shirt and even—gag—camouflage tops—see the San Diego Padres who I am pleased to report have not gone to the playoffs since they adopted this trendy fashion. Coincidence? I think not.

I dutifully rode the bus to every game; we had almost no home games. We played other army and air force base PONY League teams, and maybe even navy and marine base teams. This was a time when Japan was literally littered with US military bases. It was past the time, but only just, when every manufactured product that was exported was required to say, somewhere on its body, "Made in Occupied Japan." Yes, that is really true, but since in this time period Japan was hardly a manufacturing giant it hardly mattered. Still, lots of trinkets and folding fans and cheap rice bowls, all with that label. For historical purposes I note that this practice, no doubt created and enforced by the terms of the surrender, ended in 1954. As did the "occupation," although in daily life it didn't seem to make much difference.

Besides, the Japanese were smart enough to have watched the Korean War with, I speculate, 35% envy to see Asians beating the crap out of the white guys, and 65% apprehension. The smarter Japanese might just in some tiny space at the back of their minds remember that they themselves had beaten the crap out of the Chinese in the prelude to the Pacific War. Only the Chinese who were being killed in record numbers probably didn't see it as a "prelude." See "Rape of Nanking" and other depressing topics of Asian-on-Asian violence. The more strategic Japanese might have thought, "Goodness, if the Chinese take over Korea, it's really not that far to Japan." Fifty kilometers, to be exact. The Korea Strait certainly hadn't stopped the Japanese from themselves conquering Korea in 1905 and making it a colony until 1945 when the surrender ended what was probably the most rapacious and exploitive colonial experience of any colonized people.

Maybe King Leopold did a better job in the Congo, and if not, it wasn't for lack of trying, but the Japanese were awful colonial masters. They took all the rice grown and harvested in Korea and moved it to Japan. In exchange, they imported barley from Manchuria and fed it to the Koreans. When my family went to Korea, and when I went again later while still in school, it was easy to meet older Koreans who refused to speak Japanese even though for forty years it had been the only language taught in the schools. And they absolutely, categorically, would not eat barley.

So much for that unfortunate bit of colonial history. The point is that the Japanese could not have been totally unhappy to be shielded by the American military as they saw China slowly rising from its own set of ashes and taking on the Americans.

But never mind all this ancient geopolitical stuff. Back to the ball field!

Our PONY League team, the Washington Redskins (yeah, I know, football but we didn't care) played all our games away. Seems sort of rude but so it goes. I attended all thirteen religiously. I oiled my leather mitt before every game. I don't honestly know why this was a good idea; it's hard to imagine that this made it easier to catch balls. Wouldn't it actually have made the glove slipperier, as in more oily? But we weren't that analytical, so you oiled your glove with the ever useful three-in-one oil, and never asked, "Three what?" Then the night before the game you put a hardball in the glove and wrapped your belt around it, so that the glove would develop a better "pocket." Did this work? Doubtful, although the glove probably only cost $2.95 at the PX, almost anything would have helped. But it was the ritual, it's what you did.

I did not get listed or tagged as a "starter" in any of the thirteen games. I did not get inserted into the lineup in any of the first twelve games. In game thirteen, in the top of the ninth inning, when as the visiting team we were at bat, the coach called my name. "Bill," he said, fortunately pointing at me so I wasn't confused with the other Bill, "get in there for Charlie [or someone]." I leaped off the bench, ran to the on-deck circle, grabbed the best and probably lightest, shortest bat I could find, used it to knock against the bottom spurs of each of my shoes so as to get the mud out and be able to run faster, and advanced to the plate.

The opposing pitcher had no idea who I was, of course, nor did I have any idea if he was any good or would try to kill me by hitting me in the head with a fast ball. I suspected he would, but I didn't have any data. I stood scrunched down at the plate, and after a few practice swings, stood there.

My teammates were pretty silent, but they were always silent. Nobody was yelling "Okay, Billy, knock it out of the park!" or "Hey, Billy boy, show him what you're made of!" I would argue that the latter cheering call is not a good chant of encouragement for any contact sport.

I did. I stood there for enough pitches to be called "balls," four to be precise, before enough pitches were called "strikes," three to be precise. Mission accomplished! I dropped my bat and walked down to first base, trying to look cool. I stood on first and said to the first base coach, "Too bad he walked me, I was looking for something I could hit." Right. I was looking not to get a fatal brain aneurism from being hit in the upper forehead by a hardball thrown by a malevolent demon who cared nothing about my fate and was standing a mere thirty feet away and throwing hard things at me. He or it had the advantage of standing on a mound of dirt so it or he was pitching downhill, which added some fraction of miles per hour to the speed of the ball.

Apparently we were already losing, and apparently there were already two outs. I know this because while I was standing there expectantly on first base, the next batter struck out, although at least he swung at a couple of pitches. It was the third out, but the other guys just ran off the field celebrating, which meant they were ahead and having them take their last turn at bat was pointless. The game was over. Our box score for the inning was no hits, no runs, one walk, one man left on first.

"One man left on first." If I were ever to write my sports memoirs, that would be the title—*One Man Left on First*. They would be short memoirs.

This is a complicated explanation of our asset management strategy and why we kept at it.

Honestly, for some time we were so preoccupied with how and where to get the Covid vaccine shots, we paid attention to little else. When we did finally look at the monthly statements, and added them together, we noticed that the most recent one was $400K to $500K higher than the previous month's. This was not something that happened often, or in my experience ever.

At first, I thought it was a mistake, then I thought it was a fluke, then I thought that it wouldn't last, then I thought I should do something about it, then I wondered what that would be. I was paralyzed with success, which turned out to be the right thing to do.

By the time the pandemic had been cranking along for three or four months, we were convinced that we were not going to die shortly and in an ugly fashion. We were also foolishly convinced and that our continuing financial windfall was also not similarly going to expire. We began to look around for something meaningful to do other than scout the stores for more toilet paper. Which, by the way, was never satisfactorily explained—massive diarrhea? No one at work so all the bathrooms in the high-rise office buildings were well supplied, but everyone at home was probably not any intestinally worse off than before, but locations had changed, while supply chains were still delivering gobs of paper to Wall Street and not enough to Main Street or the suburbs.

There was much press coverage of the workers in the food and grocery distribution business and how we hoped to God they would stay on the job. Also, troublesome reports as to how workers at meatpacking plants kept getting Covid. Not really possible to cut up a pig from home.

We are blessed in Encinitas to have two wonderful grocery stores, neither of them chains. One is a small "convenience" store but it's really a mini market just up the street on the Pacific Coast Highway called Just Peachy, but everyone calls it Peachy's. They have especially good, fresh, and ripe produce and lots of other things that are not easy to find elsewhere, like pomegranate molasses. They have an interesting story, and here it is.

Just Peachy is the name of the market, a small but wonderful market that has terrific produce and an interesting assortment of international foods, especially Middle Eastern. The owner is Amir Movassat. He opened the market near us, on the Coast Highway, in 1987. He has since expanded to a market and grill on El Camino Real, which one reviewer called "another gem of a restaurant." The Facebook page says modestly:

As a family-owned business that has served the greater Encinitas area since 1987, we're passionate about providing the best foods to our community, including Middle Eastern specialty foods and seasonal produce from the finest farms in California.

And they do.

Amir is from Iran. He was born in Tehran and emigrated here by himself as an eighteen-year-old teenager, because his educational opportunities were limited there. He arrived in 1979 just before the Iran hostage crisis that started in November of that year. He had a student visa and ended up at Mercer University in Atlanta, Georgia. He knew little English.

He caught a break when after Reagan's election there was a general amnesty for Iranians in the country and he received his green card. He ended up in business, successfully. However, he had left both his parents behind, and they both died during the crisis. His relatives didn't tell him as they feared that he would come back for the funerals and would never be allowed to leave the country again. He is married and has two children, both of whom have gone to college in California, and are professionally employed—neither in the small grocery business.

The second is a large market on the south side of town, also on the Coast Highway quite close to the beach. Appropriately it is named Seaside Market. They have superb marinated tri-tip for which they are justly known, but also high-end things that again you don't find in Safeway. Anchovies packed in salt. Preserved lemons. Fresh pasta, yes fresh. Fresh pesto not canned. And on and on. There is a story here as well.

The market is owned by two brothers, John and Pete Najjar. They are the sons of an Iraqi immigrant, Selim "Sam" Najjar; they were Chaldean Catholics originally from a village called Tel Kef. The dad started a small family market in Detroit, in an edgy neighborhood, in 1963. The store was left alone in the 1967 and 1968 riots, because it had become a valued member of the community. The father was generous with his neighbors, providing food and even loans to people when they needed it. The two sons both worked in the market from an early age, usually seven days a week when they weren't in school.

In 1976 the family moved to El Cajon and the two brothers, by now young men, got a small grocery store in the neighborhood, which is in eastern San Diego. One day in 1985 a relative heard of a vacant, larger store and took them to look at it. It was in Cardiff, across from the railroad and the beach. Neither of the brothers had been to the San Diego shore or seen the ocean until then. They were working.

The store had been a Vons formerly and then a farmers market but had been closed for a year. Using a loan from a relative, Pete and John bought it, replaced some of the fixtures and lighting, and off they went. They had rounded up thirty employees and had seven thousand square feet, not much for a market. Over the years they have remodeled four times and expanded twice, taking over a small deli as well as a much larger Gold's Gym space that was originally next door.

They now have 18,500 square feet and 140 employees and are a local legend.

John and Pete each have three kids, all of whom have graduated from college (the brothers never had time to go, or money) and have professional degrees and careers. The market hires local kids from the schools and has a lot of employees who have grown up with the market. Everyone in Encinitas knows the market and many of us consider it a local treasure. If this sounds like a typical immigrant success story in America, it is.

We, like everyone else in the United States, were now with the pandemic busily ordering everything we could think of that we might need from Amazon or other less well-known places on the internet. Not toilet paper, nobody had any. We didn't want to go near anyone, we didn't want to go out, we didn't want to be close to anyone other than each other, we were in complete shutdown mode. Pretty soon our garage looked like we had become survivalists and expected a nuclear holocaust pretty much any time. Lots of dried beans, although where we thought we would get the water to cook them and the gas in the stove to boil the water in the event of Armageddon was unclear.

We should honestly note that should a nuclear holocaust be in the offing, it was highly likely to come our way. San Diego has probably the best deep-water harbor in the US. Substantial naval assets are based here. There is always at least one of the eleven US aircraft carriers sitting in the harbor, and frequently two. In the unlikely (we hope) event of such an attack, we are far enough away from the harbor that we would not be blown to bits or vaporized in the initial strike, but we would die in a couple of weeks of radiation poisoning. Or possibly we would starve to death or die of dehydration after we drank up all our bottled water. None of these are good outcomes, and all the cases of canned tomatoes and packages of dried beans and pasta won't save you once you're out of water.

Eventually we came to our senses and stopped ordering and stockpiling large amounts of Spam and canned tuna. I think we still have all the Spam; it appears to have a pull date of Dec 2050. But we had no interest in venturing afar, and we were especially sobered when the highest locations of new Covid infections in San Diego occurred in our three local Costco's. We kept our business, carefully, at Peachy's and Seaside. And canned tomatoes from Amazon.

A couple of months in, we began to think of what we could do to show our appreciation to the frontline workers. Not the docs and nurses, who were justifiably getting lionized. But the daily workers who kept the rest of the city going. What did we have that they might appreciate?

Options: Thank you notes? Have a block party? Print up thank you T-shirts? Take an "appreciation" ad out in the local paper? Wait, what about, um, money?

Well, gee, let's think. Maybe money? I don't know for sure what store clerks are paid, but I bet it isn't much over the local minimum wage of fifteen dollars an hour.

We decided to start with Peachy's. We debated the amount but figured that it had to be consequential or why bother. We came up with $250, with little analytical backing other than that it felt right. We had to find out how many workers there were, which we did by the clever tactic of going to meet with Amir, the owner. The number was eight.

Next question: how to administer this. Cash? Checks? Give the money to the store and have them give it to each employee? Amir was not keen on this and the more we thought about it we saw the specter of tax issues. Did Peachy's have to record it as income? Did the employees need to report it as wages? Did we or someone need to deal with withholding? These are not insoluble problems, but they are problems.

After a fair amount of thought we decided that we should give each employee a personal check from us, and that it would be characterized as a gift. It was also below the gift tax reporting level (now $15,000 per person per year) so that kept the IRS out of the process. We did need the names of the employees, but not their social security numbers or immigration status and we didn't ask. It was just a plain old gift. No positive "charitable deductions" for us, but we didn't care as that was not the point of this. Besides, there was no quick and easy way to make it into deductible contribution, other than running the money through a local nonprofit and we were sick to death of those sorts of institutions. For reasons already documented above.

We got Amir to tell us what day and time would make the most sense and have the most employees at the store. He also gave us the employee roster with no data on it but names. Perfect!

We wrote out eight checks by hand and showed up fully masked at the appropriate time. We handed out the checks for $250 each to the six employees who were there, took a bunch of pictures, left the remaining checks with the manager, and went home pretty satisfied. Finally, something that worked! Well, yes, it only added up to $2,000 but nobody on the receiving end complained.

We did not get any press coverage from this, but we weren't looking for any and it didn't seem to be a big enough deal to merit any. The people receiving the money were clearly surprised, happy, and grateful. You cannot often do that well.

The pandemic ground on and infections and deaths increased. Despite shutdowns, the behavior of the beloved American people was not great. Nor were there any vaccines yet. We debated what if anything we should do next. There was plenty of time to debate as little else was going on, and lots of stuff was closed, shut, *geschlossen* (German for "closed").

We decided to duplicate our Peachy's process, but on a bigger scale—Seaside Market. We called up the head of catering who we had come to know by the time-honored process of paying Seaside for some catering. She connected us to a woman named Ana Torpey, who was the head of HR. We talked her into setting us up with the manager of the store, Austin Davis, and with one of the two owners, Pete Najjar.

We met in their small conference room that was actually Ana's office. Hey, it's a grocery store. There was skepticism, as any reasonable person might expect. Here's some dude who we don't know, who wants to give our employees money, and he doesn't want anything in return. What's the trick? Is this a scam? Is he connected to a Nigerian prince somehow? Surely he wants to sell us something.

We recounted the Peachy's experience and said they should contact Amir for a check on our bona fides. Maybe they did this later. But they took us at our word and gave Ana the go-ahead to work with us on the details. There were some. This time it was 150 employees and probably thirty-five part-timers. We decided to give each full-time employee $150 and the part-time ones $100. Again, we would make it a gift from us, with no involvement of the store or the management, and thus no pesky IRS questions. We set a date a week in the future, as I didn't have enough physical checks to write 185 of them and had to get UBS to send us a hurry-up order.

On the morning of the event, Ana and I sat in her office with the employee roster busily writing checks. She would put in the names, and I would put in the rest of it and sign the checks. She collected them, put them in order, and we were ready at noon.

The manager pulled out as many folks as he could. They were, after all, still running a busy grocery store. Pete made a short speech; I made a shorter one about appreciation for their service in such a difficult time. The manager had whoever was there line up in alphabetical order and as they passed by us Ana handed me the right check. We only gave out 25% of them as not everyone was there or out being thanked instead of working. Most of them were inside doing the thing we were thanking them for.

It was a nice event—they had ordered a small tent, and they gave us a big basket of stuff from the store, including two very nice bottles of wine. Didn't have to but it was lovely. About a week later Ana called and asked if she could come by our house. We said sure, not quite clear on what to expect. She brought by a lovely mixed case of wine, and a big, framed poster board that had the signatures of all the employees on it and a big "Thank You" in the middle. It was very touching. It underlines the oldest rule in business—always associate yourself with quality people. The Seaside folks were all that, and we were happy to make their lives during the pandemic a little nicer. Probably being acknowledged for their work under trying circumstances was important, too, but acknowledgement plus money is always better.

11

The Bird Story Origins, with Apologies to *Batman Begins*

How We Got Interested in Birds While Looking for Lions

Our involvement with birds is pretty recent. As a kid I remember being in a class in New Mexico and being asked to draw a picture of a bird. I had recently seen a red-winged blackbird—someone must have helped me with the identifying, although the red wing patch and the remaining blackness of the feathers made this name fairly satisfying and easy to remember. I drew the picture, badly, as artistic talent does not run in our family. We are more "word people" and not "picture people." I took it home to show my mom, who asked politely what it was a picture of. She then hazarded a guess that it was a train engine. So much for competing with John James Audubon.

As a grown-up I probably knew what robins were but hardly ever gave it the least thought, nor did I think about any others of the bird universe. Well, maybe chickens but only to eat them. I thought bird-watchers were peculiar and odd, but harmless. When I moved to San Diego and a lovely beach house, I found that I could sit at my desk and look out on the ocean. From my deck I could see flights of brown pelicans, trailing by in a perfect line or vee, heading north or south. For what purpose I still do not know. Sometimes they would stop and circle and dive into the ocean, most likely to catch fish since it's hard to imagine any other birdlike purpose of such an activity. It really wasn't diving in any elegant, arrow-like sense of the word, it was much more like a crash. They're big birds and they are far from streamlined, but the crashing strategy must work since their numbers have rebounded since 1972. This was when the use of DDT had so affected the strength of the shells of the eggs that they laid that there was some real concern that they were on the path to extinction. The pesticide was banned and the pelicans recovered. But I had never read *Silent Spring* or really anything much about birds or bird conservation or habitat or such matters. I knew no one who was interested in birds, including any of the various women in my life.

About eight years ago I agreed to go on a safari to South Africa. We had a couple of friends who had recently done just this, and they strongly recommended a lodge that bordered the Kruger National Park and was called Kirkman's Kamp.

I was not eager to do this. I was not eager to get eaten by lions or trampled by elephants or drowned by crocodiles, or any combination of the above. It was assuredly not on my bucket list, although I don't really have one. But sometimes you do things you are not keen on, for many complex reasons. Like maintaining an important relationship.

Here is how a "safari" works. I am now an expert having been on two of them. You stay in a lodge—ours looked a little like a 1950s motel with a series of small, white, individual cabins where you sleep, and a central building where the meals are served and the gift shop and the library are. Also, the bar—let's not forget the most important part. Hey, these guys were colonized by the Brits, after all.

You get up quite early—around 5:00 a.m.—have a quick cup of coffee and maybe a bun, and get into your vehicle along with your driver and your guide. No surprise here—the driver is usually a black South African and the guide is usually a white South African.

Here is the first surprise—you don't go charging around through the bush trying to chase down some animals. The game area is crisscrossed with dirt roads or trails, and you are really supposed to stay on these trails for obvious reasons. You drive along the trail for a while until you come to a good place to stop, determined by your guide. You stop and wait and look around. You are quiet since animals apparently do not like to hear people talk. I am sympathetic in general. Soon, if your guide is any good, an animal appears, or several animals or a whole frigging lot of animals. The big surprise to me was that there were animals everywhere. Mostly they were members of the antelope/gazelle/deer ("AGD") fraternity with names like kudu and impala but there were also less frequently elephants and rhinos and leopards and other things not named after US cars. After a time, if you hadn't seen anything but members of the AGD family, the driver started the truck and drove to another place where the vehicle stopped and waited. If you're getting the picture that there was a lot of sitting around in your truck staring out at the shrubs and trees and grass, you're right.

Our second safari was also in southern Africa but this time we changed lodges every three or four days. We visited lodges in Zambia, Zimbabwe, and Botswana. We were fortunate to be in a truck with a woman named Janet Starwood who was a smart and generous person and also a very good bird-watcher. When we're sitting in the truck watching for the buffalo or the hippo to stop by, Janet is spotting and pointing out to us the various African birds that were around. Looking at these birds was way more interesting than viewing again the back of the guide's head. She even loaned us her binoculars so we could see the birds better. We got interested, and then more interested, and then we got hooked.

This infatuation was also assisted by a remarkable woman named Pam Kelly, a talented clay sculptor who we met at a function at the Oceanside Museum of Art. We were standing around the opening of something or other, disguised as art patrons. We fell into conversation and began talking energy with her husband, Paul, a clever lawyer who had done a lot of fracking transactions in Pennsylvania, where the couple was originally from. Paul's fracking deals had been good for all parties and so, tiring of the weather and the social life of northeastern Pennsylvania, they had moved to Oceanside, at least for the winter. They invited us back to dinner on the spur of the moment. It was great, and then we learned that she was not only a talented artist but a great cook. And a very good birder.

Pam had gathered a group of similarly inclined friends and led them on walks in the northern San Diego area every Wednesday morning. She was kind enough to add us to the group, and thus most Wednesday mornings will find us at a park or a riverside or a lagoon trail with Pam and others seeing what birds are around that particular day. She was careful about who she invited, but we somehow made the cut.

Soon we joined the local chapter of the Audubon Society and became supporting members of the Cornell Lab of Ornithology, the premier academic institution in the world that focuses on birds.

This interest expanded slowly. It was dramatically stimulated, however, by the release of the Cornell Lab study, done jointly with Audubon, to answer a question of seeming simplicity: How many birds are there in the United States? The study was released in September 2019. See more detail below in Chapter 12. At this point we decided that we should do more and be more focused. But that decision was driven by excellent advice we received from Roger Sant, chairman emeritus of AES and one of its two founders.

12

A Discourse on Philanthropic Strategy

Twelve World Needs and What We Are Concentrating On, or No Matter How Hard You Try You Cannot Do Everything

If you're going to give away money, there are any number of ways to do so. Unless you're just doing it just once—boom, here's all my money, good-bye—then you eventually develop an approach or a philosophy or a strategy or a plan. Or maybe you just develop a habit or set of habits. After all, it's your money, you can do whatever the hell you want with it, and you don't really have to justify that to anyone. Assuming of course that you're not doing something illegal or deeply evil. The former is easier to fix or define than the latter.

A couple of caveats: There are many forms of philanthropic activity. This essay only addresses the category of modest-size provision of financial resources, gifts in the thousands or hundreds of thousands, not the millions or billions. It addresses giving that is controlled by the owner/creator of the resources being discussed. It is not applicable to larger organizations like well-endowed family offices, the Rockefeller Foundation, or the United Givers Fund. In these cases, it may well be appropriate to select a number of categories of philanthropic activities, or the donors to the organization may have specified that their funds only be used for one or two activities. Nor do we attempt to offer an opinion on a much more complex subject—the volunteering of one's time—instead of or in addition to or in place of one's resources. All of these organizations and activities fall under the umbrella of philanthropy, and all have their own standards for evaluation. Our opinions only apply to the carve-out suggested above and may even only be appropriate for our own activities. It's a big world and there are many ways to do good.

Let us begin with one family example, that of my father, Colonel Robert Hemphill, who died in 2010 at the age of ninety-four and therefore probably cannot object to this story. Besides, it's true.

When my father got older, as often happens, his circle of activities became constricted, as did his group of acquaintances. The daily mail became more and more important to him; his computer and email skills, never strong, had eroded with age. He somehow got into a loop where he received each day in the mail many, many appeals for money, generally from "charitable" and, therefore, tax-deductible entities. He enjoyed this daily avalanche. He was living in an assisted living facility with his old dog, near my brother who visited him frequently, and I came to see him at least once a month. Nevertheless, his universe was smaller than ever—his wife was thirty years deceased, his recent companion had passed away, and he was not especially interested in making friends in his new community.

Thus, whenever he received a charitable request in the mail—"Save the wild feral burros of Placerita Canyon" or "Build a school for the blind orphans of Rwanda" for example—he sent the requesting organization twenty-five dollars. And his mail increased.

We noticed this, my brother and sister and I, and suggested that: (1) Who knew who these people were; and (2) How could he be sure that the money would be spent as advertised; and (3) He had not previously expressed much interest in feral donkeys or blind African orphans. He was unmoved by these helpful reactions. Eventually we said to ourselves it's his money and he can spend it however he wants.

And he did. It's a philanthropic approach.

There are other strategies, for example, only give money to local organizations for local problems. This is attractive. Only give money to people whom you know personally, the personal appeal approach. This is also attractive, but both maybe unnecessarily limiting and not particularly strategic.

My old boss and good friend Roger Sant, the founder of AES, has devoted much money and effort into the operations of his family fund, and has done interesting philanthropic things thereby. I make sure that I can visit him any time that I go back to Washington, and it's always fun and productive.

About six years ago I was invited over to his house for tea on one of these visits back. It was a difficult time for Roger, as his beautiful wife of many years had contracted ovarian cancer and was undergoing some of the barbaric treatments that still dominate the therapies used by the medical profession for this cancer. We were sitting in his elegant living room and trying not to talk about Vicki. I had a bit of an inspiration.

"Roger," I said, "you have had a life and a career that spanned many different kinds of activities. You were a young naval officer, you got an MBA from the Harvard Business School, you started a successful Silicon Valley company, you were a lecturer in finance at the Stanford business school, you came to Washington and were an assistant secretary of energy under Presidents Nixon and Ford, you started a nonprofit and published a seminal book on energy (*Eight Great Energy Myths*), you started AES and grew if from a million dollars of venture capital to a New York Stock Exchange 150 company. You were president of the World Wildlife Fund, you gave the Smithsonian National Museum of Natural History a large amount of money and now have an entire hall named after you, and now you run a large charitable foundation focused on environmental causes. Which of these things gave you the most pleasure, which of these activities do you look back on and value the most in your life?"

I fully expected it would be the political activities or maybe the founding of our very successful energy company.

Without hesitation, he said, "The philanthropic stuff, no question."

We discussed that for a while, and he explained more about it. Then I asked hm what guidance he would give someone who was now concentrating on doing effective philanthropic giving. He said that the best advice he could give was "focus"—pick one or two areas that are important to you personally, and then concentrate your brain power, your time, and your giving on those areas. There are an almost unlimited number of deserving things to spend time and attention on, but without this sort of discipline, your efforts will be scattershot and less effective than they could be. This seemed like pretty good advice, so with some modifications we have given it a try.

There are as many ways to give away money as there are start-up businesses in the world, or at least in California. Here is one: Using Roger's advice, pick one or two global crises, selection criteria to be discussed in a minute. Focus your giving, and then focus your attention at the same time. One of our values at the solar company that I ran was "Don't be stupid." That could apply here. It is also easier said than done. Intelligent philanthropy in any interesting size turns out to be hard work.

Let's start with the thirteen biggest global crises, as defined by us and inevitably the media. Feel free to come up with your own list, this is neither dispositive nor guaranteed to generate universal agreement. But it has a lot of stuff on it that frequently appears in the newspaper in close conjunction with the word "crisis" or "emergency," among the two most overused words in the news business and politics. Nothing anymore is just a problem, let alone a simple annoyance or a mere irritation. If your particular cause can't make the climb up to emergency or crisis status, then you are just a sad little poseur.

But one more caveat: In my opinion, any crisis worth spending both money and intellectual energy on must not have an obvious solution, especially an obvious technological solution of reasonable cost, and it must have the characteristic that an individual's application of money and brainpower can make a small but lasting dent in the problem. That dent should be able to be measured. The impact should be approximately proportional to the input money or intellectual effort. But more on this in a moment.

We begin with the global crisis evaluation.

GLOBAL CRISIS #1: Climate change/global warming. Set aside ongoing arguments about whether it is a real problem, how real, who causes it, etc. Then does it make the cut for a target for modest philanthropy? In my judgement, no—because there is little scope or room for individual action that has a proportionate impact and will be lasting. I cannot personally shut down a coal-fired power plant and replace it with a bunch of solar panels. That effort takes concerted action by a lot of people, not to mention organizations and markets. It may already be happening, which is a good thing. I did do a lot of this, at least the building of utility-scale solar plants, for six years at AES. We built fifty plants in eight countries, a total of 556 Mw of capacity. At one point we were one of the three largest solar companies in the world. That solar capacity represented 0.00139% of the world's electric capacity, but it was a start. We did it not because we were worried about global warming and thought this would fix it, but because the technology—silicon solar panels—had gotten so good that it made more economic sense to do so, and doing so competitively meant we could make generous returns for our investors. Doing well by doing good, and none of it with philanthropic money. Why give money away to support an activity that the market is already generously rewarding? You can, but it's silly.

What about electric vehicles? I suppose we could buy one, and probably we will pretty soon, but I won't buy a hundred of them—where would I put them? Since I don't commute long distances to work these days, my contribution to reducing carbon emissions, even if I walked everywhere, would be very modest. It would also be dependent on the electricity used for charging the vehicle being itself generated in a renewable manner. This is really an incidental contribution to solving global warming—not a bad thing, but not a strategy.

GLOBAL CRISIS #2: Species extinction. This is an equally or more complicated crisis than global warming. Large animals, small predators, bird populations, insects, flowers, etc. There are now, according to the U.S. Fish and Wildlife Service, 1,950 endangered species in the US alone. A whole lot more are listed as threatened. This is an unknown percent of all species in the world, as far as we can tell. Some biologists estimate that we have only discovered at best 60% to 70% of all species on this planet. The data here are notoriously difficult to gather and thus it's hard to be sure that the numbers are as dire as reported. Or maybe they're worse. If you think it is difficult to ascertain species status and numbers on land, try the ocean. Possible, but more thought and analysis is necessary. It's probably not necessary to point out that animals don't fill out census forms or send their numbers in by email to the Census Bureau website.

Here are the best numbers I have found. According to the website of the Center for Biological Diversity there are now 41,415 species on the IUCN—International Union for Conservation of Nature—Red List, and 16,306 of them are endangered species confronting extinction, the remainder being "threatened," which is like second-class status. This is up from 16,118 last year. This includes both endangered animals and endangered plants. The total number of global species is estimated at 8.7 million, give or take 1.3 million. The IUCN is the global authority on the status of the natural world and the measures needed to safeguard it. If you believe any of these numbers, then one-half of one percent of all species on the globe are endangered or threatened.

The US number of 1,200 animals and 750 plants that are endangered comes out of a universe of 21,715 total species of native plants and animals. Nearly 3,000 are animals, while over 18,000 species are plants. The ratio of endangered to the total is 8.9%.

If you really look at these numbers, it seems unlikely that the US has only 0.25% of all the world's species but 6.1% of its land mass and 5% of its endangered species. This is not a problem of data for the US alone.

Stepping back, however, there is little doubt that challenges to many species are significant, even with sketchy data. And that remedies are available and attractive. More on this in a moment.

GLOBAL CRISIS #3: Nuclear war, general war, civil war, terrorism. Yes, all bad things and ones to be avoided if possible. However, preventing war etc. is not really a field where modest charitable support makes much difference. History is pretty clear on that.

GLOBAL CRISIS #4: Nuclear waste. We supported for a time a UCSD professor who had figured out how to monitor the potential leakage of spent fuel from the canisters in which it was being buried at the San Onofre nuclear plant, as a part of its overall decommissioning, probably the most important and dangerous part. See Chapter 9. Ultimately, we were unable to get the attention of the appropriate regulatory bodies and utility officials, and eventually gave up. See Chapter 9. Not really a good focus for charitable activity, as it required too many positive decisions by too many levels of government, and we were only pushing a solution to a relatively unlikely problem. Generally, a job for government and industry, although technically very interesting.

GLOBAL CRISIS #5: Disease, epidemics, pandemics. Again, bad things. We seem to have just gone through one and were clueless about where it came from and how to eliminate it. Or how to prevent similar problems in the future. But this is the function of government, not small charitable efforts.

GLOBAL CRISIS #6: Water scarcity or shortage. This is misleading as a "problem." The planet is 97% or so made of water. The vast majority of that is oceanic and therefore modestly salty (3.5%), but effective techniques exist to desalinate either ocean water or brineous aquifers on land at modest cost. We don't have a water "crisis" or shortage, we are just spoiled at having been given lakes and rivers and rainfall and aquifers for free. The fact that now the number of humans is such that some of the free water is under challenge only means that we have a "shortage" not of water, but of really cheap water. That is not a problem for charitable action to resolve. The technology, both the organizational approach and the hardware for purification and distribution exists to "solve" this and is getting steadily cheaper. This is not fake news, but it is a fake crisis.

GLOBAL CRISIS #7: Famine, hunger. Same problem. We know how to grow food, more than enough to feed the planet. We know how to process and preserve and distribute it. The problems are not amount of food but failings of infrastructure, economic policy, and government. These are not easily corrected by charitable action.

GLOBAL CRISIS #8: Air quality. If the last fifty years of air quality research, development, and application have proven anything, it is that we know how to fix this, and at moderate cost. But again, not through charitable action. See electric cars above. Political will seems to be the problem.

GLOBAL CRISIS #9: Immigrants, refugees, asylum seekers. These are terrible problems and made larger than necessary by political extremists including some who have occupied the White House. We do know how to take people into our country and have been doing it successfully and to our ultimate national benefit for a long time. But it has never been an easy charity problem because of its many political ramifications. Also see below for a discussion of the effectiveness of building half a wall.

GLOBAL CRISIS #10: Cultural loss. The destruction in March of 2001 of the Buddhas of Bamiyan in Afghanistan by Al Qaeda extremists was a terrible thing. So was the destruction of the Temple of Bel at Palmyra in Syria by similar culprits. The fire that destroyed the roof and steeple of Notre-Dame at least wasn't because of religion. Dealing with planned destruction/conspiracy is probably a government task, not a charitable one, as is the slow desecration that bad air quality creates. Putting things back together is a reasonable charitable function, but not one that interests us. It almost always requires very large amounts of money, way above our scope.

GLOBAL CRISIS #11: Overconsumption—land, water, food, fuel, metals, plastics. By one measure or other, humans are using more and more resources per capita as they become economically better off. We are also disposing of the waste products our consumption creates in unproductive ways. This is a very challenging problem that does not lend itself to addressing in modest activities that are both meaningful and additive.

GLOBAL CRISIS #12: Meteor strike(s), as in the end of the dinosaurs. A real potential problem? Hard to say. If you knew about one with certainty and had sufficient time and access to all the resources of mankind, could you avert it? Who knows? Hollywood has continuously if sporadically been interested in this plot, starting in 1958 with *The Day the Sky Exploded* and most recently *Seeking a Friend for the End of the World* (2012). Yes, this is generally acknowledged to be a bad outcome for mankind but hopefully of extremely low probability. Not a good charitable target. Oh, bad choice of words.

GLOBAL CRISIS #13: Self-inflicted wounds. We shan't go into the deteriorating quality of human health in the US, due to such characteristics as obesity, tobacco use, drug abuse, and aversion to exercise except for foolishly destructive games like football. Creating each of these unfortunate conditions requires a voluntary act of will on the part of the afflicted person.

Despite the great need, we do not see how these conditions will be easily changed and thus it is not something of charitable interest to us.

Now for a different view, focusing not on the substantive issues or causes or pieces of the world that would be better if changed in some direction or variable, but instead looking at the mechanics.

To make a gross generalization, charitable activities tend to fall into two categories, all of which to a large degree are focused on humans, with a goal of getting humans to do something they are not doing—going to church, being nicer to your neighbors, giving food to the poor—or to desist from something they are doing—stop being racist assholes, losing weight by eating less, quitting smoking. We will leave out of the discussion the really large issues of changing behavior, which tend to be resolved by violence, systemic or extra-systemic—wars, revolutions, insurrections, assassinations, or terrorism in its many forms.

There are two interesting questions from our viewpoint:

Permanence: How can the charitable activity create permanent and essentially irreversible change in the area or cause on which it is focused? We won't quibble about the issue of how long "permanent" is and how hard it is to create permanence among humans. It is interesting to note that we have created permanent change in our nuclear energy program, changing uranium 235 into plutonium 238 inside the reactors that are at the same time creating electricity to heat and cool our houses and run our machinery. The Pu-238 is a waste product of this electricity generation, with a half-life of 25,000 years. Since it is an element, there really isn't much you can do to change it from its highly poisonous self. Unfortunately, you can, with significant effort, make it into a nuclear weapon that then has to explode in order for the plutonium to be changed into something less troublesome. Considering the annoying consequence of a nuclear explosion, this could be "permanent" but is generally thought not to be desirable.

Incremental value: Can the change desired be created in effective increments of small size, which are additive without losing impact as the size of the effort increases? Many activities require some minimum size to become effective and achieve their targeted purpose. Our first power plant at AES was under construction and 90% complete when energy difficulties arose that made its eventual operation seem likely to be less valuable than originally forecast. A lot less valuable. Our coalition of banks financing the project informed us that they were now going to stop funding the construction of the plant. There was much consternation and discussion, and we finally convinced them that a 90% complete power plant was worth precisely zero, and, in fact, was worth less than that, as it would have to be torn down if not finished, which would also not be inexpensive. If they at least let us finish it, we argued, there was a non-zero chance that they would get some of their invested capital back. Confronted with zero vs. something, they relented, and we finished the plant. It eventually returned about one-seventh of its capital to its original investors. Many activities share this "all or nothing" characteristic but this risk is usually not included in any analysis supporting the project.

To summarize, we seek to invest in causes or activities or pursuits where the given change sought is "permanent" or as permanent as we can make it, given physics and legal structures. We seek to support causes where each incremental investment dollar adds the same increment of value to the cause as the one before it, and the one that comes after. This does not mean that we are blind to all "economies of scale," but we are just dubious about them. We have seen too many times in business where promised economies of scale do not materialize even though the resources are spent. Too often the result is diseconomies of scale rather than the opposite.

Nor does this mean that we seek causes or projects of unlimited size. We just want to be able to achieve value for each dollar contributed, and if we only get halfway to the anticipated size and are required to stop by some unforeseen event, we still will have achieved 50% of the benefit we anticipated.

This results, as you think it through, that we do not choose to invest in human behavioral changes other than as a consequence of the selected project. That means we don't invest in training or education, we don't invest in policy analysis, we don't invest in seminars or hackathons or team "challenges," we don't invest in lobbying of any sort, or in religious efforts or any of the many approaches that promise to change behaviors in and of themselves. We are happy to stipulate that these all may be worthwhile activities and have some benefits. But they don't meet our standard of permanence, and they don't meet our standard of incremental cost equaling incremental benefit. And they are rarely held to a high standard of measurement.

We also do not invest in activities that simply give people something—money, other material goods, services. We do not give to food banks, we do not give to medical services for the needy (Doctors Without Borders), we do not underwrite or fund research of any kind no matter how deserving it seems—with the exception of the bonuses paid to grocery store workers during Covid. We don't support people who are "rewilding" land that has been badly treated by other people. Treating symptoms, not root causes, rarely brings lasting change and may have negative side effects. You could argue that eliminating smallpox from the world by giving people inoculations was in fact a permanent change, and one for the better, and without negative consequences. But until it was complete, it was not incrementally valuable and there was always a chance that some idiot dictator could overturn the whole thing and then all the dollars invested would have resulted in not much. Besides, research is notoriously difficult and uncertain, with successful investing requiring a real skill level that we do not possess. Five years of biotech investing taught me how difficult that is.

So much for the "nots." What do we do?

Our substantive focus is on wildlife preservation, and especially on birds. There is recent and depressing evidence that the numbers of many species of birds in the US are threatened and in decline. In a groundbreaking study conducted by the Cornell Lab of Ornithology and Audubon and published in *Science* in March of 2019, the researchers tried to answer the basic question, "How many birds are there in the US?" and the subsequent question, "Is this number higher or lower than some historic baseline?" To do this they examined population data on birds in the US, using several sources of bird data: the Audubon annual Christmas Bird Count, the USGS annual North American Breeding Bird Survey (BBS), and NASA weather radar data on large flock movements. None of these sources are comprehensive, and certainly none of them is perfect, and sorting out the mismatches and the double counting was heroic indeed. When all was said and done the numbers were not encouraging. From a 1970 base year to a 2018 end year, the number of birds in the US declined by 30%, a loss of three billion birds from the ten billion counted in 1970.

This is a startling number, and not one that the researchers anticipated. Even if the research data are off by 50%, in favor of the birds, that's still a loss of 1.5 billion birds.

There are many holes in the data. The bird circles don't cover the whole US, nor do the three thousand Breeding Bird Survey counting routes established by the Fish and Wildlife Service. Audubon counts in December, BBS routes in the late spring. Sorting out species is even harder, since the second question everyone asks, correctly, is "Are some species doing better or worse than others?" The third question is, "Why?"

The "why" answers cannot be scientifically precise but causes for the decrease in numbers include the increase in feral cats and a large number of bird collisions with the glass in building windows. But the overwhelming cause seems to be loss of habitat. This is particularly true in the case of the grassland birds, where the decline is not 30% but 53%. This is especially Midwest habitat, where the continued march of agriculture intensification and general development is claiming more and more habitat.

We come to a simple question: What can be done to save bird habitat or restore bird habitat or protect the bird habitat that we still have?

For our purposes, habitat fits our model nicely. Habitat, if carefully purchased and watched over, can be made about as "permanent" as human civilization allows. It requires no construction; it does require "maintenance" in the form of keeping out poachers, hunters, developers, subsistence farmers and gatherers, and others who would use the land for purposes inconsistent with its maintenance as avian habitat. It is useful for birds just about anywhere you can establish it, although of course some habitat is better than others. Forests beat deserts, but deserts are not without some value.

It is incrementally valuable. Ten acres of habitat is generally one-tenth as good as one hundred acres of the same sort of habitat but it only costs one-tenth as much. You can start small and buy more as resources become available. With the possible exception of transaction costs, it's all wonderfully linear as to cost and benefit.

To be fair, it is necessary to note that even in wildlife preservation, there are some limits to incrementalism. If you wish to preserve tigers, for example, a ten-acre preserve won't do it; the tiger will soon have killed everything in it and then starve to death. A male tiger's range is generally thought to be, at a minimum, 200–250 square kilometers, depending on the density of prey species. Ten acres (about four-hundredths of a square kilometer) won't do.

Finally, you can do it locally in California and it has value. Or you can go to Ecuador where many US migratory birds winter, and land is cheaper, and thus one can buy more acres for the same dollars. Well, maybe not Ecuador until they stop assassinating presidential candidates and get rid of the drug gangs.

There are all sorts of interesting second-level questions about acquiring bird habitat:

1. Should you specialize in habitat for critically endangered species?
2. Which ones?
3. How much does species X need to stop being endangered? Is habitat all it needs?
4. Where is the appropriate habitat and what does it cost?
5. How do you deal with migratory species, which includes 70% of all US species (Who knew?). For full preservation, you need habitat at both ends of the migratory path.
6. How do you deal fairly with indigenous people?

One final note: the careful reader will note that there was no discussion of marine resources and their conservation. Correct, as we do not yet know anywhere near enough to evaluate ocean life conservation needs and opportunities.

We are at the beginning of deploying resources in this manner. We are attempting to do it in a sensitive, scientifically accurate manner. We shall see how and where we succeed, and no doubt we shall also have failures.

13

We Debate the Wisdom of Becoming Drug Lords

We Decide Against It

It started with a phone call from Trish Boaz, a person new to us but the head of the San Dieguito River Valley Conservancy. She had heard somewhere—never clarified—that we were grunging around making big talk about buying and preserving habitat. That was true, even if we hadn't really bought any yet. She needed help in buying some.

The conservancy was established thirty-five years ago with the laudable goal of doing, well, conservation. Whether this meant neatly mowed lawns and playgrounds and pathways and a nature center with stuffed birds in it, or whether it was going to be a wilderness area all fenced in with no humans allowed in it and only the birds and the coyotes living there, was probably not decided initially. But they were clear enough that they had to have rights to some land in order to preserve it, whatever that meant.

Early on, probably twenty years ago, the leadership of the organization came up with a pretty good idea. Since no matter what "conservation" rubric they adopted, it would be good to have a goal, and just "we're gonna get more land and keep you suckers out of it" didn't seem to motivate anyone. Some brilliant person came up with the idea of a trail running all along the river/creek/rivulet to the ocean. They would call it the Coast to Crest Trail. In theory you would be able to make an unbroken hike from the top of mount something or other to the beach at Del Mar where the San Dieguito River drains into the ocean. This was quickly adopted by the local political establishment and pursued as energy and money would permit.

It's not worth quibbling about where the river actually begins, and it's probably not on the tippy top of a mountain, but these are "How many angels can dance on the head of a pin?" sorts of arguments. The conservancy has been pursuing this goal for twenty-plus years. When you actually look at the details it is interesting. In fact, the concept remains worthwhile, but putting it together has been slow work. You can in fact hike from the coast to the crest of Mount Something, but there are lots of discontinuities and stretches where you have to leave the "trail," as in conservancy property, and walk along a street or take an Uber to the next point where the trail starts again on conservancy land.

If you look at the Appalachian Trail critically, you will find that while much of it is connected, there are places where you have to go back to civilization and then reconnect a couple of miles later. It doesn't mean that the "through hikers" are deluded or that they are fooling the public, it just means that organizing these sorts of things is not an easy task. The "AT," as insiders call it, is 2,190-plus miles long with 1% of it in disconnects. That's twenty-two miles, and if each disconnect reconnects after a mile, then it's twenty-two breaks in the trail. The Coast to Crest Trail is less impressive. Forty-nine miles of the seventy-one-mile-long planned trail are complete today, but several major gaps remain, like twenty-two miles' worth.

Why all this only slightly interesting background? Ms. Boaz, who sounded nice on the phone, was the leadership, fine. But we didn't know her or the organization; we needed some reassurance. The first thing we did was check on LinkedIn, then we went to the organization's website for business-related stuff. Here's what it said:

> *On April 1, 2013, Trish Boaz joined the Conservancy as executive director. During these last few years, Trish has led the Conservancy's efforts to raise funding for the Riverpath Del Mar, the Pauma Valley segment of the Coast to Crest Trail, and the Birdwing Open Air Classroom. She assisted in finalizing trail alignments at Lusardi Creek and Pauma Valley, and obtained grant funding for nature education projects including the San Dieguito River Watershed Explorers and Citizen Science Programs, and habitat restoration projects. The Conservancy works with other conservation partners to acquire open-space lands. A feasibility study was completed last year to determine the best location for a bridge crossing of the river at Osuna Valley.*
>
> *The Conservancy, along with the San Dieguito River Park, were awarded an Eco Ambassador Award in 2014 for its Connecting Youth with Nature Program.*
>
> *The Conservancy's presence on Facebook and other social media sites has more than tripled, and Jess Norton, the Conservancy's conservation manager, has expanded its Citizen Science and other conservation and education programs throughout the watershed.*

It also told us that Ms. Boaz had seventeen years of senior management experience with the county of San Diego, and ten years before that at a land use law firm. It seemed to us to be all good experience and good background for the combined business management and NGO work of which she was in charge.

We arranged an in-person meeting. It all went just fine, she was personable, pleasant, and knowledgeable. We checked with her only board member that we knew and got a positive, thumbs-up sort of assessment. All good.

The state of play of the transaction was that the owner, a gentleman about whom we never got much information, was a Carlsbad resident surnamed White, who had been in the property development business. He had retired and was slowly and carefully liquidating his portfolio of assets, most of which, no surprise, was in undeveloped land. He had already agreed to sell this particular piece to the conservancy. The other good news was that he was in no hurry, so he was prepared to wait while the conservancy went through the process of raising the money. In the course of working on this transaction, we learned a lot about how conservation land financing works. Here is the short description.

With very few exceptions, conservation organizations do not raise money vaguely, put it in the bank, and then wait to see if a desirable piece of land comes along that they can buy. They don't do this for two reasons: First, it's inefficient and unattractive to be in the land buying and preserving business while sitting on a big pile of money rather than on a big pile of land. If you have ever run an investment fund, you will understand the problem. A finance guy from J.P. Morgan once explained it to me this way: The first thing you need to do to start a fund is to raise some money. This is harder than it looks. I don't care who you are, it is always harder than it looks, especially because what you're selling to potential investors is an idea, e.g., "I plan to invest in underperforming assets that our team will turn into overperforming assets and thus make you investors (umm, and us) heaps of money from our clever investments."

The unspoken part of this pitch is that you, the guy starting the fund, are fundamentally smarter and have access, legally one hopes, to information that will let you identify said assets and buy them cheaply. You will be able to do this better than the literally thousands of other very smart and hard-working women and men who also went to Stanford and Harvard Business School. And who have essentially the same access (legally) to information about these assets that you have your eye on.

This raising-money process is tedious, painful, slow, difficult, and always takes more effort and time than you estimate. How many money managers who invest some of their funds in start-up funds would you like to talk to, repeating the same PowerPoint presentation that you have now made several hundred times? Answering the same questions that potential investors have asked several hundred times? I did this a lot at AES, except we had actual projects to finance, with actual contracts to sell electricity to credit-worthy utilities, and it was still grindingly difficult.

Then, just when you finally, finally get all the money collared and all the documents negotiated and agreed to, and all the investors have signed and released their money (at least the initial drawdown) out of escrow and into your fund's bank account and you have finally gone home at one in the morning (Why do closings always take place late at night? Because the lawyers are billing by the hour?) and you have finally been able to sleep till eight and be in the office by nine instead of having a seven o'clock breakfast with yet another potential investor and at 9:15 a.m. one of your new investors calls and says, "Well? Well?" This means now that you have the money, where are those killer investments that you have been promising everyone for the eighteen months it has taken you to raise the money?

Responding that you've had the money since three in the morning and it is now only six hours and fifteen minutes later doesn't really work. Anyway, you see the picture. I am fully confident that it works the same way in the land of charitable activity.

Second, it is way easier to raise money, although never "easy" easy, if you have an asset or a project that needs the money and which you can buy just as soon as you have raised the money. I don't suppose I have to go on and on about that.

Here is the third surprise. There are several California and federal programs that will make grants to NGOs to fund purchases of attractive land that will then be dedicated and protected as wildlife habitat. I had no idea there was such a thing, and, of course, this means that the governments, state and federal, are a major source of habitat funding. But, and there are always "buts," the federal and state entities have "programs," and the programs have application processes and evaluation criteria and time deadlines and negotiating periods and criteria for giving out their money. Nothin' is easy. These programs are not quick, you don't just go to DC or Sacramento and talk to some people and come back with the money. Usually this process, recipients have told me, takes up to three years.

Let us also note that people who have something to sell generally don't like sitting around waiting for three years to see if the NGO buyer can actually come up with the money from the government. What if another unfortunate candidate with Donald Trump-like proclivities is elected and cancels the program? What if a million other things happen that screw up the deal? People selling things wish to sell them, receive the money, and go on about their business, thank you very much.

But Trish and her team have already done this. The price agreed for the property is $1.8 million. The feds and the state have already committed to fund $1.7 million of this, so Trish only needs about 5% more money, roughly $100,000, and she can close the deal, take the title to the White property, and add another important piece to the Coast to Crest Trail. As we think about it, it looks a lot like a classic financing, made up of a lot of debt and as little equity as you can get away with. But even better because you don't have to pay the government back.

We were intrigued, so after some research during which we learned all this, we called her and said that we would like to proceed. What we needed first were the project documents. She seemed mildly puzzled. "What documents are you talking about?" she asked.

"Anything that the two funders have given you. Isn't there a loan agreement or a grant agreement or something of the sort that documents the transaction?"

There was a bit of a pause, and she uttered the question that we have heard over and over in an honestly puzzled tone: "Why would you want to see that?"

Very few people in the philanthropic community seem to have heard of the term "due diligence." When we say those magic words, we frequently get puzzled stares. Ah, well.

There was a pause, and we could almost see the internal wheels grinding. She finally probably noticed that these were public documents anyway so why not? She promised to send them to us. Both documents, one from each granting agency, arrived in a couple of days by email.

We printed them out and read them, and they seemed reasonable. No foolish terms, no outlandish demands or difficult remedies, nothing that should make the transaction so unpleasant and risky as to be undoable. There should not have been any such terms, but it is surprising what you will see in documents. For a while, we were members of a local, very mid-scale country club. It has memberships for golf players, which we are not, and it also has twelve tennis courts, a very nice fitness center, and a good outdoor pool. There were two levels of membership, one for golf and everything else, and one for everything but golf. There was also a bar and a nice dining room, and several meeting/entertainment rooms you could rent if you wanted to have your own party. They would provide catering.

As we got more integrated into the community and used the club more, we began to think about using their facility, one of the party rooms, for a small party of our own, maybe a Christmas party. Not that we knew enough people yet, but we were optimistic. We asked about it, and were told that that would be fine, there was a room available. They sent us the catering menu and the drinks menu and all the associated costs. Again, all reasonable, plus the club had lots of parking in its lot. We discussed it and decided this would do nicely. We asked them to send us the appropriate contract document or term sheet and specific pricing or whatever we needed to execute to secure the room and go ahead and invite people.

We got it, and of course we read it. We are the kind of people who read the documents. As we have probably mentioned before. It was all pretty standard, except for the indemnification. The contract required that we each personally indemnify the club and its employees for any accident or claim made by anyone harmed during our function. There was no limit on the indemnification amount. There was no exception for gross negligence or willful misconduct not by our guests, but by the club's own employees. If one of our guests got drunk and when leaving the club drove into and knocked down the club's sign, we understood that we would probably have to handle that. Ditto if one of our guests got drunk and threw a deck chair into the pool; that would be on us. But if one of the club's help serving our party was careless and somehow managed to burn down the whole club, we were responsible? With no limit on the damages? This was silliness; no facility ever makes such a demand in its documents, and no person in their right mind ever agrees to such a term. No sense putting your entire net worth at risk just so you can have a Christmas party for fifteen people you don't yet know all that well.

We met with the club's management and pointed out the problem. He seemed unperturbed. "This is our standard contract," he explained unhelpfully. "No one ever objects to it," he added unbelievably. He didn't offer to modify it to something reasonable. He didn't offer to "check with company management." So that was that, and we held the party at home. Thank goodness no one threw a deck chair into the swimming pool, which was aided by the fact that we don't have a swimming pool.

That documents hurdle having been passed with Trish, we asked when we could go see the property. More evidence of slight befuddlement. "Do you really want to?" we were asked, as if Mrs. Boaz couldn't believe such a request. Note that we were not discussing a visit to the Arctic tundra in the dead of winter to seek out the elusive snowy owl. The White property was right next to Lake Hodges, a popular fishing and hiking area and public park, a mere fifteen miles and thirty-one minutes away from Encinitas along a well-traveled highway called the Del Dios Highway. Which according to Google means the "highway of God" although while it's a nice enough road, the "of God" part is a bit of an overreach.

"Well, okay," she agreed reluctantly, "I have to set something up." She got back to us several days later with a proposal to meet at a small dwelling just on the north side of the property. We would park there and walk next door to the property. The advantage of this was that the home had a number and a mailbox on the Del Dios Highway so you could actually find it. The White property was bordered on the east by this highway, but there was no mailbox or gate or any such identifier.

Several days later, on a lovely San Diego day—moderately warm, cloudless, sunny—we drove out to the designated house at the appointed time and waited for Trish to show up. She did a few minutes later, bringing her older teenage daughter with her for reasons never explained. But since the daughter just sat in the car the whole time, it didn't matter. Parenting seems to be different now than when I was being parented.

The property was laid out in a long rectangle, thin on the north-south dimension and longer going east-west. Across from the eastern boundary (the road) were a couple of houses and then the lake. The property sloped uphill from the road and ended at the top of a large north-south ridge. It also had within its boundary a smaller but distinctive and rugged east-west ridge that divided the property roughly into two even thinner east-west pieces.

We started on the northern half, next to where we were parked. There really weren't any trails, so we picked our way through the chapparal vegetation, avoiding the junipers and hopefully the snakes, if any. It was pretty uneven and rough going. It was also dry and rocky but not impassable. We did see the occasional bird, we crossed a small dry creek bed, and that was about it. Trish asked halfheartedly if we really needed to see the other side, and if so, recommended that we not scramble up through the dense brush and climb over the ridge, but go back to the cars and drive back a little way south on the highway and go in from there. We assented.

The southern half of the property was pretty much like the northern half—dense brush and scrub vegetation, the occasional dry and short tree. But in this case, there was a trail leading into the property. We began walking on the trail as it wound west and modestly upward. The turns and increasing elevation blocked the view forward.

At about a hundred meters in, we made a small turn and there alongside the trail was a messy sleeping bag off to the side and some empty food tins—chili mac and other delights. "Oh," said Trish, "this must be a homeless person hanging out here, we'll get this cleaned up." Seemed an odd venue if one were homeless—where did you get water? But okay.

We kept going on the twisty trail. At about nine hundred meters in, the trail turned steeply to the right. Once we got around the bend, we saw a stretch of the ridge running ahead of us to the right. We also saw that someone had dug three large platforms or shallow caves into the ridge, the middle one offsetting the top and bottom one, and each of them about eight feet above the one below it. Each level had several large, industrial, black plastic barrels placed on the floor of the platform. Connecting the three levels and barrels were two long plastic troughs. Some liquid could clearly be moved from the top to the middle to the bottom platform. At the edge of the bottom platform was a pretty large 5 kW generator, and some car batteries not hooked up to anything. In a pile to the right of the generator were a junky assortment of many empty one-gallon cans of some industrial chemical. But no one was there.

We stood there, stunned. "What the hell is this?" I muttered.

"Thank God nobody is here," L responded, "let's get out of here."

"Trish," I said, "we need to get out of here before whoever was working this site comes back."

"Oh, wait, take my picture," she said, for reasons we could not understand. We really wanted to leave, but before we left, Trish insisted that we take a picture of her standing in front of what looked like drug manufacturing paraphernalia. I wondered at this, and wanted to ask her if it was to help the Mexican narcos track her down. But I bit my tongue as I was really mostly interested in getting the hell out of Dodge.

We then quickly hustled back down the trail to the car and the highway. I could not quite figure out what we were going to do if we met someone coming up, but luckily no individuals appeared. Whew.

Slightly out of breath at the bottom, L remarked, "I've seen *Breaking Bad*. I think that was a meth lab."

Trish was disbelieving. "We'll get some volunteers out here to clean this up," she said cheerfully.

We had professional environmental work in our background. "Trish, you can't just pick up the cans, put them in black plastic bags, and call it a day. You need to have at least some environmental people come out here and see if there has been any soil contamination. This site drains right into Lake Hodges."

I was still plenty nervous and suggested that we get in the cars and get the f*** on the road. We also asked that Trish call the county sheriff to come and evaluate the site. She didn't seem convinced.

That afternoon I went on the internet and started looking around for "meth labs." Seeing *Breaking Bad* really wasn't enough to make me a full-fledged drug lab detector. After not much searching I found a U.S. Forest Service site with lots of pictures and a heading that read something like: "Warning—Drug Manufacturing Sites" and had lots of pictures. All the pictures had hardware and plastic containers and chemical cans similar to what we had just seen that morning. Below all the pictures was this legend: "These sites are dangerous. Do not touch anything and leave immediately. Call us with the location and a description of what you have seen as soon as you can. Repeat: Do not stay in the vicinity of sites that look like this, these are drug manufacturing sites run by criminal enterprises."

I sent the Forest Service brochure to Trish. The next day she got back to me with a message that said they believed that this site was being used to raise native plants.

I replied, as patiently as I could, "Trish, this is not a nursery. I have been to a nursery. This is a drug site."

A couple days later we told her that we were no longer interested in a donation to help buy the White property. About a month later we heard through the conservation grapevine that the conservancy had raised the money elsewhere and completed the transaction. Did they ever do an environmental assessment to determine if there was a problem? To this day I do not know.

The part of this story that is especially disturbing, setting aside its adventure value, is this: Had anyone in the organization done any advance work on the site before agreeing to take us out there? And now, which answer do you like: (1) No, this was the first time that anyone from the conservancy had shown the site to anyone. And the surprising discovery was to be explained how?

(2) Yes, they had done the advance work, visited the site ahead of time, but had not seen the south side of the property, or had seen it but had not been bothered.

In my AES career I must have built close to one hundred power plants, all over the world, some in dangerous and undesirable places. I never built a plant where I had not personally visited the site ahead of time. You just don't. For obvious reasons.

I do have to say that as a result of this adventure I began to think that if I made more site visits to evaluate potential bird habitat, I might consider going armed.

14

The Andean Condor (National Bird of Ecuador) Raises Its Ugly Head

There's a First Time for Everything, Even Ecuador and Matt Clark

For goodness' sake, the Andean condor is even bigger than our good old American, almost extinct but not quite, condor, and probably just as ugly. Bird people, and countries, might need some marketing guidance in choosing signature birds.

When about five years ago we started getting serious about habitat, we started chasing down all the national nonprofits with "bird" or "birding" in their names. This naturally included Audubon since everyone knows that John James Audubon was the country's first and premier bird enthusiast. Also shooter. You didn't think he painted all those pictures out in nature, did you?

We eventually ran into an organization called Nature and Culture International, led by an executive named Matt Clark. Even more peculiar is that their headquarters is right down the road from us in Del Mar.

He seemed legitimate: he had a very nice website; he had E. O. Wilson, the famous insect scientist, on his board; and Jane Goodall, the famous chimpanzee enthusiast as well. Well, Wilson was dead, so he was of necessity moved to emeritus status. We read some of the PR stuff in their website, then called them up and invited Matt to meet us for coffee in Del Mar for a habitat discussion. We presume he checked with someone or looked us up on LinkedIn, as he agreed. Or maybe his office was out of coffee that day. One never knows.

It turns out that they raise money and make habitat investments, almost exclusively for bird habitat and almost exclusively in Central and South America. At this point we had not met anyone else doing this, so we were intrigued. He explained the key drivers to this particular bird preservation strategy:

1. 70% of all American birds migrate every year.
2. If you're an American bird, and your DNA says migrate, you're highly likely to go to South America. Africa is too far, and China/Indonesia/Australia is even farther.
3. If you just preserve the North American part of a bird's range, then when it takes off for Latin America and finds that its traditional nesting/fledging forest has in the past six months been cut down, that's a problem. You need to preserve both ends of the dumbbell.
4. Preservable land in South America is about a hundred times an acre cheaper than outside of Las Vegas.

So that's where Matt and his team focused their efforts.

I have done overseas projects before, and they come with their own special concerns. The list is long and anyone who reads the newspaper can come up with 90% of the entries: corruption, terrorism, shaky rule of law in general, expropriation, poaching, lack of law enforcement, unclear enforcement of contracts, lack of skilled personnel, and on and on. I have probably left out ten or fifteen other problems, starting with language difficulties.

But we discussed all this and there were good if not great answers, especially for, yes, Ecuador. In fact, Matt was at that moment working on a very nice habitat project called Nangaritza, for which they had agreements to buy and conserve. It was two side-by-side parcels in the southeast corner of the country. It was an area where a lot of rogue gold mining was going on, which was destroying the value of the land in a big way. There was a good local partner who could handle the local parts of the preservation, and the whole thing—all two hundred-plus acres—was priced at $100K. A sale would allow Matt and company to take over the land, put up fences, hire rangers, and preserve an area that was, as they always seem to be, critical for saving the endangered blue-throated hillstar. A bird found nowhere else in the world, with an unfortunate tendency for hanging around gold mines—no, I made that up.

We were hooked. We had just recovered from our unsatisfactory effort with the San Dieguito people and we were eager to do something to show that we were serious.

We asked Matt to send us the documents so we could at least do a little due diligence. He did, we read them (at least the ones in English), and it all seemed fine if you ignored the fact that we had never seen the sites, never been to Ecuador, never done a land deal for habitat anywhere in the world, and never worked with Matt before. Picky, picky, picky. We didn't know anyone on his board of directors, either. This may sound in retrospect like a recipe for disaster, or at least for a disappointing relationship. It probably is, and we do not recommend it. But he was charming, and we weren't having much local luck what with the meth people and all. Matt's agent, named Castro (I wasn't sure if this was a good sign or a bad sign, but he probably wasn't Cuban), was on the case. We could not go visit the site due to Covid restrictions, but what the heck. After embarrassingly little due diligence, we sent him $95K and change for the two parcels.

Soon after this he notified us that his agent in Ecuador had closed the purchase of one of the parcels and he had used half of our funds for this, as previously agreed. He wanted to wait on any press release until the entire set of parcels had been purchased, but he had run our press release language past his board of directors, and it was approved. So that was nice, especially given our subsequent disagreement with the Cornell Lab of Ornithology discussed in the coming chapters. The careful observer, however, will note that this left half of our funding sitting in Del Mar, waiting for the second parcel to close and the funding to be needed.

We had agreed that we wouldn't announce anything until the whole piece of land was sequestered, so we didn't. And we waited. And waited. We received occasional messages from Matt that Mr. Castro was pushing things, but that this was Ecuador and things did not always move expeditiously. Okay, we get that, we've done business all over the world, and besides, things don't always move quickly in the United States. Try getting an air quality permit for a coal plant in Hawaii, for example. I have and it didn't.

Let's cut to the chase. In November, ten months in, we met with Matt and said, in brief, that if there was no movement on the second parcel by the end of the year, we would like for him to send us back what remained of our money. Note that he had no obligation to do this, at least no binding legal obligation. We had signed a brief document when we made the initial donation, but it said nothing about this alternative, nor did that possibility occur to us at the time. Rookie mistake.

By late December, there was still no movement on parcel #2, so we called Matt and asked him to send back the remaining funds. We did make it clear that we were still very interested in him, his organization, and the parcel not yet purchased, and whenever the deal got done, we were ready to fund. To his credit, Matt promptly sent us a check. This story could have ended differently, and it was an interesting and cheap lesson. I should have learned this from all my financings in the energy business, but somehow I did not. We know it now. Your leverage ends, no matter what the docs say, when you fund the project. This is especially true in the philanthropic arena where agreements are much less carefully drafted and administered.

We breathed a collective sigh of relief and said to ourselves, okay, let's not do that again. This can be #2 on our Golden Rules of Philanthropy: never give anyone the money ahead of time; #1 of course is always visit the site. Which the careful reader will note that we hadn't done in this case either. Live and learn, usually expensively, fortunately not this time.

15

This Philanthropy Stuff Ain't So Easy

Ecuador Again, but This Time With ABC

If you decide that you are now a big-time philanthropist and your focus is on conserving bird habitat, then what do you do? If you answered, "Call the Nature Conservancy," go directly to jail, do not pass go, do not collect two hundred dollars.

It's an interesting story. The organization was originally set up about fifty years ago to do good by purchasing threatened pieces of real estate that had environmental value, which generally meant value for preserving wildlife. For a long time, until around 2002, the organization did just that. It raised money from donors who were in favor of its goals, it assembled a professional staff to make sure it could determine comparative values of one piece of land vs. another, and it did quite a lot of good work.

I got to know something about them because my old boss from many years ago, when I was working at the Office of Management and Budget, was a great guy named John Sawhill who became their CEO when he left the government. I was at that time setting up a charitable remainder trust, a tax-delaying strategy that required that you put as the beneficiary of your trust a legitimate 501(c)(3) organization. More on this later.

In 1995 I did all that was required and contributed a slug of AES stock at its then high value.

But life is more uncertain than one would like, and five years later John Sawhill unexpectedly died at sixty-three. The organization did a search for a new president and came up with a Goldman Sachs partner named Mark Tercek. He was relatively young and interested in a career change and moving to Washington where the organization was headquartered. He also turned out to be interested in changing the business focus. Instead of the boring, old, and very successful process of preserving threatened pieces of real estate, he decided that they should focus on "policy." It was DC, the land of policy, and you could convince yourself that making environmental laws and regulations was a much more productive use of time and money than buying real estate. Also, more sexy and you got way better press coverage.

He shook up the organization and the board and ran around doing policy for the next twenty years. I cannot name a single piece of law that his efforts were responsible for getting passed, but then I stopped doing "policy" when I left the government.

Despite my previous commitment to them, the Nature Conservancy was no longer in the habitat business, Ecuador didn't work very well, and forget the San Dieguito River Valley Conservancy. Back to basics. How do you find habitat you can purchase and conserve? Are there specialist real estate agents who do habitat for a living, and if so, who are they? The answer to that is "not exactly." It turns out that there are several NGOs in addition to our list above who have focused in on the issue of avian habitat preservation.

At about the same time we were contacted by a smart, young ornithologist named Joel Merriman. He turned out to be the son-in-law of Ken and Dottie Woodcock, old AES colleagues of long standing. Ken had been our head marketing guy at AES and had brought in a number of projects that had seemed unlikely to the rest of us smart executives. The best example was late in one year when Ken came back from one of his marketing trips, in this case to Hawaii.

At this point in our existence, we were a company that did big, coal-fired power plants, and nothing else. We had five under our belts and so felt pretty good about our skills and our approach to the electricity industry. Ken galloped into the CEO's office where we were having some sort of meeting and said with great excitement, "There's a bid at HECO [Hawaiian Electric, the utility serving the island of Oahu]. Responses are due soon, they want a gas plant downtown, but I want to bid a coal plant on the other side of the island in an industrial park, and I think we can win!"

We all looked at him with disbelief. My dad was at that point living in Oahu and working for the speaker of the legislature, so I had been there a bunch of times, and figured I knew a bit about it.

"Ken, are you nuts? Nobody burns coal in Hawaii. Never have, never will. Besides, where will you get the coal? Surely not on the islands."

"No problem, we can get it from Indonesia."

I asked with as much restraint as I could, "Have you looked at a map of the Pacific Ocean lately? Indonesia is not close."

"Yeah, but the state has just built a big harbor at Barber's Point, near the industrial park, and they need customers. It's perfect for a coal unlading port."

Much similar discussion proceeded, with us smart executives trying to convince Ken that this was a bad idea. But he was inconvincible. Finally, Roger Sant, the chairman, said, "Okay, Ken, you can bid on this, but you can't use any AES resources. You can get your wife to type up the bid response, and you can go to Kinko's to make the copies and charge it on your own credit card, but you can't tie up anybody here on this silly exercise."

Ken left delighted. Good marketing guys are only good marketing guys if they have incredibly thick skins and an optimistic nature that is never daunted. It helps if they win one every so often, too.

In six weeks, Ken came dancing back into the office. "Guess who's going to Hawaii?" he trumpeted in his classically Ivy League, somewhat nasally voice. He didn't wait for us to guess. "We are! We won the bid, and we are going to build the first coal plant in Hawaii!"

Of course, there were those little details like negotiating the power purchase agreement that we would use once the plant was built so we could sell all the electricity to HECO at a lovely, guaranteed price. We had to develop and submit the air quality permits, and then nurse them through the island bureaucracy. Which, it's fair to say, had basically zero experience with the control technology and the emissions of a big, solid, fuel power plant.

This is a longer than necessary diversion from the main point, which is that Ken was a jewel and managed to pull off business deals that the rest of us never could have imagined doing. He also had two lovely daughters, one of whom ended up married to the guy who called me, Joel Merriman. I had sent a Christmas letter to Ken and Dottie, in which I had mentioned our recent fascination with birds and preserving bird habitat. They in turn shared this with Joel who was visiting them for Christmas with his wife, their daughter. Families do that sort of thing I have been told. Joel was working for a company called the American Bird Conservancy.

If you go to their website as I did, here's some of what you'll find:

> For more than 25 years, American Bird Conservancy [ABC] has been standing up for birds and their habitats throughout the Americas. We're proud of our bird conservation results. But **the need is great**. Many birds are experiencing major population declines and need our help more than ever.
>
> Our strategic approach to conservation drives all that we do, and the results are measurable: We've made significant strides to prevent the extinction of the most endangered birds, conserve important bird habitat, reduce top threats to birds, and build an Americas-wide community of bird conservationists.

It sounded pretty good to me, and so I spent time on the phone with Joel, and then with Mike Parr, Joel's boss and the head of ABC. The more we discussed what they wanted to do, and had been successful doing, the more it seemed like what we had been trying to find. A major portion of their work was in South America, again for the reasons mentioned earlier—more bird for the buck.

When I asked about specific projects on which they were working, Mike asked me how I felt about Ecuador. Despite that fact that I had never been there, we had already crossed that bridge with the Nature and Culture

International people (see Chapter 14). Mike then told me about their current most important project, a 57,000 square kilometer preserve that they were seeking to establish with their local partners, a firm with the unlikely name of Jocotoco.

"Aha" I said, "so they realized that Coco Loco was already taken?"

After a while I stopped being snarky and looked up the organization. Here is how they describe themselves:

> **The Jocotoco Foundation** is an Ecuadorian conservation organization that was founded in 1998 to protect the newly discovered *Jocotoco Antpitta*—a highly range-restricted bird species with fewer than 1,500 individuals. Since then, Jocotoco has established a network of 16 conservation reserves totaling over 23,000 ha (57,000 acres) protecting some of the world's most endangered species by conserving their remaining natural habitats. An emphasis is placed on species and habitats not already protected by Ecuador's extensive National Park Systems (20.3% of terrestrial and 12.07% of Marine territory). Jocotoco's actions work to compliment the efforts by the Ecuadorian Government to project Ecuador's globally significant biodiversity.

The project, generally called "Choco," Mike explained patiently, is the name of an area of northwest Ecuador that's mostly rainforest, although there is also lovely mountainous terrain since the Andes are to the east, and you get all the different habitat regimes that changing altitude gives you. It could not be better for preserving various different species since many birds are found only at certain altitude levels. I surmised that I would remain confused between Jocotoco and Choco for a while longer.

I confessed my ignorance on this matter, which was large.

Mike further explained that they usually didn't do projects this large. They had worked with Jocotoco as a local partner on several other projects, and this organization now had eleven habitat preserves that it had established. But this new one would be kind of a crowning glory.

Then the hard part: the seller was a timber company called Botrosa that had decided that the timber business was no longer what they wanted to be in, given the decade-long depression in lumber prices. They were liquidating some assets while they decided what else they wanted to do. Perhaps they already knew; that was never part of the story that was told to me. The total cost of this acquisition was to be $15 million. Of that, the Jocotoco organization, no slouches they, had already secured a commitment from the Rainforest Trust for $8 million and had a grant proposal in to some other organization for several more million that they were assured would be approved. But they were still short several million.

This seemed to us like the kind of deal that made sense, and where we could be the last money in, the money that was needed to get to funding and purchasing the acreage. After not very much thought, we committed to put in a million dollars at closing. But this "commitment" was not very solid as we made it clear that we needed to see and review all the documents and, more importantly, we needed to visit the property and meet with the Jocotoco people to get familiar with their organization, their abilities, and their working style.

We worried that ABC would not find this acceptable, or that they would want some sort of binding agreement. Or maybe they would want us to fund into an escrow account. Or provide audited financial statements. Or any one of a number of other financial requirements that we would expect to see if we were the deal proponent. After a fair amount of internal hand-wringing, and since there were only two of us it wasn't that many hands to wring, we finally said, "Screw these people. We are not making any commitment that is legally binding, and we are through with doing things that encumber money for projects that may or may not ever turn into real acquisitions. If our nonbinding, email-quality commitment isn't good enough, then they can go find someone else with a million dollars to invest into a bunch of bird-friendly forests in a country they have never visited."

The money to purchase these 53,000 acres of land was mostly raised. "Raised" as in funds or organizations or donors like me had committed to fund the acquisition when it got to the point of closing. What you do not do, although it took me a while to learn this, is you don't give the money to the NGO until all the legal work is done, all the due diligence is complete, all the permits have been received, all the sales and title transfer documents have been drafted and agreed to, everyone is satisfied that this is what they expected and agreed to at the beginning of the process. Whatever changes have been made, and there are always changes along the way, are still consistent with the original idea of preserving a certain slice of land with a lot of birds on it at least part of the year.

The more Mike and his staff shared information and documents with us, the more comfortable we got with the proposed transaction. It finally occurred to me that what we were doing here was a "project." A stand-alone deal, which after a lot of effort converted a strand of tropical forest ready to be cut down into a piece of bird habitat that would be purchased and protected essentially forever. Never cut down, never turned into farmland or into gold mines or into meth labs or into condos for rich vacationers or any of the myriad other uses that would negatively impact the things that made it valuable for birds. Like all projects, it had its own risks and uncertainties along the development process.

As I thought about this, I looked back at my AES and energy experience, where all we did were projects. Okay, that's an exaggeration; after we completed the project, we actually had to operate it and make electricity, but that part was way easier than getting a project through the difficult and complicated process of being ready for construction, and then being constructed. It was arguably where much of the value was created. Of all the projects we started, no more than half ever got to the finish line, closed their financing, and got built. Project development is a specific set of skills, but the process is pretty much the same, power plants or bird sanctuaries. "Well shoot," I thought to myself, "I can do projects. I can't necessarily research bird DNA or put a cast on an injured bird or catch birds in mist nets and tag them with microchips and small batteries so their migration paths can be followed, but I can do a project."

After more work and more conversations and more reading of documents, we got comfortable with making a funding commitment. To be honest, what we said was a bit conditional. We agreed to fund a million dollars of the purchase price of the Choco project at closing, but there were a bunch of conditions precedent that we needed. First and most important, we needed all the money to be in hand from all the other funders. To do this perfectly would require setting up an escrow account into which we would all fund. The escrow agent would have very clear instructions to release the funds to the property owner or owners from whom we were buying the property if and only if all the funds were in hand. All the other conditions (permits, documents, etc.) would have to be satisfactory to all the funders. When and after those conditions had been met, we were then to close and fund. These requirements were not unique, they were what one would expect in any multimillion-dollar real estate transaction.

We had another condition—we had to go to Ecuador and meet the sponsor and see the property. I wasn't completely clear how I would "see" 53,000 acres, but I figured I would work that out later. Maybe rent a helicopter? Ride around in an ATV? We would have to do something, but I was also sure that I wasn't the first person ever to decide to do a site visit before buying a large piece of land. We signed on to a nonbinding, unenforceable, not litigable piece of paper that said what I have just written down. We didn't have to submit our bank statement or a private financial statement to prove that we had the money. This might have been due to the AES connection, which was what had gotten us into this deal in the first place. Again, in any transaction like this one, there is always a certain amount of trust necessary between the parties, or nothing ever gets done. You verify as much as you can, you only do business with recognized parties with track records and websites and reassuring executives, and then you close your eyes and jump.

Along the way, you can expect surprises. Guaranteed. You have agreements to cover all the surprises you can think of, but there are an infinite possible number of surprises, and we're only talking about the bad surprises here, and you cannot write an infinitely long letter of intent with remedies for each kind of bad behavior, although your lawyer would be happy to try.

As things went merrily along, we got a surprise. Of course. As noted above, the seller, a lumber company named Botrosa, had decided to get out of the lumber business, sell off some assets to do-gooders like Choco backed by funders like us, and go off on his merry way into another line of work, maybe plastics; it was never especially clear. When the deal was put together and priced, the value of the forest was essentially tied to the price of lumber.

I have never been a forester or dabbled in lumber except at the Home Depot. I don't even like home improvement projects unless someone else is doing them. Besides, I am not any good at them, although if called on I can usually change a burned-out light bulb. Under duress, I can paint a bedroom wall, but not well and not without substantial complaining. I didn't know beans about the timber/lumber business. However, like all areas of commerce, as you get into it, the detail and the complexity expand as you sink deeper into the details.

It turns out that lumber is a commodity like soybeans or natural gas or cotton. It is measured in units called board feet, defined as a theoretical piece of wood twelve inches by twelve inches by one inch. How you look at a tree and derive this number isn't clear but never mind. It is priced in units of 1,000 board feet. Just like 1,000 Btus of gas or barrels of oil or bushels of soybeans. I don't know about cotton. When the initial deal was made, the price of lumber was low and had been low for some years. Let us acknowledge that "low" and "high" are to some extent in the eyes of the transactor.

In fact, if you go to the Chicago Board of Trade there is a nifty graph of the twenty-five-year history of lumber prices. It looks like this:

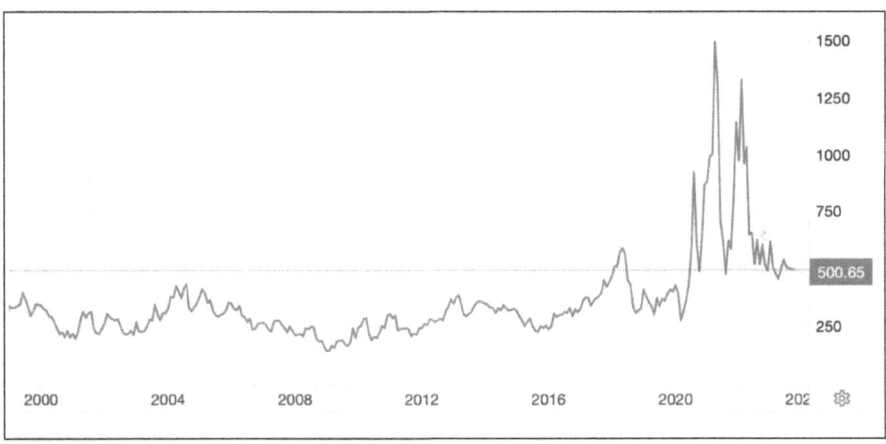

The price noted above was in the $300 to $400 range. And no one expected it to rise, since it had been hanging around $300 plus or minus since the year 2000 and maybe before but I didn't look that far. But then suddenly it did. It got to $1,500 about a year after the initial agreement was signed. The seller finally said, "Uh, we never expected lumber to get this valuable, so we're not so sure that we want to sell all this forest to you Jocotoco guys." Probably not in those exact words since he would have said it in Spanish to begin with. The seller didn't offer to go ahead with the transaction if we doubled the price. He probably figured that we wouldn't or couldn't or both, and he was right.

The Jocotoco guys scrambled. This is what you do when your deal falls apart unless you are the party blowing things up. It is not unheard of for deals to fall apart. In fact, it might even be the norm. If you're lucky, they fall apart early and cannot be salvaged. While you have spent some time and money, you haven't spent a lot and told your board and your friends how wonderful this is going to be to own the biggest power plant in Bazulgorsk. But it is still troublesome for one of the major players to close up his notebook or his computer, stand up dramatically from the conference table, look around the room and declare, "This deal is dead."

The first time I heard these dire words was on our initial project, Deepwater, a 180 Mw cogeneration plant sitting on a site on the Houston Ship Channel. It was to be built by Bechtel, burn petroleum coke that we would get from the Arco refinery next door, and sell the refinery process steam and electricity to Houston Lighting and Power. At $275 million dollars, it was complicated, but there has never been a deal in history that cost more than $50 million whose proponents won't be happy to tell you that it was complicated. Maybe we're programmed by evolution to deal successfully with complexity.

Anyway, the financing structure involved a lease with GE Credit, a construction loan from J.P. Morgan and seven other banks, and a tax-exempt bond to finance the pollution-control portion of the plant. The transaction had to be closed and the bonds sold by midnight of that year, or the legislation expired authorizing such bonds, and on and on. Complexity, coupled with the fact that we at AES were dead out of money and needed the $3 million fee we would earn at closing or we would not be able to make payroll the coming January. None of the participants, including us, had ever done a nonrecourse financing of this size on a power plant. Complexity, tension, and first-of-a-kind deal. Sure, bring it on.

About seven days before closing, as we were all sitting in a very large conference room at J.P. Morgan, someone, probably GE Credit, walked in, threw some papers on the table, and said thunderously, "This deal is dead!" My heart sank. I couldn't believe what I was hearing, and as I looked around the room everyone else seemed as stunned as I. In truth, I was reading my own despair into the faces of the others.

Scrambling, side meetings, hurried conferences, slight tweaks to the structuring proposal, calls to various home offices and lots of whispered two-person conversations ensued. The problem that GE had was solved and suddenly the deal was alive, and we all went back to reading and marking up documents. The deal was resuscitated and closed as it needed to at 11:00 p.m. on New Year's Eve. And I don't even remember what the problem was. That's how these things work.

Back to Choco. The problem here was not some arcane manner of legal interpretation of a depreciation schedule. The problem was that the darn lumber price had skyrocketed as noted above, and no amount of deal term tinkering was going to convince the landowners to stick with their original price.

The Choco team promised to find some other land just as good and put the project back together. This after they had told us donors that this was the absolutely best conservation land in all of Ecuador. But we didn't blame them, we just said, "Sure, see what you can do." The best part of this story is that we had finally learned, and we had not given them one cent of the promised funding. We were sorry it all did not appear to be working out, we liked the project, but we were not advancing any funds into a deal that might not close. All deals ever crafted might not close, until they close or blow up. Good lesson. Besides, going to Ecuador for a site visit in the middle of the pandemic would not have been easy. Hmm, it does appear that this preserving bird habitat is more complicated than we first thought.

About a year plus since this episode, there was finally a new proposal from the Jocotoco folks. Mike Parr, braving Covid and who knows what else, had flown down to Ecuador to confer with them. They had indeed been busy in the area, and were starting to find, qualify, and then purchase smaller parcels with the goal of eventually assembling them into a bridge between the Botrosa lands, when/if they came back on the market, and the big existing reserve to the east. The funds who had committed to the Botrosa project had decided to support this new effort with half of their committed funding, and to reserve for two years the other half to be used on Botrosa if it came back from the dead. They invited us to join, and Mike wrote a very good report explaining the new direction, why it was a reasonable approach, where these lands were, and included maps and pictures. It's nice to deal with professionals. He asked us if we would like to consider this.

Here is what his report said:

Rio Canande Reserve Report—American Bird Conservancy, 1/28/22

Mike Parr and Daniel Lebbin visited the Rio Canande Reserve, managed by American Bird Conservancy's local partner Jocotoco Foundation (Fundación de Conservación Jocotoco), and surrounding lands in January 2022 to assess land acquisition options for reserve expansion. The Rio Canande Reserve protects the largest and most important stretch of lowland Choco rainforest remaining in northwestern Ecuador and is home to many globally threatened species, including the Brown-headed Spider Monkey, Great Green Macaw, and Banded Ground-Cuckoo. ABC and Jocotoco Foundation originally proposed to purchase lands owned by the Botrosa logging company to expand the Rio Canande Reserve. The Botrosa lands offered a rare opportunity to secure large holdings (~23,000 ha/53,000 acres) of low-elevation (<300m) rainforest from a single seller to connect key portions of the existing reserve and connect the reserve to indigenous Chachi territories and the El Pambilar Wildlife Sanctuary. Jocotoco and their supporters were able to fundraise the $14M (in hand and pledges) to purchase and manage these lands, but Botrosa backed out of the deal after lumber prices spiked. Botrosa is not currently extracting timber from their lands we sought to buy, but instead is extracting timber from lands owned by the Chachi communities under agreements with them. Botrosa is unlikely to sell their lands in 2022, despite timber prices starting to approach prior levels and our interest in purchasing. We are hopeful that this deal may arise again in future years, yet we are unable to predict when they might sell their land.

Meanwhile, Jocotoco has been pursuing an alternative land acquisition strategy to purchase the same amount of land further to the east to consolidate a corridor connecting the existing reserve to the Cotacachi-Cayapas National Park, including the use of $7.5M in funds originally raised for the Botrosa lands. Rainforest Trust is currently holding part ($5.5M) of its funding for two more years in hopes that the Botrosa deal might be revived.

Under this alternative strategy, Jocotoco would purchase roughly 230 parcels total to reach 23,000 ha, and they have ~170 properties remaining to purchase in order to reach this goal. Jocotoco now manages 9,959.80 ha at Rio Canande Reserve (which includes about 3,000 hectares purchased in 2021), has negotiated 5,608.00 hectares for purchase (which is in the process of titling and will be purchased once titles are completed), and has 5,875.00 hectares remaining to negotiate (and title) shown in the maps below. These alternative lands are more expensive ($14–15M for land acquisition for 23,000 hectares) and have slightly different conservation value. The alternative corridor tends to be slightly higher in elevation, and most of it has not been logged and therefore retains certain key tree species in higher abundance and larger populations of key animal species including the Brown-headed Spider Monkey and Great Green Macaw. A recent analysis of threatened birds shows the corridor to be of higher priority than Botrosa lands for birds and provides more connectivity for wildlife to shift their ranges up in elevation into the Cotacachi-Cayapas National

Park under predicted climate warming scenarios. During our visit, we were surprised by the high density of raptors in the entire area (Botrosa lands, El Pambilar Wildlife Sanctuary corridor and Rio Canande Reserve), as we saw all three species of local Hawk-Eagles. This is a good sign of healthy prey densities in this region. The highest conservation priority currently is to prevent additional logging road construction within the corridor to prevent opening up new areas to timber extraction and subsequent settlement by farmers cultivating cacao, balsa, and cattle. ABC recommends using your pledge to expand the Rio Canande Reserve through land acquisitions that consolidate the corridor between the Rio Canande Reserve and the Cotacachi-Cayapas National Park now to prevent further road access and to protect the high conservation value of this area.

The motives for landowners in the corridor to sell are as follows. Less than 5% of all owners live on the land. Most of the land parcels that Jocotoco Foundation is acquiring are remote, requiring several hours of walking in often difficult terrain, from the nearest road. Such land is not productive for cacao production or other agriculture. The only economic value is the timber that can be extracted using a rope-pully system we observed during our trip. Yet, income from timber harvest is marginal, as owners (unlike Botrosa) have no permit to sell outside their state. They further lack knowledge of long-term forest management. Hence, the lack of economic opportunity is the reason why landowners are willing to sell to us. They use the funds they receive to buy smaller, more accessible lands closer to their homes. Jocotoco Foundation has received several messages from sellers thanking them for acquiring lands.

We sat down, read the above, and had something of an insight. Late in coming, but better than nothing.

"If I was the company staff lead working on this project, and decided that it was what we wanted to add to our portfolio, what would I do to convince our board of directors to invest?" I asked myself.

Myself thought for perhaps a minute, then said, "Write up an issue paper to be presented to the board." Well, of course. We were only doing it for ourselves, but it seemed a good discipline, in which we had perhaps been a little lacking in the past. It's nice to have your own money to invest, but it can sometimes make you a bit lazy.

We put together a short paper on the new proposal, and it is displayed below.

Rio Canande Reserve, Northwest Ecuador
ABC/Jocotoco Foundation
Draft 21 Feb 2022

Positives
Attractiveness of Site and Conservation Area
The Choco area has high population of scarce as well as plentiful birds (three species of hawk eagles observed on Parr trip). Although Ecuador is one of the smallest countries in South America, it has the fourth-highest bird diversity of any country in the world with 1,659 identified species. This is only surpassed by Brazil, Colombia, and Peru, significantly larger countries. The US, for example, has 1,107 bird species.

> Ecuador possesses twenty-six differentiated habitat types, each one with characteristic flora related to altitude and precipitation levels. Among them are three of the world's ten biodiversity "hot spots," namely, the humid forests of the northwest (the Choco area), outside faces of the mountain range, and the Amazon forests of the northeast.
> The area has several endangered populations of mammals and birds (brown-headed spider monkey, great green macaw, banded ground cuckoo).

The recent national election went off smoothly by South American standards. New administration's view of wildlife protection/habitat conservation is yet to be determined, as they're busy trying to get rid of the gangs. Which is understandable.

The specific area is bordered on the east by very large but higher altitude national reserve (Cotacachi-Cayapas National Park), on the west by the existing Rio Canande Reserve already owned by Jocotoco, and to the north the indigenous Chachi territories and the smallish El Pambilar Wildlife Sanctuary. The Botrosa area is to the west and south. It is likely eventually to be logged if nothing else happens.

Current Situation Creates an Opportunity
The Botrosa deal for 53,000 acres for $15 million has fallen apart because Botrosa withdrew as lumber prices went up, but there are many smaller pieces of land with equivalent [??] conservation value between the lowland Botrosa property, the Rio Canande Reserve, and the National Park and there appear to be willing sellers.

The target area is a bit of a patchwork and has roughly 230 smaller parcels; Jocotoco has already purchased sixty of these sites.

Local Sponsor/Site Manager
The Jocotoco Foundation already owns and manages fifteen wildlife refuges (57,000 acres) in Ecuador. ABC has partnered with it on several [many?] of these and is listed on Jocotoco's website as an important partner. The website lists thirteen other North American and European conservation organizations as "partners" as well. But not anyone we know.

Jocotoco and ABC had raised $15 million in pledges (including us for $1 million) to purchase the Botrosa property before Botrosa backed out.

Major funders who had supported the Botrosa purchase have agreed with the change of strategy and have allowed Jocotoco to draw about half their money for the small holder purchases. The remainder is being held for two years in anticipation that the Botrosa opportunity will return.

We slightly know one Jocotoco board member, Heather Hodges, former US ambassador to Ecuador.

Timing/Urgency
The area is at some development risk that the project(s) will prevent. There has been squatter clear-cutting/agriculture along the few roads in this region. It is likely that this project will continue to progress on an incremental basis with or without our contribution.

Intangible Benefits
Assuming that we can be as connected/informed as we want, we will learn a great deal from participating in this effort.

Negatives

Complexity
The project will have to initiate and manage a number of transactions/parcels, approximately 230.

> The small holder's price per hectare is higher than the original Botrosa deal, mostly due to higher transaction costs and maybe other factors.

Lack of Local Knowledge

We have never done business in or even visited Ecuador. Nor have any of our close business connections. If we contribute $1 million, this will be our largest land deal to date by 20X.

Lack of Impact

We will be the smallest funder in the project and thus will have little impact on project selection, deal terms and conditions, etc. It is unclear and probably unlikely that we could make a contribution that was tied to a specific property and have a press release that specified or identified this. Besides, the current effort does not appear to be set up that way.

Political Risk/Corruption

There is political risk in Ecuador, as there is everywhere. One scale (theGlobalEconomy.com) ranks Ecuador at four on a scale where one is least risk and seven is most.

> The Corruption Perceptions Index ranks countries and territories based on how corrupt their public sector is perceived to be. A country or territory's score indicates the perceived level of public sector corruption on a scale of 0 (highly corrupt) to 100 (very clean). Ecuador ranks 39 on the most recent (2000) ranking. This is not great.
> Is there any evidence in the area of cocaine, marijuana, or other cultivation of illegal plants; any meth labs?

Who Are These Guys?

We have never done a transaction with either ABC or Jocotoco. We have never met anyone from Jocotoco. We have never met the CEO, Martin Schaefer. Curiously, he lives in Germany. We don't know the story behind this.

> We are unlikely to be comfortable visiting Ecuador in the near future given ongoing Covid risk. However, 75% of the population is "fully vaccinated" without booster, and 15%

have received booster shots. On the other hand, the CDC has just issued "do not visit" guidance for Ecuador.

Reputation

After all this discussion and our earlier commitment, if now we do not do something, we run some reputation risk.

Alternative Courses of Action

- Do nothing—too big, too far away, conservation action already underway so our contribution would be of minor impact, we have no experience with ABC or Jocotoco, any PR or reputation benefits limited by Ecuador location.
- Commit to $1 million and fund now—big number, same negatives as above, but demonstrates real commitment, probably a sound conservation investment, has a much lower cost per acre than California projects.
- Commit $500K but with conditions, especially a site visit. Less useful to the project and budget planning, we could still pull out due to local conditions. We could also make this less than a commitment and emphasize the need for more information/comfort with the country, the sponsor, and the project details. This probably means funding no sooner than next year.
- Commit to participate in the Botrosa acquisition at a $1 million level as before if/when it comes back—shows some good faith, gives time to visit Ecuador, expand our knowledge of partner and area.

We discussed this some more and decided that maybe we should send a draft to Mike, since he knew the area better than we did, and he had written the great trip report quoted earlier that got us re-interested in the area. Besides, he deserved to know what we were thinking, so that when the next opportunity came along, we would start from a better joint knowledge base. And honestly, we had little faith that the Joco people would be able to do what we were suggesting.

Be careful what you ask for. Within two weeks of sending out the analysis, Mike and Joco came back with exactly what we had suggested as our ideal. The proposal was for three pieces of property totaling 150 acres for just over $100K in the area where they were buying other land and working to assemble the "bridge reserve." They even included maps of the area and the parcels, and further invited us to come to Ecuador since we were still quite clear that we needed to make a site visit before donating any significant funding to the effort.

But by this time we were overcome by deal fatigue. And the political news from Ecuador was starting to turn ugly. We just couldn't get up our previous enthusiasm for this project in its changed configuration. Spending $20K in travel costs to go to Ecuador to evaluate a $100K deal seemed less and less sensible, so we declined as courteously as we could. And I still hadn't gotten my trip to Ecuador.

16

Far Above Cayuga's Waters Where Birds Fly, Unless They're Pelagic, In Which Case They Just Sit on the Water

We Hook Up with Cornell and Sara Barker and Try to Donate Money to Buy Land along with Land Trusts, and Even Go See Several Candidates

The Cornell Lab of Ornithology ("CLO") is quite likely the most important lab in the world that focuses on birds. Unlike famous universities where you can argue in general whether Yale or Harvard is better, there's really no one in second place when it comes to birds. When you look up "best universities for ornithology" you get the usual Stanford/Harvard/UC Berkeley/UC Davis list and, strangely, Fashion Institute of Technology. But nobody holds a candle to the CLO.

They are a $45 million organization with two hundred employees. You can even see a picture of each of the two hundred except that some have instead chosen to be represented by a bird graphic. We assume that despite this oddity—were they absent on school picture day?—they are also people as you can get their names and email addresses should you wish for some reason to harass them. But don't do that.

Here is what they say about themselves on their website: "Our mission is to interpret and conserve the earth's biological diversity through research, education, and citizen science focused on birds and nature."

On the About Us page they add: "Conserving birds and biodiversity in the 21st century is a complex endeavor that requires innovative science and technology, a detailed understanding of ecological and social systems, and the ability to implement sustainable solutions at global and local scales."

Keep this in mind as you read the rest of this and subsequent chapters.

The lab is also responsible for several bird-watcher-focused developments that are excellent. The first is an app called Merlin Bird ID, which helps determine just what exactly the bird is that you are looking at, or more likely just saw, because then it flew away as do all birds that are really worth looking at. With the Merlin app, you input bird size and color and where you saw it—flying, in a tree, on a bush, on the ground. Because this is the internet and you are using your cell phone to do all this, Merlin also knows your location (and thus the bird's) as well as time and date. It processes all this data and gives you a list of the most likely bird, which you then can either select or ask for more choices. This is way easier than the old-fashioned way of stopping, digging your bird identification handbook out of your backpack, paging through it, and making a tentative identification. Merlin is good, quick, and accurate. But wait, there's more.

Merlin has recently added a characteristic where if the bird is still around and is making noise, you can point your cell phone at the sound, even if you can't see the bird, push your button, and Merlin will listen, then search its memory of bird sounds and tell you literally immediately what the bird is. This part is especially good: if the sound you recorded has more than one bird song mixed in it, Merlin will separate the songs and tell you which two or three birds you have recorded. And it will ignore car noises, airplanes flying by, sneezes, and other irrelevant sonic interruptions.

This is all the result of a very large effort to collect and record bird songs and build a neural network that lets Merlin do just what I have described above. This was only recently completed by the lab, which is understandable. We were told that they have more than a billion individual clips of bird song in their database, with said bird song identified with a bird. They had to assemble and label these and write the comparison software, etc. Lots and lots of grinding effort to make what seems like a simple identification program.

Of course, since we're never satisfied, what we'd really like is to be able to send a picture to Merlin and get back an identification. You can technically do this, but you have to take a picture and download it, send it off, etc. There are several plant sites as well—Google Lens will do this for plants essentially instantaneously. But almost all plants I have ever wanted to identify are standing still, not flying around, and will let you get pretty close to them so you can get a really good picture of a leaf or a berry or some bark. Not so good if you find that you have been scrabbling around in a bunch of poison ivy, but those of us who are susceptible to this noxious vine have long since learned to identify it from a distance, without outside assistance.

In addition, the lab, about fifteen years ago, working in partnership with the National Audubon Society, developed and runs what is basically a listing website for the birds you have seen. You walk through the woods or grasslands or plains or even putter around on a small boat and note what birds you have seen. Bird-watchers are notorious list keepers, with the weirdest of them keeping something called a "life list," which is an attempt to see how close one can come to seeing one of every species on earth. This is not easy as there are about 10,300 species to see, and they don't all live in California, which is annoying.

This program is called eBird and it cumulates all the entries that obsessive bird-watchers send in to it, and then you can access both the numbers and the date of the siting. You can search by bird or by location. Say you're going to take a hike along a certain swath of the Appalachian Trail, and you'd like to know what birds are around for you to look for. Put in the location coordinates, or import them from Google Maps, and a bunch of small red circles will pop up at the location or along the route you have specified. Each red circle is an eBird submission made by a diligent bird-watcher, listing what she or he saw, species and numbers thereof, and the date and time and location.

Right now, you are probably asking yourself if there's anything good on Netflix rather than reading this tedious delving into the depths and mechanics of bird-watching. More likely, you're asking yourself, "Why would anyone keep such a list, thus adding a didactic effort to what was supposed to be a nice, non-tedious, no effort, and noncompetitive walk in the woods?" Then why would said list maker in fact submit it to the lab, thus making it in essence a public document? You do not get rated on it, there's not a contest to see the most birds, there are no prizes given or recognition awards awarded. You assuredly can't make any money doing it.

So again, why do it? Okay, wait, that wasn't quite correct; if you make enough entries, you can become a Big Birder, but never mind.

I don't really know why bird-watchers seem to be quite this anal or maybe precise is a fairer word. But ponder this. Several years ago, I had a conversation with one of the lab scholars who essentially with several others invented eBird in the early 2000s. I asked him out of idle curiosity how many eBird submissions they get annually, expecting the answer to be in the hundreds of thousands.

"We expect that this year [2021] we will receive a billion eBird reports."

Whoa! There are about seven billion people in the world. There are also, depending on your source, about seven billion cell phones in the world, although this source says confusingly that this represents only 85% of all people owning a cell phone. Thus, some 15% of all cell phone users have two cell phones? We don't know why.

That is as if every one of out of seven or so people in the world sent in one eBird submission in 2021. This seems unlikely. There cannot possibly be that many bird-watchers in the world. In fact, you can call up a global map of eBird submissions and see that there are lots and lots and lots of reports from North and South America and Europe and North Africa and Australia and South Asia but few from Russia or China.

You can draw many different conclusions from these data, but one conclusion is that there are a hell of a lot of people sending in eBird reports every year. In fact, the serious bird people with whom I have been on short local bird walks *always* send in an eBird report of the walk, even if it's only "two house sparrows, six rock pigeons, and a couple of crows."

I rest my case on the importance and capabilities of the Cornell Lab. You can see why we would jump at the chance to go on a bird walk with some of the professors from Ithaca. And we got such a chance, as a couple of Cornell Lab researchers came to our area in 2019. They paired with local alumni to do a bird walk and we were included. Another interesting fact: the lab is located on a road called Sapsucker Woods and everyone who goes to Cornell knows about it even if they can't tell a bird from a bison or a Baby Ruth.

More interesting facts: yellow-bellied sapsuckers (the wood's namesake if you've lost the thread here) are fairly small woodpeckers with stout, straight bills. The long wings extend about halfway to the tip of the stiff, pointed tail at rest. Often, sapsuckers hold their crown feathers up to form a peak at the back of the head. They are larger than a downy woodpecker and slightly smaller than a hairy woodpecker. I presume they are found in northern New York but didn't check.

On a walk through the forest you might spot rows of shallow holes in tree bark. In the East, this is the work of the yellow-bellied sapsucker, an enterprising woodpecker that laps up the leaking sap and any trapped insects with its specialized, brush-tipped tongue. Attired sharply in barred black and white, with a red cap and (in males) throat, they sit still on tree trunks for long intervals while feeding. To find one, listen for their loud mewing calls or stuttered drumming. That's all I know.

Thus armed with data, we go off to the San Dieguito Lagoon, starting at its Nature Center, to do the walk with the lab researchers and local alumni. The lagoon has the obligatory sign up about "what animals will you see here" and "don't step on the rattlesnakes" although since this is a lagoon with some narrow, dry land trails running through it, chances of rattlesnake encounters seem pretty unlikely. Water moccasins would be more like it, but I do not think they have been allowed into California. According to the helpful website "non-native water snakes of California":

> Within North America, snakes in the genus *Nerodia* are native to the eastern and southeastern US, eastern Canada, and Mexico. Unlike the cottonmouth water moccasin (*Agkistrodon piscivorus*), which **has not become established in California,**

[emphasis added with relief] water snakes are not poisonous and do not present a threat to human safety.

Just to clear this up, all nine species of the genus *Nerodia* are called water snakes because they live in water. I do not believe that they have gills and thus are not water fish snakes or fish snakes or something like that. So don't worry about water snakes as you go bird-watching, although why would you since every bird-watching expedition I have ever been on to date does not include wading through water while watching for birds. If it did, I wouldn't go.

The San Dieguito Lagoon is about 110 acres, a decent size, and has a good trail system, one that we have hiked before. It is not what you would call a pristine woodland habitat. It's a large rectangle bounded on the west by the Coast Highway, on the east by Interstate 5 and a serious railroad track, on the north by Manchester Avenue, and on the south by a bunch of houses and condos. Look, it's California, not the trans-Siberian wilderness.

It does have a range of reasonable birds. We see an Anna's hummingbird or maybe an Allen's hummingbird, which if the light is right shimmers with a very bright purple radiance, essentially iridescent. Hummingbirds are a bit hard to see, or really to take pictures of, as they dart about and don't work any one flower for any length of time. But they're not especially worried about humans, probably because they fly so doggone quickly, and make the most amazing turns and zigs and zags as they do so. On our walk we come across one that is staying still, and does so for a remarkably long period of time, thus allowing everyone in our party with a camera, which would be everyone but me, to get many, many pictures of this nice little bird. The Cornell scientists are especially gaga over what is to us a pretty usual bird appearance. Maybe no hummingbirds live in the cold and ice of Ithaca.

We also see egrets and some shore birds and some little brown birds and some gulls. We are very close to the ocean, it's on the other side of the Coast Highway, so gulls are hardly a surprise. Or a novelty. But the other reason for going "birding" takes over, which is it's a nice day, the weather is pleasant, and we're outdoors doing nothing productive and chatting with others who share our peculiar intertest in birds, and we don't feel guilty about goofing off like this.

The walking ends and we go off to lunch with one of the Cornell bird scientists and with one of the development people. I have long been fascinated as to why what the money-raising people do is called "development." Why aren't they just called financiers or sales or bankers or something more clearly related to their employment function, which is to ask all the graduates they meet to give the university money? I don't think they should be called beggars, but they are generally proposing a transaction wherein you give the university (or church or museum or any sort of NGO) some money and they give you nothing. Maybe you get a mention in one line of their annual report, along with all the other suckers who gave them the same amount of money. If you give them really large amounts of money it's possible you can get a building named after you, or at least a conference room or a gallery in a museum. You probably don't get to design the gallery or the conference room. You only get to influence what you are "getting" if you are Warren Buffet's buddy named Charlie Munger and you have for God knows what reason decided to pay for an entire large dormitory at the University of California at Santa Barbara, except all the dorm rooms have no windows. There has been a large discussion about this, which we won't go into—"prison" anyone?—but they are building it using his money and architectural taste. We use the term "taste" with reservation.

During our lunch with the development guy and the science guy we slyly make clear that we're not endowing a building anywhere for Cornell or for any other university. We explained that it's bird habitat that we're interested in, going through all the arguments found earlier in this book. They seem a tad disappointed. Perhaps it's not true that everything about everyone is already accessible on the internet, including your net worth, all you have to do is look it up. Or maybe it is true, and they just didn't do their homework. I know for a fact that in the early 1990s a publication called the *Virginia* magazine ran an article about who the fifty richest Virginians in the state were. I was one of the ones featured. We had just gone public at AES, so we had some paper wealth. That was long ago but I suspect that if you looked carefully you could find it. But never mind all that. Times and stock values have changed.

The Cornell people got over their disappointment, and described for us a grant program they had that handed out money to land trusts for things like staff development and training. We must have looked somewhat slack-jawed at this description, for several reasons. First, we had no idea what a "land trust" was, never heard of one, never visited one, never got into a fight with one, nothing. Second, we thought we had been clear that we wanted to fund the acquisition of habitat, and not "soft" stuff like training and research and lobbying.

We responded, politely but clearly, "What's a land trust?" We got some confusing answers that I will not try to reconstruct. Here's the real answer, courtesy of the internet. Land trusts are a particular kind of nonprofit legal entity with specialized assets, in this case, yes, land. It is an organization that, as all or part of its mission, actively works to conserve land by: (1) acquiring land or conservation easements (or assisting with their acquisition), and/or (2) stewarding/managing land or conservation easements.

Here is the rest of what we have learned. There are lots of them, but they tend to be geographically specialized, focusing on a particular area. There are over one thousand in the US, forty-five in California. If you have land in your estate and you don't want it sold when you die, you can donate it to a land trust. If you have a collection of original Picassos and want them to be preserved but available to the public and art scholars, then you leave them to an art museum who has the talent and staff and space and resources to protect and display them. Same with land. By leaving or donating to a land trust, you get the tax benefits that you always get in contributing to 501(c)(3) entities. Just as you can put conditions on a donation of a painting to a museum, i.e., never sell this, you can do the same with a land trust donation. Now you know.

The land trust program run by the Cornell Lab only did the things mentioned above; it gave money to land trusts to help them do their jobs better. There were $5,000 grants for training and $15,000 grants for capacity building, whatever that is. The whole program ran at about a $200,000 rate and was managed by a bird person named Sara Barker, to whom they promised to introduce us.

Then we asked rudely, "Why don't you do purchases of habitat with this program?"

Because we don't have the money, they candidly replied, which seemed a reasonable answer.

"Well, what if we put up some money, could you add habitat acquisition to your land trust grant program bag of tricks?" This reaction to this question is about as easy to predict as asking a kid if he'd like a candy bar.

"Why, yes, I do believe we could consider that," responded the development guy.

The science guy was losing interest since we weren't talking directly about birds. He went back to playing with his camera to see how good his pictures of the hummingbird had turned out.

"I will see that we get Sara Barker to call you, and you can discuss with her what you have in mind and how we could help you with that," the development guy, enthused. This was an assumption that we actually had "something in mind" more than "buy some bird habitat," which at the time we did not.

About a week later we were introduced via the dreaded Zoom call to Sara Barker, a pleasant woman with a slightly diffident manner. She explained how she ran the entire land trust program as a grant program making six or so annual grants, some of the smaller ones, some of the larger ones. She had been doing this for three or four years and had developed relationships with many of the land trusts. Since there were one thousand of them, we suspected that these were not likely to be close relationships. However, if you have money and you are trying to give it to a selection of a modest-sized group of institutions, there's no reason for the institutions not to be nice to you—return your calls and messages, and every so often even toss off a short grant proposal and hope that the lottery wheel's arrow stops at your colored square. NGOs, which don't have large endowments from wealthy donors and haven't somehow developed into national organizations with lots of members, seem to live on grants, mostly from various governments but also from foundations private or public, and other folks like the Cornell Lab.

It turned out that we had caught her at a good time, as the next cycle of the annual grant process was to start soon (three months—"soon" in NGO language as we learned) and she thought we had time to write up a description of the program and work out the program details. After all we had to:

1. Decide who to make eligible for our grant(s)
2. Figure out what we wanted
3. Send out an announcement
4. Read the responses
5. Decide and fund

The lab cycle for this was six to nine months. No, I am not kidding. Sara pointed out that there were many second-level decisions to make, such as geographic eligibility.

"California," we said.

"No," she responded, "we need to have a subsequent call to discuss details like this."

We were still in our "courting" phase of the relationship, so instead of saying, "No we don't, it's California," we said, "Sure."

It went on like that for several more weeks and calls.

Here is where we finally ended up on the grant announcement document: Who? Land trusts, but not just any land trusts, only land trusts who were "accredited." The National Land Trust Alliance, an interest group of land trusts, runs an "accreditation" program that rates land trusts as to whether they clean their floors regularly and brush their teeth after every meal. I am making that up, but the association checks their accounting, and whether they are monitoring the properties that they hold in trust, etc. You can't be giving your money or your land to just anybody, you know. There's a little bit of "who will watch the watch dogs in all this" and a distinct lack of faith in markets, but these are nonprofits monitoring other nonprofits and if they believed in markets, they would have joined Google.

Where? Anywhere in California, that is, anybody who is an "accredited land trust" in California. Or more precisely anybody who is an accredited land trust and wants to use the money to buy more land. In California. The land trusts don't seem to cross state borders. We didn't ask about this. As noted earlier, there are one thousand of the things. Would it be more efficient if there were a hundred of them? Probably, but we were, remember, still courting. Best not to ask.

How much? Not more than $50K. We planned to make two grants and see how it all worked. After all, neither of us, neither us nor the Cornell Lab, had ever done this independently before, nor had we ever worked together. The courtship was going well, but unless courtships go well, you never get married. And given the US divorce rate of 50%, even good courtships don't produce perfect and long-lasting relationships.

What for? Buying land for habitat. We were also willing to entertain conservation easements, since Sara and everyone we talked to said we should, and we accepted this advice without careful analysis.

We pause here to examine this a bit further. What, you may ask, is a conservation easement? It is a legally enforceable agreement executed by you, party A, the landowner, to sell party B a piece of your rights on a certain piece of property. It is different from what is called for some reason "fee simple," wherein you, party A the landowner, sell party B, the guy who wants to buy your piece of land, all of your land and all the rights that come with it. Like, the right to build whatever you want on the land you have just bought, depending, of course, on all the local and state and federal rules that govern who can mess around with land and how and when and with what permissions.

An easement is, at least in this case, a real estate right, like the right to run a road through the piece of property. Or build a house or plant some corn or shoot all the birds that are foolish enough to land on the property. All of these and many other rights come with fee simple ownership. But what if you dislike development of your land and you wish to have it preserved into the future and forever? Then you can sell the development rights, now separated from the ownership rights, to some conservation-minded individual or group who in turn pledges to keep on not developing the land forever or in eternity, whichever comes later.

Generally, the original landowner (party A) can get paid for this since it diminishes the value of his land and why would he do that if he didn't get paid?

I don't know who thought this particular application of easements up, but the general concept has been around for a long time, this is just a specialized application. It has become more and more popular since (it is argued) you the conservation nut can get the same result you were looking for, i.e., no development on the property, for less cost than just buying the whole darn thing. And you the landowner, who is, let's say, running cattle on his 1,500-acre ranch in the high sierras, and has two sons with families living on the ranch with him, to whom he intends to leave the ranch to when he goes into that place where they keep forever and eternity, can make some money by selling something that you don't ever intend to use. And from the conservation side, it's cheaper than buying the whole piece of land in fee simple.

Many land trusts have made use of conservation easement to accomplish their purpose of preserving big chunks of land. One we dealt with, California Rangeland Trust, only uses conservation easements, and does not buy any land or anything in fee simple.

Is there a catch? There's always a catch.

The conservation easement usually allows the landowner to keep doing with the land what he was doing to make a living. If he or she is a rancher, then they get to keep raising cows and selling them to Grand Union for hamburger for you and me to buy. The transaction is more difficult than that but essentially that's it. But the easement probably allows the landowner to run a certain number of cows on this property, say five hundred. But what if he's had a particularly successful year and his heifers have enlarged his herd to 525 total cows. You cannot sell calves profitably until they are around six months old. So, he is in violation of the agreement. And what if he has agreed to leave a portion, maybe 25%, of his land fallow and not raise feed on it but let the birds thrive. Now he needs more feed for the extra twenty-five cows. It galls him to buy more feed, which is expensive, and he can raise it more cheaply on the land that is right there, and he has the machinery to plant and harvest it, and the help and the place to store it, so . . .

Generally, the easement doesn't require the landowner to self-report if he violates a term of it, and if it did why would he? The easement holder usually has the right to visit the land annually, probably with some notice, and look around. Count the cows, check the acreage being farmed, etc. You ever try to count a herd of cattle? Especially if they're all cowing around in a bunch here and there? And how good is the easement holder at estimating the exact size of a field under cultivation, by eye? You can probably get a surveyor out to measure it, but that's expensive and time-consuming. If the rancher is not so bright, he might decide that he needs another storage building to hold the extra feed, so he builds one. But the agreement specifies that he can only have so many buildings, and the easement holder can probably count buildings. Enforcement at the end of the day will require legal action and the remedy of specific performance and more enforcement, and so on.

These agreements, like so many contracts, work fine when everything is going well. They have an infinite number of ways that the landowner can violate them, and you cannot write an infinitely long agreement listing all the things that the landowner is not allowed to do, or that he must do, since naturally we have both potential sins of omission and sins of commission here.

Because the requirements run with the land, when the original party dies or sells his ranch, then there's a whole new party to deal with who knew—if he had a decent lawyer—that there were a set of limitations on what he could do, but probably either thought he could ignore them or get away with some or he could renegotiate.

Let us not even raise the issue of bankruptcy and whether an easement can be set aside in a bankruptcy proceeding. We had enough concerns with easements as it was. The result of all this was that we decided and subsequently communicated to landowners and land trusts that we were not going to fund projects that relied on conservation easements. Simpler to understand and transact, and more permanent. We hope.

We came to this conclusion *after* we had okayed the document that Sara planned to send out to all the California land trusts. Oh well..

After a reasonable amount of negotiation, the invitation to submit proposals was released January of 2021 with all the terms and so forth spelled out as above but in more formal language. We asked for responses to be submitted no later than March 1, and promised to award and fund in July. We made the application form as brief as we reasonably could. Then we waited and left the question answering about our document to Sara, since she was the program manager and had the relationships with the land trusts.

At the first of March, as requested we received five proposals. They were all written in reasonably clear English and mostly complied with the terms of our program. The good news was that we could understand why they wanted the money and how they planned to use it. Each proposal suggested that they could use the whole fifty grand, thank you very much. Nobody asked for less, and why would they? We were at first disappointed that we got only five proposals. Then we took a few breaths and said to ourselves: "This is a brand-new program. It is being funded by people no one in the land conservation or ranching business has ever heard of. Cornell has never had such a program before. There are only forty-five land trusts in California, and we received legitimate proposals from five of them. Unless my math has deserted me, that was a response rate of better than ten percent for a first-time program." Looked at from that perspective, we decided to quit whining and be grateful that we had that many sensible responses.

Here in summary are the five applications. The entire applications and the reviewers' comments can be found at Appendix A.

1. Willow Creek Ranch Conservation Easement. This is a large ranch in Lassen County, family owned by a family willing to sell an easement prohibiting any future development of the ranch's 2,700 acres. Negotiation on the easement had just begun, with eventual expected price in the $1.5 million range. Our $50K would be both early money and small. But worth a visit.

2. Elkhorn Slough Foundation acquisition. Acquiring a 2.4-acre property inholding in 3,000 acres of surrounding, already-protected lands. Price would be $375,000. The site is near Watsonville, CA, about halfway between the coastal towns of Santa Cruz and Monterey. A lot of money for a small piece of real estate. It also became clear when you read the whole application that the property had already

been acquired, using funds borrowed from a private donor, and what the foundation was now doing was raising funds to repay this loan. Nothing wrong with that but being a "takeout" lender did not add to the total amount of land being conserved, it just substituted our money for the other guy's money.

3. Saving Mount Diablo's "Missing Mile" of conserved land. This area, near the San Francisco Bay, would have added 154 acres of a conservation easement on a privately owned set of trail rides for horses to the existing 20,000-acre Mount Diablo State Park. It would open up this land for more public use, but the total easement cost was $1.04 million so we would be a small piece of the financing. And a trivial addition to the existing conserved area. We never quite figured out why it was the "missing mile."

4. The La Sierra Acquisition project, a seventy-five-acre property to be owned and managed by the Mountains Restoration Trust, a land trust of Los Angeles. Total price was $1.32 million, which had already been raised. Our funds would be used for the "stewardship" requirements of the purchase, that is, cleaning up and caring for the property. No more land, just maintenance.

5. Santa Rita Ranch acquisition by the Land Conservancy of San Luis Obispo County. This was the biggest property of the lot, at 1,715 acres and $7.6 million. It had already been acquired but using up the land trust's existing funds, which they wanted to have at least partially replenished. The property had been besieged by developers on its borders so the acquisition was a good conservation "save." But it needed attention, especially because of significant invasive plants.

Sara had organized a group of her colleagues to read all the applications and provide comments (included in the appendix) before she forwarded the applications to us. Seemed slightly odd, but it was her program. No one seemed to be in a hurry on all this. After a while the comments came back. They were generally of the opinion that Willow Creek Ranch, Santa Rita Ranch, and La Sierra in the Santa Monica mountains were the best of the five. She asked us to read all the applications and all the comments and provide our comments. She asked if we could get all this done in three weeks. Because we were still in our "good sport" phase of the relationship, we bit our tongues. What we wanted to say was, "Three weeks? Jesus, it's just short applications and shorter comments and there are only five of them. We could do all this in three days or possibly three hours, not three weeks." But we didn't say that.

When we went through them, we came on the main difficulty that most of the applications had for us, a conceptual problem that we had not focused on. If you go back to the description above of the clever bridge financing strategy, we liked being the bridge financier for two reasons: first, we could deploy our money quickly and then if all went well, get it back when the state and federal grant money came in, and use it again and again for the same purpose. Second, for the right project, we were adding new habitat to the total score of protected habitats in the US, and the project arguably wouldn't get done without our financing.

Coming in as a takeout financier is fine as a financing strategy in business deals, but these weren't business deals. Boy, were they not business deals. Being the second guys in didn't add to the overall inventory of protected land. There wasn't any "multiplier" effect, although using that term here is a trifle off point.

The second problem we had with some of the applications was the second-cutest girl at the dance syndrome. While the grant applicants were happy to have us, they clearly had other options and people that they had used before, and no doubt preferred to dealing with them rather than a bunch of ex-energy geeks with no credentials and a bird woman from way back in northern NY. They wouldn't mind dancing a dance or two with us, but you got the feeling that once they had our commitment in hand, they could go to their traditional and usually local financing sources and play us off. This analogy is somewhat flawed since price really played no role here, but we were competing on more than price, we just didn't realize it.

The assessments were pretty simple to make. In the end we ruled out the "Missing Mile" project on the basis of no sense giving money to the already rich. The Elkhorn Slough proposal was not highly ranked because it was a transaction that had already taken place, and all we would be doing was repaying part of a loan that had been used to buy the property in question. Plus, it was only 2.4 acres, pretty small by anyone's definition. But at least we had some decent proposals and now it was time to check for meth labs.

17

Perhaps We Are Not As Smart As We Think We Are

The Grant Program Grinds On, to Include Site Visits

We were left with three projects—Santa Rita Ranch, Willow Creek, and La Sierra—and two pots of money since we had committed $100K with a maximum of $50K per project.

"Okay," we said, "Time for the site visits." The grant applications had mentioned this little fillip and the applicants had all agreed. Why in the world would you not? But agreeing in theory and setting this up in practice took some doing.

All of this was made substantially more difficult by the fact that this was late May of 2021, and we were still in a big, frightening pandemic with little end in sight. We no longer had "assistants" to do the heavy lifting of airplane and hotel reservations. Okay, no problem, once in the distant past I was able to make reservations, and besides, who in their right mind really wants to be in an airport or an airplane or close to anyone they don't know, which includes all but probably a hundred or so of the earth's total population of seven-plus billion people. Besides, we were suffering a large attack of cabin fever.

The good news was that we were mostly going to drive, and that our clever decision to limit the program, at least for the first year, to California, meant that we really could drive, and make a big circle through the state, beginning in and returning to our home in Encinitas. Then we looked at the distances and decided that we would risk at least one leg of the journey by air.

As it finally worked out, we flew from LAX to Reno, which was the closest airport to the initial stop in Lassen County to see our first candidate, Willow Creek. From there we then rented a car and drove another two hours north, made the visit, then went west to the ocean, then south to the other two sites, both very close to the Pacific Ocean. We planned to turn in the rental car in Los Angeles, reclaim our own car, and drive the two hours back to Encinitas. The pandemic at this point was fourteen months old. And not getting any better.

The only real issue was the hotels, so we did some internet research and picked out ones that either looked fine or were stuck in the great middle of "not luxury/not Days Inn" where much of the US motel inventory resides. We also bought a map of California although it turned out that we hardly used it. Waze is very much better than paper maps especially if you know more or less where you're going and have some flexibility to your time schedule.

We were also a little excited as for the last twenty-five years we had traveled all over the world but never really taken a "driving a car, old-fashioned road trip." We decided that given the weirdness of the time, we should provision ourselves more than we would generally do. With healthy provisions that would keep, like red wine and Cheetos. And some cheese. And make 7-Eleven stops from time to time to replenish our inventory. This may sound a little either naïve or strange, but we really had read lots of stories about stores closed and restaurants not open and on and on. Oh, yeah, and a bottle or two of water for the car. At least we didn't take my Ka-Bar combat knife or any water purification pills, although I thought about it. We weren't camping, after all.

On the 16th of May, we checked one last time to make sure Northern California hadn't chosen this particular time to burn down and we took off. We did keep the CAL FIRE website URL handy in case we smelled smoke.

Our first revelation was the LA airport. It is the second-busiest airport in the US with 84.5 million passengers per year. If you are mathematically inclined you will quickly note that this is 231,507 passengers a day filling eight terminals, or 28,938 passengers per terminal per day. We thought maybe they would all stay home like responsible citizens that they were not and keep themselves and us safe from disease, allowing us to dance about the airport without a care. I didn't think there are any dancing movies about airports but there could be if it weren't for all those doggone people.

LAX was not deserted. It was pretty full of disgruntled people, actually, poorly dressed overall. One reason they were disgruntled was the flights kept being delayed and the airline desks were scantily staffed as the staffers were no more eager than anyone else to deal up close with angry people whom they did not know. We were equally uninterested in such close contact even though we had been fully vaccinated with two shots of Moderna in late February.

The other source of disgruntlement was that most of the concessions were closed. Not just understaffed—closed, smacko, shuttered up and locked and nobody home. You could not buy a newspaper or a cheap murder mystery or a bag of Doritos or a Coke or a lovely "I Love LA" souvenir T-shirt; it was all shut down. Because we were all adhering to the previous rule of "show up 2.5 hours early" there were lots of rule-followers sitting in all the chairs or else standing around. It was pretty unattractive. And you surely could not get a beer, even though it was 4:30 in the afternoon, time enough by our clocks for happy hour to begin.

"Aha," we said ruefully, crowded rooms with questionable ventilation, lots of people all of them breathing, most wearing masks but not all, and we're stuck in this hellhole for another hour and a half until the airline lets us load into a more refined version of this same nightmare. And why exactly did we think we needed to risk serious illness just to give away our own money to people we do not know who will use it for things we are not sure of and cannot really monitor?

That was a sort of a glum view of our situation, but the only real other choice was to say, "Piss on this, bad idea, let's go home." Probably if we were completely rational this is what we should have done, but then our old friend, Mr. Shame and Embarrassment, took over, the one that whispers in your ear, "Yes, but what will others think of you?" Of course, the "others" were just a bunch of folks at Cornell who we had never met in person and really could not be called exactly "friends"—maybe "acquaintances" or "professional colleagues" or "coworkers." Not friends.

We got on. The plane took off and flew through the air and landed safely. No one offered us a glass of fizzy water or a cheap beer or a truly awful glass of wine. It was Southwest. Peanuts disappeared a long time ago. We had no excuse not to keep our masks on the whole time, and besides we wanted to, and we did. We were in the minority.

We picked up a rental car at the airport in Reno, despite all the internet whining about how difficult it was to find such a thing. And Reno is not a big airport, as well as not being a big town. I used to come here for board meetings of an ill-fated venture investment in batteries of which the less said the better. Chemistry worked fine, even better than expected, but they could not figure out how to manufacture them. Batteries showed up to customers in a pack about the size of a milk carton, but they were always plus or minus a half inch in one or the other dimension. Not so good if you have already fabricated the battery box into which these cells are to be deposited. Couldn't they measure them before they left the "factory" you may ask? There were many questions. It was a start-up, starting up in a city whose claim to fame is it has the second-most slot machines after Las Vegas. So there.

We drove two hours to the capital of Lassen County, a city named Susanville. Not clear if the accent was on the first syllable—"SU-san-ville" or the second—"su-SAN-ville." I am pretty sure that the French pronunciation was not used—"su-san-vee."

We learned much while we were in what's-its-name ville. We learned that the town was founded by a lumber guy named Isaac Roop. He and his sister. She, of course, was named "Ville," no just kidding, she was named Susan. Neither of the parties in question ever married, and they lived together for their entire lives, too busy building up S-ville, one presumes. In its heyday they were a lumber sort of place. Cut down all the really big trees and hauled them off to a sawmill and sent all the planks and board and railroad ties and other lumber things off to the rest of California and probably the US. But ... once you have cut down all the really big trees in twenty years that took two hundred years or so to get so big, and since you don't practice modern forest management i.e., replanting stuff and waiting two hundred years to harvest it, then there is a predictable but unpleasant future to this area. It's four thousand feet high and has very cold winters and hot, dry summers. No water to speak of. It has slightly more than fifteen thousand people, and as far as we could tell when we arrived and checked into the Red Roof Inn (fanciest place in town), 90% of them appeared to have gone on vacation or died of Covid.

It was eerie. The streets were vacant of cars, although they had all the things you expect of a street—pavement, lanes, occasional stoplights still working. But no cars. You could have walked down the middle of Main Street, and there was only one real street in town, and been in no danger of getting hit by a car or a logging truck. You might have been hit by a prison van carrying prisoners. The city/county had lobbied hard and now was the proud owner, or custodian perhaps, of not one, not two, but three prisons of consequential size. Sixty percent of the town's workforce was employed at the prisons. Not logging, not mining, not ranching, but being what the brits call "trustees," prisoners keeping the other prisoners housed and quiet and behaving themselves and inside. At least we hoped so.

In an effort to cater to tourists, the city government had arranged for nine murals to be painted in large mural size on nine of the vacant walls off Main Street. We knew this not because we were smart but because there was a brochure given to us when we checked in, promoting the nine "Famous Susanville Murals." There was only one real place to eat dinner in the town discounting the one McDonald's, and it was too early to go to "the Lumberjack." It's self-promoted features: "Large portions, friendly staff, and good home cooking!" Well, who could resist that? Its special is the Chainsaw Sandwich. I do not believe this is a sandwich either made of a chainsaw or made by using a chainsaw, but I cannot be sure.

With the evening meal thus decided, we drove up Main Street to the location of the Famous Murals. I worried that we would have trouble finding a place to park. This turned out not to be a worry. The Famous Murals were all located within the last three blocks of town before Main Street turned off into the forest and became a two-lane state road. They were not exactly Michelangelo quality, more comic book or graphic novel, but big. They showed settlers doing various settler-like things like cutting down big trees and celebrating when the railroad came to town. No indigenous folks, no surprise. There was one Famous Mural with a very big headshot-type picture of Isaac Roop and his sister. They did not look handsome or pretty; he looked annoyed, and she looked lost. So much for the city history. We went back to the Lumberjack for the predictable dinner and a couple glasses of not too good California jug wine.

The next morning as planned, we drove out to the Willow Creek Ranch, the first of our three finalists in the grant program. The ranch was the home to three hundred cattle and a flock of human beings. There were also some birds, including two sandhill cranes who were a long way from Nebraska. The ranch was long and a bit narrow and bordered on one side by Doyle Grade Road and on the other by a Bureau of Land Management wildlife refuge. We found this out by missing a turn and driving around the refuge for a while. They didn't have any cranes. Doyle Grade remains a mystery, although he (I presume it's a "he") has a completely blank Facebook page. I didn't know you could do that.

Just to prove that stereotypes don't always work, the ranch was owned and run by a very nice guy named Jack Hanson and his wife, Darcy. He didn't wear a cowboy hat, or even a John Deere baseball cap. He didn't ride a horse; he did his wrangling on an ATV. He had gone to Stanford and majored in business economics. He was about my age, so I asked him the inevitable question. Yes, he had gotten drafted but chose the combat engineering branch of the army, possibly not noticing the first of two words describing what he was getting into. We exchanged Vietnam veteran stories for a while. I liked him; he was a nice combination of decent, smart, and down-to-earth without some gooey faux folksiness. He wasn't tall, always a plus in my book.

He had two grown and married sons and a modest clutch of grandchildren, and they all together lived in a sort of housing compound with three separate houses and ran the ranch. The ranch from a business standpoint was a "cow/calf" operation, which he explained meant that he had female cows ("heifers"), a couple of bulls, and then calves that were being grown in order to become steaks and hamburgers and perhaps bone broth or mucilage. I am not sure on the process. Anyway, he raised the calves until they were big enough to "harvest," their word not mine, and then they would go off to somewhere and be "harvested." I wasn't entirely clear on whether this cycle had overlaps or what happened to the heifers when they could no longer produce calves, but I imagine that one can speculate. No milk from the heifers; he only sold calves when they were no longer calves.

Jack was a delightful person, very open with us, very proud of his ranch and the operation, happy to drive us around in the ATVs and explain some of the vagaries of the business. He was careful to clarify how the cows were all pastured, not fed in feed lots, and that he rotated them around to various pastures in order to have the pastures regrow their grass. He did sometimes help the grass along by adding seed to the plots that were being set aside for regrowth. It all looked pretty complicated, and I didn't even ask him about the economics of the various operations as that was not our interest here.

After the tour of the land and the buildings (one barn included a pair of barn owls of which he was quite proud) Jack and his sons and wives hosted us to a big lunch in the middle of their yard. Lots of homemade things like potato salad and other salads and bread (homemade) and butter and homemade jam and of course beef. Not sure if it was theirs or some other rancher's, but it was all very good. And, lest we forget, apple pie with ice cream for dessert. It was gracious of them and let us get a more unofficial feel for what kind of people they were.

They were as curious about us as we were about them. We were asked lot of questions about why we were doing this, what were we looking for, how long did we expect to continue—"Until we run out of money," we answered honestly.

One of the most interesting quirks of the business occurred in the winter. Given how far north they were, and the four thousand feet worth of altitude, the winters were unpleasant. Not much pasturage left in December and January in Lassen County. Jack explained that they had two choices since apparently the sales cycle didn't square exactly with the calves being ready to market on the first of December. They could elect to put out hay, or something like hay, for the winter but they would then have to raise it and harvest it and store it and so on. Or they could buy it from someone else and feed it to their herd. The alternative was to put all the cows in trucks, take them down to Sacramento, and have them pastured there for three or so months on someone else's ranch. Obviously Sacramento was far enough south that the "winter" was not a problem.

"You give all the cows a winter vacation?" I asked.

"Well, I guess you could call it that," he responded, "but I gotta tell you, loading three hundred not-very-cooperative cows into large trucks is not much like a vacation for us."

The proposal was for a conservation easement to be applied to the whole ranch and also become part of the deed. The suggested easement was pretty standard, we were assured. The other party to the easement was a California-wide land trust called Rangeland Trust, and they actually had one of their senior guys out at the ranch to help show us around or to make sure the Willow Creek guys didn't say anything foolish. Given our complete lack of experience in the business, I wouldn't have recognized or been able to discriminate between stupid and brilliant, so I think they were safe. Our funds would go to Rangeland Trust and be part of what was needed to purchase the easement from Jack and his family.

The terms of the proposed easement were straightforward, as discussed above. We were assured that this was standard, as was the estimated price for the easement. But it was still early times on this deal, nobody had committed to anything except getting money from us. We did have one advantage, which we had decided among the two of us: we were not putting our money in until we could be the last money in, or until we could do a real closing, with escrows and all. While this may seem obvious to the casual reader, generally the people we speak to in the NGO/conservation business do not especially like this. And why would they? Money today is always better than money next week. "Commitments" don't always turn into real money. We had learned this the hard way, sadly the best way to learn things, although painful.

But back to Willow Creek Ranch. We were driven all over the property after lunch. Not on horseback, thank goodness. Actually, I don't think they had any horses, just ATVs. We saw the current year's herd of calves, each of which to my untutored eye looked to be the size of a small locomotive. Calves, huh? They were jet black and didn't seem interested in getting out of the way of our modestly sized and powered ATV, which was not much bigger than a golf cart. Perhaps someone had told them of their eventual destiny. And in another evidence of good management, each calf had a white ear tag with a black number in it, and the tags were big enough you could read them without having to peer deeply into the animal's ear. Not names, just numbers. What is a good cow's name, anyway—Bessie? Bossie? Hubert?

We did not discuss things like price and deal terms. Which was a good thing because I don't know what we would have said. The Rangeland proposal was that they would negotiate a conservation easement for the ranch, get the terms and conditions and price set, and then at closing we would come in with our $50K, along with a bunch of other money that was not yet assembled. At least that part was okay as to timing.

And how was this price to be set? Rangeland wasn't buying the whole ranch, remember, only the ranch's rights to further develop the property. The agreement in simple terms was that either it stayed a ranch of the same size and environmental impact and number of buildings and number of cows, or less, to include shutting down entirely. The Rangeland guy told us that there would need to be an appraisal done of the value of this easement, and that would provide the negotiating basis.

Appraisals play a large role in this business, we discovered. That has to be especially true of something like a conservation easement, in which the purchaser is buying the absence of something, that is, the absence of any further economic/environmental development of the site. What's that worth? There aren't really a lot of convenient market comps for this, so it's a lot of analysis and judgment and comparative but inexact examples of similar transactions, but never really in the same place or market, same size, same limitations, etc. All real estate has some of these same limitations, but there the limits are pretty extreme. Everyone agrees that a conservation easement is worth less than a fee simple sale of a property, with a range of 40% to 60%. But even determining the sale price in a small market with few transactions isn't so simple. Both buyer and seller tend to default to the appraisal, at least as a starting point.

When you boiled it all down, we had made a trip to see a ranch and we were thinking about making a commitment to an unpriced transaction with unknown terms, conditions, and limitations. But at least we had seen the site and met the management. And our commitment would be a "soft" one; if something odd came up we could honorably back out. At least that was what we thought. This might not have been exactly Cornell's view.

At a reasonable hour next morning, we got up and headed to the lobby of the motel, as they had advertised "breakfast provided." If you define breakfast as a very stale small bagel, no cream cheese or butter, and a paper napkin loaded into a brown paper bag, then you will not be disappointed by their rendition of "breakfast." It's not that we were exactly expecting eggs Benedict and certainly not *oeufs en cocotte Florentine* (eggs in ramekins with spinach), which by the way I have never had nor made, although they don't sound bad, but the translation is frequently "shirred eggs," which is where my interest rapidly declines. A little orange juice would not have hurt. They did have awful coffee, the staple of almost every cheap motel I have ever stayed in, and there have been many.

Of course, we went down a block to McDonald's. There have been many bad things said over the years about McDonald's, and as I write this a Wall Street raider is taking them to task about their treatment of pregnant pigs, but I don't care enough to read whether he is for it or against it. What I will say is that they infallibly make a very good breakfast as long as you stick with the "sausage something" and stay away from the "bacon something" and get the "meal" that gives you hash browns in the shape of a pre-Columbian ax-head but flattened and fried, as well as a cup of decent if not great coffee. And all for less than five bucks. I'm a fan.

As we finish off our breakfast, wringing the grease off our hands and dripping it onto our jeans instead, despite using five brown paper napkins to remove the first layer, I note an interesting fact. I have lived in California at an early age (Novato—my dad was stationed at Hamilton AFB outside SFO); San Jose for one summer between years at Yale and another similar summer in Vandenburg AFB; Los Angeles when I went to graduate school at UCLA; and now San Diego for eight years. I have visited here a lot, especially San Francisco and associated surroundings including through the wine country. I have driven across the state on I-80 from Carson City, Nevada, through or past Sacramento to San Francisco or downward to Los Angeles. My solar company built an $800 million solar plant in El Centro; my friend John and I climbed Mount Whitney. But I had never really been north of the Reno/Sacramento/San Francisco line before, ever.

There are a lot of people up there! And if you're driving from Susanville over to Mendocino, you will find that not only are there clusters of people from time to time, usually in towns, there are a boatload—a large boatload—of mountains that run north-south while you are attempting to go east to west. And the roads are all two lanes; I didn't know that California had any two-lane roads left except to get from your house to your garage. It is two separate sets of really large mountains, the Sierra Nevada and then there is the Mendocino Range closer to the ocean. The two-lane road leaving Susanville to go tortuously over the two mountain ranges (and just for completeness through the Mendocino National Forest) to Mendocino (the town, not the mountains or forest) where we had innocently booked our reservations for the evening. This is State Route 32.

As soon as you leave downtown Susanville, you don't get to a suburban block, you don't pass an auto supply parts store, you don't see a motel; you see a steeply rising and curving road that leads immediately into really big trees that some deranged forest ranger has planted right next to the road. And a welcoming sign that says: CA-32: DANGER, FREQUENTLY CLOSED DUE TO SNOW; CHECK BEFORE TAKING. When you pull up Google Maps you will find to your amazement, not that it's snowing in March, thank God, but that there is no other east to west road listed on the map for two hundred miles in either direction. You could drive two hours back to Reno on a reasonable road but that's going southeast and you need to go west. It is more than a little daunting.

But what the heck, this could be an adventure; remember the pioneers came through here, at least the dumb ones who didn't just stop in Nebraska and say, "Shoot, that's enough for us." Only a small number of them ended up eating each other and I don't think I see Donner Pass on the map, so let's go! Besides, I checked on Google Maps for the route to Mendocino and there's only one, and it's this one, but it's only three hundred miles, which should take no more than six hours.

It did not take six hours. Not only did you have to drive across the long, winding road through the Sierra Nevada, then you got to the flat part of the route and drove and drove past many, many flat agricultural fields where they were growing something—onions? Turnips? Catnip? Who can tell? And in March it was hard to tell since only modest bits of green were sticking up cautiously. Not vineyards, those I can recognize, and corn when it's five or six feet tall, but it was none of these. Finally, as the six hours were about up and we were ready to be in Mendocino, there was another whole bunch of north-south mountains in the way, with only again a single, two-lane winding road through it, and the inevitable large trucks who also needed to get to Mendocino. Large truck capital of the world?

No turnouts and no intermediate stops like diners in the movies for the truckers to stop at and go inside and have a cup of coffee and a slice of pie and chat up the cute but middle-aged waitress whom they know by name—usually Marge—and thus get out of the way so I could resume our lightning-like pace of forty-five miles per hour, not the twenty-five miles per hour that you had to do once you got behind a large truck. This mountain range, by the way, is called, with little imagination, the Mendocino Range, and it is in Mendocino County, and we are headed to the town of Mendocino. I presume if the county had a lake its imagination-challenged first explorer would have named it, of course, Lake Johnson—just kidding, Mendocino. These mountains are also part of the North Coast Range and are not quite as big as the Sierra Nevada. The range includes the Mayacamas, Sonoma, and Vaca Mountains. Which are all located somewhere around there and maybe I drove through them as well; I cannot be sure. I did a little map research when planning the trip, but I clearly did not do enough mountains research. Did you know, for example, that the Mendocino Range has 301 named mountains in it, most of which I have driven up or around? The highest is named Anthony. It must be a boy mountain. For some reason none of the mountains is named Mendocino. I cannot imagine how Mr. Mendocino missed this chance.

Well, wait. Who was Mr. Mendocino anyway? Our source of knowledge of course is Wikipedia again, which explains in one place that "Mendocino" is Spanish for "of Mendoza" and shortly thereafter announces that the stupid place was named by unnamed early explorers in honor of Anthony de Mendoza, but isn't that already "of Mendoza?" There is also a Mendocino Headlands State Park in case you're interested, but no beer we could find named Mendocino. Forest and mountains yes, beer no. Wrong priorities.

We finally get though the tedious mountains and embedded trucks, the last hour driving in the dark. There was some bad language included, in the manner of "Don't these frigging mountains ever end?" We reached the city of Mendocino, and it turns out that I have not only not done my mountain research, I have also not done my population research. Mendocino has 855 people, none of whom work past five, and it's now almost six.

We find what has been billed as a "hotel" but turns out to be collection of four separate houses with some rooms for rent. It is called the Blue Door Inn but does not have a blue door. We are greeted with "Well, we're glad you got here, we close at six." Huh? What kind of hotel closes at six? If we got here at six fifteen, what would have happened?

We do not wait around for the answer to these questions but rush over, three blocks away, to one of the other hotel buildings that has our room in it.

Well, it may, or it may not, since the key that has been given to us does not open the firmly locked door standing between us and a place where we hope to finally sit down and relax for a little. We rush back to the main building and the "office" and catch them before they close. We note politely that a nonfunctioning key, or possibly a nonfunctioning lock, is not welcoming. The desk person is puzzled. "The key is supposed to work," she explains. We agree but point out that many things during Covid that are supposed to work do not, this being only one of them. She consults with the other person in authority there. They finally decide to give us a room upstairs in the same building where we are desperately standing. We lug our luggage (so that's where the name came from!) up the very narrow stairway with a landing halfway up. I ponder the question of a fire escape in this clearly old and clearly wooden building. There are none of the lighted EXIT signs to be found, and only one way into or out of our room. Which has a gas-fired fireplace that seems nice but is turned on and cannot be turned off. By the time we find this out, of course, both the desk people have decamped.

But there's more fun awaiting us. We were assured by the write-ups that the lovely coastal setting of Mendocino has all the charm of a New England seaside town. We wander around the three streets and down to the park along the water's dangerous cliffside edge. No swimming here unless you wish to be dashed against the rocks, which I do not, not now and not ever, New England charm or not. I don't see that rock-dashing is part of New England charm. I look around for lobster boats but see none. It's also windy and cold, a direct charm steal from New England coastal towns in the nine months of winter. The place is also full of Airbnb's— it looks like every other house is one.

Here is the best news. The 855 residents have all decided to eat out this evening, and to do so before six thirty, which is what it now is. Two of the charming restaurants are closed because of Covid or simple distaste, and the other two have half of the 855 people inside eating dinner or trying to attract the attention of the two waiters, and the other half standing around outside waiting for their reservations to come up. This is a mite discouraging. No, we can't sit at the bar—twenty-seven people already are and 119 people are standing behind them waiting to pounce on the stool of any bar sitter who makes a false move, like hanging up his or her coat or going to the bathroom.

I have an inspiration, of sorts, believing that survival skills are always useful. "I saw a gas station with a convenience store attached when we drove in here, let's go back there and get some snacks and maybe a beer." We jump into the car, drive ten minutes back toward the road of the trees, and find the establishment, which, in conformance with the Mendocino code of conduct, closed at six.

We know when we're beaten. We retreat to our quite warm room and find, thank goodness, that it has been provisioned with a small half-bottle of drinkable red wine and some stale crackers. No wine opener of course ("Get one at the front desk" says a note on the end table) but one of us (me) always travels with a Swiss Army knife, and never ever buys a Swiss Army knife that does not have a corkscrew and by the way some small scissors. We have been traveling with some cheese and some nuts on the formerly laughable off chance that in the fourth-largest economy on the face of the earth we will come across a location where food is not available after six. We open the wine and eat the crackers and nuts and cheese. It's not great, but better than chewing on the rug or our leather shoes that are not in fact leather. Besides, I don't believe those stories about pioneers eating their shoes. Even the laces? Maybe each other, not their shoes.

Morning came in our hotbox of a room, but the further good news was that there was no hot water for the shower. At this point I was taking no "amenity" for granted. Sure enough, the "breakfast" in the "bed and breakfast" was not ready in its brown paper bag until eight thirty and we had to get moving, so we bagged it. And in an hour found a McDonald's.

We were on our way to the Santa Rita Ranch in San Luis Obispo County, and we figured that we could get there in seven hours if we hustled as it was 382 miles according to Google and we had San Francisco in the way. But the good news is that you can go around the Bay Area on interstates, and if you time it right it is not as noxious as LA. Of course, nothing is as noxious as LA, so that's a false comparison.

There were, however, NO mountain ranges to cross and NO two-lane highways as the only road to take. We didn't even get lost. When we rolled into the Hotel Cerro after only one false turn, which was easily corrected, we were tired and apprehensive. But the place was wonderful, new and modern and lovely. The only problem was again, the non-open syndrome. The hotel's fancy California modern cuisine restaurant, called with a somewhat surprising lack of imagination "Brasserie," was described by the hotel itself as a "cool, brick-lined eatery serving casual French cuisine alongside wine, craft cocktails and local beer." The San Luis Obispo restaurant guide said, "The cuisine at Hotel Cerro focuses on the natural flavors of our region. With an uncomplicated cooking style, the local ingredients are the hero of every dish." We checked in, got to our equally cool, brick-lined casual room, and headed downstairs to the Lumberjack challenge—would the food be better than Susanville's best? How could it not?

We shall never know. The restaurant was closed, our research in vain and our anticipation crushed. We crawled over to the hotel desk and asked if there was someplace around there we could get a cheeseburger. They took pity on us and said that there was a pretty good Italian restaurant just up the street. It was called Buona Tavola. It might mean something in Italian but we didn't care. We went there, they had room, it was pretty but not prettied up, and the food was imaginative enough to be interesting and sensible enough to be edible. No gels or seaweed in decorative shapes or the large intestine of some small mammal. We were delighted!

Our luck ran out with breakfast, of course. It was supposed to be part of the deal and since we had carefully scheduled a later-than-usual start time for our site visit—ten o'clock—we were looking forward to room service, fresh pastries, freshly brewed coffee, and maybe even a side order of—dare we say it—bacon! And sitting around reading the morning paper and making thoughtful remarks to each other on the state of the world.

Well, no. Brasserie was still closed, but lots of coffee shops were around in the hotel general area. But, oddly for a college town or maybe any town, nowhere to find a paper. Geez Louise, the continuing decline of American civilization to which we were now unwilling witnesses. And not even a nearby McDonald's. The good part was that we had, after two days of pretty intense travel, scheduled a non-travel day. We had directions and a generous schedule so after some grumbling and some 7-Eleven coffee and something called, um, wait—it was so bad I cannot remember what it was called, some gruesome 7-Eleven concoction—we went off to see the second of our three sites, the Santa Rita Ranch.

The California coastline had treacherously arranged more mountains between us in San Luis Obispo and the ranch, which was just east of a smaller town called Templeton. I have driven from Paso Robles via SLO and Templeton probably fifty times and never really noticed that there are some mountains along the way. Some illegitimate descendent of the Mendocino mountains or maybe the San Luis Obispo mountains. Anyway, we were back in what were perhaps "suburban" mountains, between Templeton and the ocean.

As noted earlier, the ranch was a 1,715-acre piece of property, rolling and rugged and mostly wooded with a small river, naturally called the Amazon (no, the Santa Rita Creek), running through it. There was a small dam on this river that had created a lovely, long lake, and there was a house on the lakefront, although it had never really been inhabited. It had also never really been a ranch, as in a place to raise cattle, so much of the vegetation was coastal sage and riparian oak, beautiful stuff. There was some pasturage, probably no more than fifteen acres, and one of the previous owners was allowed to put about twenty-five cows on it, but that would be over soon, and it only applied to a very small piece of the acreage.

We met Kyle Walsh, the conservation director, right at ten, as promised. We got into his Jeep or Forester or something woodsy and started driving around. Walsh was the number two guy at the land trust and a dedicated conservationist, and also smart and knowledgeable. We stopped to see different parts of the property probably six or seven times, got out of the Jeep, walked around. At one point, probably the highest point on the site, Kyle pointed toward the west and said, "See that?"

We looked, but without further direction than Kyle pointing generally toward the ocean it was hard to tell what he was singling out—a bird, an important tree, a cloud shaped like Okinawa, what?

"There's Moro Rock!" he said triumphantly.

Sure enough, when you looked in the right direction and squinted, you saw a moderately sized rock, a Sugarloaf manqué, over in the ocean, or actually right on the shore with most of it in the surf. It is maybe equivalent to a very small five-story hotel shaped like a mound. The Morro Bay website refers to it as "the Gibraltar of the Pacific." This is a tag line invented by a real moron who has never been to or even read anything about Gibraltar. Morro Bay is a crumby little beach town blip on the Coast Highway. If you do your research, you will find that Portuguese explorer Juan Rodriguez Cabrillo named the rock "El Morro" in 1542 when he passed by but did not stop. Because there's no harbor, and precious little else. In Spanish, *morro* means "hill." Hence Morro Rock translates as "hill rock." Well, that's interesting, in a mis-spelled sort of way.

The tour of the site continues. At every place where we stop and get out, we flush a flock of birds, too many flying away in various directions for us to try and identify. I do not know how Walsh arranged this, did he have them all caged up and then released by beaters at his signal? It was very impressive. He even arranged for us to see a badger, not very close but certainly close enough to identify as it waddled off into the undergrowth. A badger! None of us had ever seen a badger in the wild! Given that badgers have a reputation as being mean-spirited, and besides they have long claws and real teeth and are not vegetarians, the distance for seeing him was about right. Besides, we were not in the market for badger habitat, but the nice thing about establishing bird habitat is that you get other stuff as a bonus. I could do without the snakes, but you get the point.

Walsh turned out to be intelligent and committed. He was also in charge of the work to upgrade and "re-naturalize" the site—my words, not his. At one point we passed three workers (couldn't tell gender as they were in hazmat suits) busy applying some sort of herbicide to an infestation of thistle. He mentioned what kind it was, bull thistle I believe, which they were trying to get rid of. Some quick research reveals that there are three noxious thistles in California, all three from southern Europe. In addition to milk thistle (*Silybum marianum*) there is Italian thistle (*Carduus pycnocephalus*) and bull thistle (*Cirsium vulgare*). None of the agriculture sites I checked has a single kind word for any of these. There is also a native and endemic California thistle called (surprise!) California thistle. Its Latin name is *Cirsium occidentale var californicum* and is a perennial herb native to the Santa Monica Mountains—which is where we are heading next. No one likes it either. And no one mentions the globe artichoke (*Cynara cardunculus var. scolymus*), also known by the names French artichoke and green artichoke in the US, which is a variety of a species of thistle cultivated as a yummy food. Botanists are so crabby. I am pretty sure the herbicide people weren't squirting poison on artichokes.

The rule of thumb I am slowly learning for bird habitat is simple: water, open space, forest. This property has all three and a smart and dedicated land trust managing it. Okay, they were being nice to us because we were offering them money, but after a while you begin to be able to sort out differences between organizations. For example, it's good to be helpful, but also honest. At one point somewhere on the property he stopped us, and we got out and he pointed to a hill across a small valley. There was a white splotch on the side of the hill, not big, maybe one acre, hard to tell. "I just wanted you to see that this is here," he said.

"Okay, fine," us landscape experts responded. "Uh, what is it?" It looked more or less like a natural rock outcropping.

"That's a former limestone mine," he said. "Hasn't been used for forty years, but one of the previous owners let the local cemetery come up here and cut slabs out of it for tombstones. There's little we can do to fix that."

"I don't suppose you can go and buy back the tombstones," I remarked because I find it hard to keep quiet at times when I really should.

The tour ended with handshakes and thanks all around, as well as promises to answer any further questions that we might have subsequently. We were highly impressed.

We drove back to downtown San Luis Obispo, a much nicer small city than I had remembered. We wandered around and supported the local businesses by miscellaneous shopping. Then, because we are not really dumb, we made reservations and went back to the exact same Italian restaurant at which we had eaten the night before. It was still wonderful.

The next morning, we needed to be off to the Santa Monica Mountains, found magically next to Santa Monica, but three-plus hours from SLO. We had a morning appointment to meet a person from the Santa Monica Mountains land trust at the site by ten. We detoured from our normal policy because we couldn't find a nearby McDonald's, and instead tried the local 7-Eleven. This was not a good idea—do not let your children do this unless they wish to die of sugar poisoning and horrible coffee.

We rendezvoused with our host, Charles, and he used the organization's key to let us in through a locked gate. We were up on the top of the range and on Mulholland Drive, which runs more or less north-south on the top of the ridge of mountains that separates LA and Santa Monica from the San Fernando Valley. This road is famous in the movie world as a David Lynch special, as in, "Damn, what's going on here?" You realize that the French loved the movie, giving it one of those Palme d'Or at Cannes in 2001, and critics had a different opinion. According to Wikipedia, it uses "Lynch's characteristic surrealist style and has left the general meaning of the film's events open to interpretation. Lynch has declined to offer an explanation of his intentions for the narrative, leaving audiences, critics, and cast members to speculate on what transpires." Yes sir, nothing I like better than a movie that doesn't make any sense. If I wanted that I'd just watch the local city council meetings.

This particular part of the aforesaid road has been closed, gated and, as mentioned, locked. We can get in because we're with the land trust guy. But the road is very steep at this point, and we are at the top picking our way on a sort of off-road trail that parallels the road and is also very steep going down. There is also very little vegetation. The area burned several years ago, and this is LA where it really doesn't rain very much so there has not been much regrowth. There are occasional blackened tree remains alongside the trail and maybe some weeds of indiscriminate parentage, but not much else. It also looks like rattlesnakes could live here, although why even they wouldn't seek out somewhere nicer like Beverly Hills is not clear. I begin to wish we were wearing snake gaiters, even though I have only read about them and am not entirely clear what they are. I do not think they are what snakes wear to keep their socks up, however.

Our Charles does his best to point out the good points of the property. At the far bottom of the trail is a mobile home park that the land trust is having a fight with because they seem to have encroached on some of the land of the site. We see one blue jay in our first thirty careful minutes on the trail.

Our guide points out a former trail that was used by the stage coach in times past. It is difficult to discern. Equally difficult is to figure out why the stage just didn't go over to the valley and head on up to San Francisco that way. And then we hear a distant grinding, roaring sound that rapidly grows louder and louder until I begin to search the sky for a B-52 that is about to make an emergency landing right on top of us. It is VERY LOUD and getting closer.

Charles is not concerned or has gone deaf. Finally, we see, beside us along the closed road, two truly crazy skateboarders, crouched low on their boards, zooming down Mulholland Drive at probably fifty miles an hour, leaning into the curves and having a great time. Their hearing must already be gone, I conclude.

"Oh, yeah," says Charles nonchalantly, "they're not supposed to be here, but the gate doesn't keep them out."

"Won't getting killed keep them out?" I ask, only half in jest. They are really going fast, and I don't remember if skateboards have brakes of some kind. Maybe you just drag your toe like in roller-skating?

I am ignored and we continue our journey through this burned, dusty, birdless piece of remarkably unattractive real estate. I am careful to make sure that Charles is in the lead and will get bitten by any snakes first.

Eventually we turn around and climb back up the same trail we have skidded and slid down. It is not any easier than you would assume, as in, not at all easy. Hot, dusty, but fortunately snakeless. The site, once we understand the boundaries, is basically forty-five acres on the side of a very steep mountain. Too steep to build on except by highway engineers, who then reconsidered and closed the road. Did I mention the fire two years ago?

None of this was clear from reading the application and doing a bit of map research. Aha! This is why you do a site visit. Now I never have to come back here.

By the time we finished up it was around noon. We had planned to drive on to downtown Santa Monica, not more than an hour away, and spend the night at Shutters on the Beach, a lovely hotel we were fond of. But we had also planned that this site visit would take longer than it did. And we had been on the road now for more than a week with various adventures and misadventures. We looked at each other. We looked at our watches. We decided we could be home in four hours, even counting driving through LA. We had already paid for the hotel so that's a sunk cost. And no doubt the cats were wondering where we were. This is a cat owner's fantasy. Cats are only likely to be concerned largely because they are worried about getting fed. Since we had arranged for someone to feed them, there was no chance they were concerned. As everyone who has ever had a cat knows. We turned the car south and headed back to Encinitas.

We discussed the three sites on the way back. It didn't take much discussion. The Santa Monica site was a big NO, for all the reasons cited above. Too ugly, too burned, too steep, bad neighbors, too few birds. The Santa Rita Ranch was a big YES for just about the opposite set of reasons: beautiful, not burned, great mixed terrain, impressive staff, water available, no close neighbors let alone ones encroaching on the site, lots of birds. The badger also helped but didn't sway the judgement.

Willow Creek was a toss-up. We loved the people who were smart and impressive and seemed dedicated to managing their site for both cattle and wildlife. But they were at the start of negotiating their agreement with the Rangeland Trust, and everyone agreed that the final conservation easement would be in the vicinity of $2 million. This made our measly $50K fine, but not impressive. We would be first money in with no clear schedule of when, or even if ever, the deal would close. The big money would have to come from the state or federal wildlife grants, a process uncertain as to timing and amount. Could take two years, could take five years, could take never. Having some of our funds tied up, even on a loose "commitment" basis, was not attractive.

We didn't firmly decide on Santa Rita Ranch at that point for one reason: because we had never actually seen the proposed conservation easement document, let alone the final document. When we visited the ranch, we asked about that and were reassured that it would be "pretty standard." But that meant nothing to us since we had never seen any agreement, let alone a "standard" one. More work was clearly necessary.

18

We Cement Our Partnership with CLO, but Unfortunately Choose Mucilage Rather Than a Better Kind of Adhesive

We Probably Should Have Used Elmer's Glue-All

Back at the Encinitas homestead we arranged for a conference call with Sara Barker, the program manager. She and a Cornell Lab development person named Christopher Miller had been our main points of contact for this whole endeavor. Probably we made a mistake in not connecting with someone higher in the organization to make sure that all the bases were touched, and the institution was in favor. But everything up to this point had gone smoothly, and besides, what NGO doesn't like someone to come to them and offer money? We didn't even want a building named after us.

Sara had already notified the two grant applicants whose applications we had decided against that they were no longer in the running. And after not very much discussion, she agreed with us that the Santa Monica Mountains project was not worth pursuing further. She duly notified them that they, too, had not made the cut. That left Willow Creek and the Santa Rita Ranch.

This is the point at which the train began to depart from the tracks. At first gradually. Sara suggested that now that we had two potential winners, we should go ahead and send the lab the $100K it would take to actually make the grants. By this time on our steep learning curve of philanthropy as administered by nonprofits, we were at least far enough up said curve to have learned a few things. The principal thing we had learned was don't give anyone the money until the deal is ready to close. Of course, Cornell would like to have the money right now, with none of the details finalized. Of course, as they told us, that was how all their programs worked. It would enable the lab to get the tedious administrative work of receiving the money and putting it in an account out of the way. And assuring the potential grantees that the funds were in hand.

Tedious? Exactly how tedious could depositing a check in a bank account be? And waiting the five days or so for it to clear? That seemed unconvincing.

The issue of our credit was never raised directly, just indirectly by telling us that this funding ahead of time was their usual procedure and they didn't understand why we found this not to our liking.

We thought about having a long discussion about the numerous reasons why this was a bad idea. First and foremost, what if the potential grant recipients balked at some of the terms and conditions that we assumed would be put in the grant agreement? What if they then balked hard enough that we (and Cornell) decided not to fund them?

What if Sara negotiated a grant agreement that was fine with her but not fine with us? Could she go ahead and fund them while we sat in the corner being mad and feeling stupid?

What if Jack Hanson at Willow Creek had a heart attack and died, and his kids said hell no, we're selling this ranch to a developer to make into three-acre ranchettes?

What if Willow Creek and their land trust sponsor, Rangeland, were never able to raise the federal and state wildlife grant funds to complete the purchase of the conservation easement?

After some more thought we decided that funding a conservation easement was too different from purchasing a piece of property. It basically set up a regulatory structure that placed a good deal of trust in the landowner to abide by all the conditions in the easement. But the party on the other side of the deal had to monitor this behavior. Too much room for disagreement, bad behavior, hurt feelings, and lots of monitoring expense. So, Willow Creek was out, despite the fact that we had enjoyed our brief visit there.

We continued our discussions on funding Santa Rita with Sara directly. We also said, as politely as we could manage it, that we actually didn't give a rat's patootie about what they did with other donors, we weren't other donors. And if this were to have been a condition of Cornell teaming up with us, they should have disclosed it at the beginning, and we could then have taken our resources elsewhere.

To all these what-ifs, Sara and Chris's answer was, in essence, "We will take your generous funding and apply it elsewhere to the benefit of birds." Not "We will consult closely with you and then spend it only on project of which you approve" and certainly not "We will immediately send the money back." All accompanied by a chorus of "This is how we have always done it, after all we are the premium bird laboratory in the world and people stand in line to work with us."

We held our ground, as politely as we could manage. Sara decided to go ahead and negotiate the grant agreements for us to approve, and Chris slunk off to the development offices, no doubt to tell stories about how darn difficult it was to find donors who were easy to work with.

We started with the Santa Rita Ranch agreement. As mentioned earlier, the land trust had engaged in a reasonable financing practice. They had raised a pool of money that they kept for opportune purchases of property. Once the purchase is complete, they then either refill their coffers with grants from the state and feds, or they do a round of general fundraising from their usual sources, or both. Their application suggested that our funding would be used for this, and for the work on the property that was necessary to return it to its native state. But little detail was provided on either of these two uses.

The good news was that they owned the place, so there was no uncertainty about funding a project that might never go forward. Our basic idea when we entered into this process with Cornell was that we could come in and be the last step in a fee simple purchase. But nobody asked us to do that, exactly.

We discussed this several times among ourselves and the Cornell Lab people. The concern was lack of specificity on how the funds were to be applied, and how we could somehow assure ourselves that if we contributed to replenishing their acquisition fund, they didn't just take the money and go to Vegas. As you will probably note, this is the other side of the coin of the issue discussed above. How do we know that we will get what we think we are funding? There is no good answer to this, as the grant document is not a contract and probably is not enforceable if the grant recipient engages in bad behavior. No one really talks about that, but in our business history there have been many instances of parties to a contract deciding not to honor parts of it to which they had previously agreed. The answer in business is you sue the bastards, and this has been known to happen even with the nicest relationships. It's not a good answer, but it's what makes contracts work.

After more debate than was probably useful, we concluded as follows: We would ask them to allocate one half of the money to replenish their acquisition fund, and the acquisition fund had to continue to make acquisitions for wildlife habitat. Since this was the land trusts' reason for being, this didn't seem like much of an "ask." Besides, since money is fungible, there was no way that we would ever be able to tell if they followed this practice. The bet here, if there was one, was that these were honorable people devoted to doing what had got them the Santa Rita Ranch, and we were betting they would continue. We just didn't know exactly what our $50K would help fund, or where or when.

Half of the funds were to be used for working on the ranch to get it back to "natural habitat" state, whatever that was. It was not meant that they had to take out the dam and drain the lake and tear down the three-bedroom house that they planned to use for environmental education. It was okay to keep funding the hazmat people to poison all the thistles. Making sure that they were not endemic California thistles, but instead those bad guys from Italy, of course.

The back and forth and the drafting of the agreement took several months. This seemed a bit odd to us, but we were not the actors here, although Sara did keep us apprised on how it was going and occasionally asked for our comments. It was only a ten-page agreement and not legally enforceable at that, so there was not a lot to comment on. Finally it was done and ready to be executed.

We still had not transferred the money.

Good thing. Next came the issue of the press release. We really are not publicity-seeking ego-nuts. There are lots of reasons to keep one's affairs private, or at least not aggressively publicized. If we were a public company, then of course we would have legal disclosure obligations. I dealt with that for many years at AES. But we're not, so we don't. But we are doing other things than habitat, and one of those is helping make our local political system work better than the abysmal results it currently rings up. We have tried the customary approaches of providing comments on proposed actions, testifying at public hearings, and modestly funding candidates whom we think would be better than the current bunch of clown cars running the city. California has constrained the amount of money one can contribute to candidates for state and local office to $4,900 dollars. Many local jurisdictions have ratcheted this down further. In Encinitas, the limit per candidate is $250. This is not very much money. It is made less constraining by the Supreme Court decision called Citizens United, which essentially said that a person or an organization can spend however much money it wants to on a candidate/campaign, but that this activity may not be "coordinated" with the candidate and her or his campaign. This has given rise to something called "independent expenditure"—committees that raise and spend money but without any communication with the candidate. Weird, but that's how it works.

We tried this unsuccessfully two years ago. We have since determined that we would be more successful if we were better known in the community. So we come full circle. Funding wildlife habitat isn't really a political activity, certainly not a local one, but it is a nice charitable thing to do, and one of which we are proud. We are also grateful to have been lucky enough to have successful careers that now allow us to spend money on this activity. We wanted to be mentioned in the press release on the Santa Rita Ranch.

We communicated this need to Sara and Chris early on, and got the "oh sure" response that we did not realize at the time did not in fact mean, "Yes, we will mention that this whole stupid program would never have been undertaken but for the fact that the two of you put up all the resources therefore."

"Oh sure" actually meant "We'll handle this, you go sit in the corner and be quiet and you'll see the press release when it comes out." Nothing further was discussed about this matter while we went through the whole process of sending out the program notice, receiving proposals, evaluating them, driving around California doing site visits (on our own dime) and finally picking the first recipient.

Once all that stuff was done and the grant agreement successfully negotiated and executed, we naively said, "Okay, it's time for the press release, would you like us to take a crack at the first draft?" This seemed to us a helpful offer, we've written press releases before, we know who the lab is, we know who the land trust is, we've been to the site, we know the amount of the grant and the source of the money, this cannot be more than a couple of hours work, if that.

We were meant with a somewhat frosty reception for this generous offer. Something along the lines of "The lab always drafts its own press releases."

"Okay," we said, "but we need to give you the sentences about us that we need to have included." We sent them the following four sentences:

> The $50,000 funding for this project was provided by a California philanthropic couple, Robert Hemphill and Leah Bissonette. They live in Encinitas, California, and focus their charitable activity on finding and preserving important bird habitat, especially in California, but also in select international locations. As well as their philanthropic activity, Leah and Bob are founders of a local activist group, Concerned Citizens of Encinitas. This nonprofit organization works to bring responsiveness, transparency, and accountability to local political decisions and programs.

Pretty aggressive and self-aggrandizing, right? I could have added another phrase to the last sentence: " ... so far with little success" but that seemed too much.

The response was strange. Chris said in essence, "No one mentions donors in their press releases. And we don't plan to do so in ours."

This seemed odd to me. No, it didn't seem odd, it seemed completely untrue. I went on to the internet and checked out several other NGOs who had recently done something funded by somebody. And guess what—the donor's name was ALWAYS plastered all over the press release, usually in the headline, e.g.: JOE SMITH GIVES UNIVERSITY OF CALIFORNIA $5 MILLION FOR CANCER RESEARCH.

I sent the examples back to Chris and Sara. No real response. No, that's not right, they did have a response, which was hardly an acknowledgement: "Isn't it time you sent us the money?"

Mrs. Hemphill didn't raise no idiots. We sent back a response that said, politely, we are not going to fund this grant until we see the final press release.

Bad judgment on the development front: Chris had in addition the previous week sent us a solicitation for the Chairman's Council of the lab. You got the usual benefits from signing on, but the price tag was ten grand. We said what the heck and put a check in the mail. But in the short time since then, we had been increasingly dumped on by the development people, so I called up the bank and asked them to stop payment on the check. Fortunately, it had not yet cleared so this was possible, and they did it. Then I called the only development person who had been nice to us and told her that the check was on hold until the press release got done the way we wanted it. I asked her for the name of the head of development for the lab, which turned out to be a woman named, remarkably, Bramble Kimble.

I looked her up on the internet, oh useful source of much information, and it turned out that prior to coming to Cornell, she had been the head of development for the Nature Conservancy in Washington for more than a few years. Useful coincidence: when I worked at the Office of Management and Budget in the Jimmy Carter administration, my boss was a former McKinsey consultant and then pharmacy company CEO named

John Sawhill. He was a terrific guy and became a good friend and supporter. When he left the government, he stayed in Washington and became CEO of the Nature Conservancy for some time. During his tenure, Ms. Kimble had worked for him. Aha! I decided based on this linkage, and the fact that we were getting nowhere dealing with the lower-level people, I should call her and ask for her intercession. We are arguing about a press release that perhaps eleven people in the whole country will ever read, for God's sake!

I did eventually connect with her. She was polite and concerned and sort of knew about the project, but not the important details. She remembered John Sawhill with real reverence and enthusiasm. She listened carefully to our description of the situation and the roadblocks that the lab people had thrown up. She agreed to dig into the situation and get back to me.

In a couple of days, she did so. They were willing to add our language to the press release, but they needed it to come at the end, and it would be in smaller type than the rest of the release. I said that I had to see what she meant so she needed to send me a copy of what they were proposing. The truth was that I no longer trusted the program people to do what they said they would, and we were absolutely not going to fund until we had things the way we wanted them. It was our only negotiating leverage, and we weren't giving it up until we had our way. After all, nothing else had worked with them.

She sent it to us, and we read it. It was factual and not especially inspiring, but okay. Our four sentences were in fact at the end of the release, and they were in eight-point type, which looks like this: this is eight-point type.

It's pretty small compared to the twelve-point type that is the size you are now reading. I thought about how crappy this was and considered fighting on, this time to get our sentences in the same size type as the Cornell bits of the press release. I did get the feeling that if I did that, I was crossing some sort of self-defined "jerk" line and getting into jerk territory, and no longer residing in Legitimately Offended Donor Territory.

We gave up, said it was fine, please send us the instructions for wiring you the money. Which we did. We also released the hold on the $10K for the Chairman's Council contribution.

Sure enough, although Cornell sent the press release to all the local San Diego news outlets that we provided names and addresses for, not a one of them picked it up. Good thing we hadn't been counting on wads of free press coverage to kick off our campaign for governor.

19

Harvesting the Rewards of Success!

Sung to the tune of "When Johnny Comes Marching Home"

There is more to the Cornell story.

We had finally finished with the funding of the Santa Rita Ranch through Cornell and were honestly, despite all the problems, feeling quite pleased with ourselves. This is always a risky feeling, but it's so nice. . . .

Shortly thereafter, the head of development had one of her minions ask us to join the Cornell Lab's Chairman's Council for the coming year, which we had done before. You were required to make a donation to the lab of $10,000 per year but were assured that it was a great honor, limited to a special few, lots of other benefits. This and our other dealings should have raised alarms, but it did not. We're obviously easy when it comes to donors. We joined again and gave.

Part of the benefits of being a member of the Chairman's Council is that you get invited on special trips that they arrange. The lab uses one of the high-end wildlife tour companies, Victor Emanuel Nature Tours, usually shortened to VENT. We had heard of Victor Emanuel Nature Tours when several years ago we went on a birding trip with a bird viewing company called Rockjumper to the South Pacific. I did not write up that trip—laziness? bad judgement?—and that was probably a mistake. But here's the summary: great birds, sketchy accommodations, horrible food. And we were still charged the luxury price that we have come to understand is $1,000 per person per day. In this case that included cold showers, which are at the top of my personal list of things to be avoided at all costs.

When I spent my obligatory year in Vietnam as an infantry officer with the 1st Cavalry, most of the time in the field there were no showers at all. We were, after all, running around in the boonies trying to find the enemy before he found us. This meant sleeping under shelter halves or ponchos, eating C rations, and sometimes washing in streams we came across. Although checking first to see if there were leeches, which there usually were. And after one especially unpleasant experience, checking first upstream a bit. We didn't do that initially. Then one day while half the platoon was bathing and the other half standing guard waiting their turn, one of the standing guard guys wandered off. This was never a good idea, but discipline is hard to maintain twenty-four hours a day. He was still within sight of the rest of the platoon when he came hurrying back, announcing that there were two dead bodies in the stream just up a ways. Hurried exits by all the bathers.

When I came out of the field, I was in brigade headquarters, which may sound lovely. However, unfortunately there was still a war on, and the brigade was chasing the North Vietnamese Army (NVA) around, so we moved the whole shebang frequently. We did get to sleep in large ten- or twenty-man tents that leaked when it rained. It is possible they were left over from WWII. We had the engineers to provide us decent drinking water and water for washing, but no hot water for showers. Every night, or honestly maybe every third or fourth night, you would grit your teeth and take a quick cold shower. When after nine months I went on R & R to Hawaii, I probably spent more time in the bathroom taking many hot showers than I did in bed with my wife. And I swore that when I got back to "the World" I would never again take a cold shower. Never again.

Then came the Rockjumper trip to the south Pacific. First stop, Samoa and Uncle Dave's Eco Lodge, a crappy little sort of motel where the walls of the bathroom did not extend to the peaked ceiling, so privacy/modesty were not really possible. That I could have lived with. But no hot water. Not just none in the evening or none in the morning or none at certain unpredictable times of day or at specified times of day. None.

Added to this was the delightful lunch menu. When you're out in the woods or the jungle trying to find the elusive Taveuni silktail you don't have time to stop and find a McDonald's and besides, there aren't any. Okay, fine. But you got to the start of the bird hike in a small van (there were only six of us plus our guide) so there was carrying capacity for picnic-type fixings. What we got was white sandwich bread, a slice of American cheese, and water. No potato chips, no mayonnaise, no tiny Snickers bars for dessert, and certainly no pickles, and not even Kool-Aid let alone a cold beer for lunch to drink.

For a while we went along with this thinking it might be a problem with the supplies in Samoa. But then we got to Fiji, and it was the same, and in Vanuatu it was the same. We finally groused about this to some of our fellow travelers, all of whom had been on more bird trips than we. We were informed, somewhat haughtily I thought, that: (1) real birders are there for the birds and do not expect any better food or accommodations than we were getting, and (2) if we really were such short hitters that we couldn't stand not having beef Wellington on good china served for lunch, then next time we should try Victor Emanuel Nature Tours. I made a careful note to do just that. "Spelled with one 'm' or two?" I asked, not entirely in jest.

Apparently, the Cornell Lab's Chairman's Council agreed with us on this one.

Soon after the Santa Rita project was funded and the press release sent out and we had sent our money in to join the council, we got a message inviting us on an upcoming Chairman's Council trip to Monterey Bay. It was a four-day excursion and included both bird outings and a boat trip in Monterey Bay to see pelagic birds (of course) but also incidentally whales. "Boats" and "whales" are two key words for us, kind of like the opposite of a "safe word" you use if you need to get out of the middle of some weird recreational bondage. I only know this from watching television.

The trip was arranged by VENT, so that was a plus. The plan included staying at a lovely lodge in Carmel called the Bernardus Lodge and Spa.

There were daily bird trips and one day devoted to zooming around Monterey Bay in a boat, chasing birds and whales. You did have to pay all your own transportation and food and lodging costs, but local transport, boats, and trip leaders were included. And the leaders were both from Cornell Lab and from VENT.

It did look good, and much of it was outdoors, and we were pretty tired of being Covid captives, so we signed on. Besides, the drive from San Diego to Monterey was a pretty easy one. The event was largely as represented. There were senior lab personnel there and three or four VENT people, all of whom proved very knowledgeable about birds and not bad about fish and whales. The food was very good. You could not have found a white bread sandwich if you tried. Which we did not. And every evening after dinner the lab director, a recently appointed academic named Ian Owens with a very impressive record, would give a slide presentation on the lab, its priorities, the future of birds, etc.

There were eighteen of us Chairman's Council members making up the audience. The group didn't skew young; maybe one-fourth in the under-fifty range and the rest of us older. Remember, you had to cough up $10K just to get invited, not to mention the rest of the cost. Everyone we met was smart and accomplished and pleasant. The one that we liked best was a woman named Heather Hodges. We met her later in the second day, at the evening cocktail hour. After some standard introductory banter, it turned out that she lived in Ohio, did not appear to be married, and was retired from the State Department. She seemed a pretty standard-issue Midwest American, and that's a compliment. Her last posting had been in Guayaquil, Ecuador, which is how she said it.

Because I have made this mistake before and regretted it, I did not ask her if she had been an administrative assistant or what. Instead, I reached high and asked if she had been the DCM (deputy chief of mission, the number two person in every embassy).

"No," she replied pleasantly enough, "I was the ambassador." Okay, not a complete bungle on my part, but I could have just not tried to show off about how I knew embassy jargon like "DCM."

We went on to have a really interesting conversation about her time when the WikiLeaks scandal fomented by the notable Julian Assange was blowing up. Apparently, it blew up in Ecuador as well as in countless other embassies. Heather had sent classified but straightforward cables to her counterpart in Washington, and these were among the many documents that Assange published. The then president of Ecuador was of course mentioned in them, in a straightforward way, warts and all. He was offended to have his warts listed and categorized, and after some storming about, he made her persona non grata. Thus she became the first and so far only woman ambassador in South America, and the first woman ambassador anywhere, to be designated PNG. This is a nontrivial accomplishment.

Note also that she introduced herself as "Heather Hodges." I have met more than a few retired ambassadors, and I have NEVER met one who did not introduce himself as "Ambassador Smith" or "Ambassador Jones," even though they hadn't been near an embassy in fifteen years. But not Heather. And her name tag didn't say "Ambassador" either. Such humility is rare but delightful.

She knew the Jocotoco group in Ecuador that we had almost worked with before the deal came unglued. She liked them and, in fact, had joined their board of directors once she had stopped being an ambassador. She obviously rated them highly or else why join the board and risk one's good name and waste your time? She knew about the project and was in general quite encouraging about the country. It was a surprise and a delight to spend some time with someone who knew both birds and Ecuador.

The agenda for the trip was simple: Birding trips to various Monterey locations on two of the days, and a whale and bird-watching trip on the bay the third day. Breakfast at the lodge (very good and generous), lunch at some location nearer one of the birding locations, again good food and well provided. Each of the three evenings started with a cocktail party for an hour, then an excellent dinner, then a presentation by the director or one of the senior staff members.

The bird trips were fun, since several of the lab people lived in Monterey and, being bird people, knew just where to go. In particular, they took us on the second day along US Route 1 to look for condors, the largest bird in North America, possibly in the world, although the Andean condor is a contender. Basically a scavenger, it roosts high on the coast range that borders the ocean in that area, generally known as the Santa Lucia Mountains. It mostly eats washed-up whales and other large but dead sea animals. You might be a really big bird, but it takes quite a bit of time to completely eat a whale. Even a small whale.

A condor, when viewed up close in the aviary at the San Diego Zoo Safari Park, home to several disabled condors, is pretty darn ugly. It directly resembles a turkey vulture, not one of nature's more beautiful creations. It has a big hooked bill, and no feathers on its head, so its head is an unlovely shade of reddish pink. The lack of feathers enables it to use its large bill and rip apart whales and stick its head inside to eat and not get its feathers dirty. It is unlikely that watching this process would make one yearn to be turned into a condor. Or a dead whale. But when it soars over the cliffs and hills it is pretty darn majestic, as it relies on the thermals to carry it aloft, thus conserving its energy for ripping things apart.

The whale and pelagic bird trip was a knockout. Pelagic turns out to mean "sea living" and refers to birds like albatrosses and shearwaters and lots of other birds that live almost all the time on the ocean. There is that pesky problem of having a nest and some eggs to preserve the species, but these nesting sites are usually on steep, rocky, and ugly islands that no one really cares about, and thus make good sites for the brief period of mating and fostering the young until it's out to sea again. It probably goes without saying that if you are a pelagic bird, you mostly eat fish. No surprise there. You may also eat other birds from time to time, but no one likes to point that out.

The trip was on a small boat, of course, never my favorite, but following the logic, you have to be out on the ocean to see stuff that lives on or above the ocean. Dramamine has made this less challenging than when I was a kid. We spent almost all day on the ocean and saw a lot of birds that really none of us landlubbers could identify, and nothing particularly colorful. But birdwatchers don't always have to be spotting trogons or birds of paradise to be happy. They just have to see *some* birds, and we did.

More to the point, the trip sponsors advertised whales. We have routinely seen whales in the waters outside San Diego, as they make their annual migratory journey to the Gulf of Mexico where they give birth and fool around. This happens on January and February and by mid-March it's over. The trip back from Mexico is not as orderly and thus doesn't provide any particular windows for whale observation. No, I don't know why. That said, this "whale watching" cruise was in October, so I had little expectation that we'd see anything. Well, maybe some dolphins, they're always accommodating.

Sometimes your lack of real knowledge catches up with you. This was one of those times. The whales we see migrating down to the gulf are gray whales. But there are other kinds of whales who do not seem to have adopted the grays' schedule or preference for accommodations. Humpbacks are one of these, and they are even easier to see than grays because (1) they are larger, and (2) they do have something of a humped back. See them we did, in ones and twos, as we cruised around Monterey Bay. It turns out that Monterey Bay is really big and deep so it can accommodate lots of sea life. You can be easily out of sight of land (not my personal favorite feeling) and still be just in the middle of the bay. We chugged around and saw lots of whales, and then as a grand finale, we spotted three humpbacks who were following and hunting a school of sardines. We watched this from pretty close for probably a half an hour, longer than you ever see gray whales. As a finale, all three rose to the surface and then dived, giving us a perfectly synchronized view of three tail flukes, all nicely lined up, as they dived down to continue sardine feeding. It was a great site and very impressive. I am glad that Captain Ahab didn't kill all the whales. It's useful to note that the discovery of petroleum had something of a positive effect in keeping whales alive, as opposed to being hunted and refined into oil to use in lamps.

Back from our day on the bay, we got ready for the final evening of the trip. The previous two nights the director had said lots about his plans for the lab, but nothing at all—nothing, nada, *rien de tout*—about how nice it was for all the guests on the trip to have given the lab all the money they did, thank you very much, please keep it up. I could have written that speech, as could any donor.

We got changed into presentable clothes and wandered off to the evening's cocktail party. Emboldened by a glass of wine, we decided to seek out the director and ask him about our Santa Rita Ranch project. All we could figure out that made sense was that he was new, he wasn't fully briefed on all the lab's activities, he hadn't had time to read all his briefing books, etc. We finally collared him and moved him off somewhat from the crush of cocktailers. We started by congratulating him on his appointment and by noting what a good relationship we had with Sara. Then we bluntly asked him if he had heard of the Santa Rita Ranch project that we had just funded through the lab.

"Yeah, I've heard about that," he remarked almost dismissively. There was an uncomfortable silence while we waited for him to say something—anything—nice.

Finally, we said politely, "From your remarks about your priorities on the previous two evenings, it doesn't seem like bird habitat is at the top of your list."

"There are a lot of people who do habitat," he replied. "There are a lot of land trusts out there. I don't think we should be doing that." He then turned away and went over to talk to someone who was more in line with his priorities, whatever they were, which clearly didn't include us.

We were both surprised and downcast by this assessment of a program we had worked more than a year on and had every expectation of continuing. Nope. We were done. Usually when I've gotten fired, it was by people who were giving me money, not by people I was giving money to.

We had plenty of time on the way home to lick our wounds and try to sort out what had happened and where we could have done better. This was after we got through calling the director a dick and a shithead and a stupid jerk in a fancy suit, and not even that fancy a suit when it came down to it. We didn't think that the idea was flawed, or the execution in some way lacking. We had done a lot of work on our own dime to make sure that we selected good projects with dedicated and capable people to make them work. We had worked carefully with Sara, and we agreed on all her substantive matters. Our conclusions were threefold:

1. It wasn't enough money. It was enough money for at least some grant recipients to be interested and to submit proposals. It was enough money for Sara to be enthusiastic about this new part of her program. But wasn't enough money for the development people to be very interested. It wasn't Jeff Bezos-quantity money. Chris Miller, our allotted development herder, told us so during the impasse on the press release. "You're not contributing enough money to get your name on the press release," he explained dismissively on one of several acrimonious telephone conversations. I leave it to the reader's imagination to imagine how well received this was. We had, in fact, planned to expand the program and make a larger commitment in the future, but it appeared that if the amount was less than multiple millions, the lab and the university couldn't be bothered.
2. Sara wasn't high enough in the organization to get internal encouragement, or to have anyone even pay much attention to what she was doing. The lab's annual budget is $37.5 million, and all the money Sara was managing, including our prospective $100K, was maybe 1% of that. They didn't even give her enough overhead money to come with us on our trip to the three California sites we were as a team evaluating. Not a good sign.
3. We really didn't know anyone else in the organization. We had no "executive sponsor." No godfather to protect us, no mentor. What we probably should have done—at some point in the process—was ask for a meeting with the director to make sure that he was on board with this new effort. But it was Covid, we weren't keen to fly all the way across country to Ithaca (no direct flights by the way) for a thirty-minute meeting and a head pat. The director was new, having joined during Covid, so he hadn't been spending much time in the lab much less getting familiar with all its many programs. Besides, everything was going smoothly until the press release, so why should we have been worried? "I guess we won't make that mistake again," he said ruefully.

20

The Cornell Lab President's Council Story, Second Installment

Is it Really Good Never to Learn from Your Mistakes? Only If You Like Looking Stupid, I Suppose.

Despite the fact that the lab director had fired us after our successful investment in saving the ranch at San Luis Obispo, we were still members of the Chairman's Council because we had given them our ten grand. And if the Monterey trip was any indication, the trips that were offered to council members were really quite nice.

About a year later there was another such trip, this time to the Pantanal in Brazil. It is covered in a letter to my aunt that is found later in the next book. Suffice it to say that it was also wonderful, although the food not quite as good.

Then it came time for us to renew our membership with the Chairman's Council for a third time—to be members for 2023 this time. Promised were trips to Nebraska to see the sandhill cranes and a trip to Portugal to see whatever birds live there, the former in the spring because that's when they are on their way from Mexico to the Arctic where they will breed and raise their young for a while. They make a stopover in central Nebraska, which is corn-raising central, and they eat all the non-harvested corn in the fields, then fly on. We have been there, and it's great and there really are a whole lot of birds during the right period—something like 150,000. These birds are also big and easy to see, and they stand still so you can look at them. Portugal, I am not so sure.

I got the usual polite letter reminding me that this contribution is an annual thing, and they'd like me to get with it. But I have become more demanding as I get more involved in the mess and peculiarity that is US philanthropic giving. As discussed earlier I am no longer so comfortable with the model: give us some money, don't ask questions, and we'll do good things with it, and then you can see your name in the annual report (at the back) and look at all the pictures of the starving children or starving birds that we have helped.

Since I now had a lot of experience with the Cornell Lab people, and since the head of development, the wonderfully named Bramble Kimble, had been with us on the great trip to the Pantanal in Brazil, I thought I could express a few thoughts to at least her before forking over ten grand on a "hope and hype" basis.

We had earlier sent Bramble Kimble and her development colleague Melissa a nice message congratulating them on the most recent issue of the lab's semiannual magazine, called *Living Bird*. In that message we also said:

More important is an issue of philanthropy. We have noticed that in the realm of large gifts, (Bill and Melinda Gates, MacKenzie Scott, etc.) precision as to proposed uses and accountability as to results are more and more the expectations of donors. That emphasis does not seem to have yet trickled down to smaller donors such as we are. We would be interested in your ideas for such programs or projects for the lab to which our Chairman's Council contribution could be connected. In all of our philanthropic activities we are trying for support that includes transparency and accountability. We would be happy to have a conversation about this at your convenience.

No response.

I think that was polite and it was surely honest. Frankly, we cannot be the only people in the world concerned about what NGOs and 501(c)(3) organizations do with our money, be these contributions large or small. Thus, in response to the appeal for funds, we sent Bramble and Melissa, the person actually assigned to deal with recalcitrant "Chairman's Council" people like me, another similar message:

> Dear Bramble and Melissa—
>
> We are interested in continuing to support the lab at the Chairman's Council level. We are particularly interested in work using eBird data to update the three billion bird-loss study. We think you may already be planning for such projects. We would like our $10,000 donation to be used exclusively to support such work and to that end we would like an explanation of how the project would be implemented and specifically how the funding would be used. To be clear, we are not interested in donating to a general fund or to overall lab administration. We understand that those are legitimate and appropriate costs, but we are only interested in donating to a specific project/series of projects, and we would like our donation restricted to such projects.
>
> Let us know if this works for you and, if so, please provide a description of the proposed project(s) and the funding/expenses plan.
>
> Thanks,
> Leah & Bob
> PS: We are still having happy thoughts about the Brazil trip.

I made sure that the tone and the language were comfortable just in case I was going off the deep end here.

This was not well received by the lab. The return email, which I won't bother quoting, was polite but said, basically, we don't bother to track such small donations and provide the information you are seeking. If you would like to consider a substantially larger contribution to the ever so important (okay, my elaboration here) work of the lab, we could consider what activities you were interested in funding. Otherwise, just send us the money and shut up. They were more polite than that. But that was the substance of their response.

I wanted to send back a three-page rebuttal and argument, clarifying our position, and buttressing it with other opinions and practices. There was another point of view, probably more realistic. That viewpoint noted that the lab had already fired us once and that was when we gave them $50K, not $10K. Walking away and finding other opportunities seemed a more productive course. So we did. Besides, we had already been to Portugal and didn't think it was all that great. So there.

21

Can't Anybody Here Play This Game?

A Summary of Sorts

Just to summarize if you have gotten lost in the details: We have to date (not counting what follows) had interesting relationships with various parties who are in the land conservation business, or who seemed like they should be in the land conservation business. Looks can be deceiving. They and the results are:

San Dieguito River Valley Conservancy: We wanted to give them $100K as the final financing for a nice 110-acre undeveloped piece of land near Lake Hodges in western San Diego County. Everything looked fine until we literally stumbled upon the presence of a meth lab, previously undisclosed to us and apparently unknown by the president of the conservancy. Other than that, what did you think of the play, Mrs. Lincoln?

Cornell Lab of Ornithology: A long and disappointing relationship wherein we convinced them to go into the land conservation business, an area that they were not previously in. We set up a joint grant program to find projects that did just that. We worked all through the structuring of the grant proposal, sending it out, getting responses in, evaluating the responses, making site visits to three of the five, selecting the one best and actually funding it to the tune of $50K. Very shortly thereafter, the new lab director, without the slightest conversation with us, fired us and shut down the program. Thanks for the dough, now get lost.

When we tried again on a more limited basis to direct the uses of our charitable giving to the lab, the answer was a polite but clear "Hell no."

Another nice effort but no score: We got connected by a referral to the Escondido Creek Conservancy, a local NGO that focuses on preserving the watershed of the Escondido Creek. This is a small creek in Escondido but turns into a larger creek as it meanders west from its start in the Laguna Mountains until it empties into the Pacific Ocean via the San Elijo Lagoon. The head of it, Ann Van Leer, is a capable woman with a nice sense of business. We met with her in Escondido for lunch and got on well. Later that month, she and the board chairman, Leonard Witmer, arranged to take us on a ride-along to look at the parcels that they were yearning to acquire. These were all in the eastern part of San Diego County. One thing that she emphasized was that in the land acquisition and conservation game, patience was necessary. A lot of patience.

Several months later, she asked us to come look at a parcel of 117 acres called Bear Valley, only because it was on Bear Valley Road. I guess it was also in some place called Bear Valley but there ain't been no bears in these here parts for probably a hundred years. Which is generally okay with me. The land also bordered I-15 and the family who owned it was discussing selling it. They had acquired it several years earlier on a whim (and a tub of money) that having a "country place" would be a great idea. It was that, and it was also a lot of work and cost to maintain. They were "thinking" about selling. They had in mind $2.5 million, more of course than they had paid for it (less than $2 million). It was a nice piece of land, but like almost all parcels near urban centers, it was hardly an undisturbed wilderness. About 25% of it was leased out to a neighbor who was growing something—maybe corn—on it. There was a small house on it, and a cleared, one-quarter-acre home site at the highest point from which, if you squinted hard, you could see a sliver of the Pacific Ocean even though it was probably fifteen miles away. In addition, the previous owner had decided that raising ostriches was a dandy idea and bought a bunch of them. He also cleared some land for corrals and put up a lot of wire fencing.

His gift was not ostrich ranching, it turned out, and eventually all the ostriches died or were sold to other people who also thought that having ostriches was a keen idea. Is this a great country or what?

But then the family decided that they really didn't want to sell yet, possibly waiting for the reincarnation of Elvis Presley, so that whole idea went back into the files.

Next Ann discussed with us something called the Bremmer property, a fifty-acre vacant lot near Lake Hodges. Again, the patriarch of the family had bought this as a rural retreat, but he eventually died before any retreat quality lodging could be constructed, or really anything much. The widow wanted to sell the property but didn't really need to and had significant expectations. Ann had convinced her to let the conservancy hire an independent assessor to do an assessment of the property, but she suggested that it would be nice if we paid part of the cost of this.

That seemed okay, so we did, and he proceeded. In the meantime, she arranged for me to go out and see the property, which I did. It was mostly steep, completely undeveloped, although a nice ranch house was at the north side property. But the owner was very interested in having the property sold to the conservancy and gave me a complete tour. A complete tour of an undeveloped property really doesn't take a lot of time.

The most interesting part of the whole thing was that when we got to the top of the hill, we could look out to the east and see Lake Hodges. And the Del Dios Highway. Yes, it was bordered on the east by the famous White property, home to the meth lab, that we had looked at several years earlier. But I walked all over this one and there wasn't anything illicit. Lots of scrubs and bushes and rocks and dust, which all was good and what we wanted.

The assessment finally was completed. It came in at about $750,000, which was around what Ann expected. It was not what the owner had expected, since she thought it was worth probably $2 million. Hence, no deal, at least not now. Patience, patience.

A small footnote: There are, it turns out, several well-funded state and federal programs where you can get grants to help purchase properties to turn into conservation sites. Usually, you can get up to 90% of the price, so you always need the 10% of "private" money. But one interesting catch is that the grant rules are that you cannot spend more than an independent appraisal of the value of the property. Not an awful restriction, and a reasonable constraint. Hence the need for the assessment. And the result of a deal that couldn't proceed, at least at this time.

Audubon Society: They do lots of good stuff, more along the lines of advocacy and lobbying and education than land conservation. We got very interested in their conservation ranching program and supported it in a modest way. It's kind of a backdoor way of doing bird conservation, but the need is large and it's clever. However, they are not likely ever to go buy a piece of land and preserve it, it's too big a step.

The Nature Conservancy: A group that got their start doing just what we have in mind—buying land and preserving it for all time forward. Way before I got the bird bug in California, I admired the Nature Conservancy for their credo, as it seemed at the time of action instead of words. My admiration was inflated when John Sawhill, my boss at the Office of Management and Budget, took over the job of president of the organization when he left the government in 1990. At the time, AES was going through an amazing growth spurt, both in terms of new projects and acquisitions and as to its stock price. We had gone public in 1990 at $2 per share (ten cents when adjusted for splits and additional issuances) and had reached the remarkable level of $50. This meant your approximately one million-plus shares, earned or acquired at a very low basis (a few cents per share), were now worth more than $50 million. But if you sold them, you had an enormous capital gains tax to pay.

Some genius had come up with a tax-advantaged transaction called a "charitable remainder unitrust," frequently shortened to CRUT. How this works is simple: you take some amount of stock, put it into the trust, which is held by a trustee. You pledge, and the trustee agrees, to give whatever is left in the trust to a charitable organization when you pass on. In addition, the trust is required to pay you some amount annually of the trust's income, in most cases 2% or 3%, so you have some income while you are alive. The trust can sell the shares and not incur any tax. Thereafter, the trustee manages the trust for the mutual benefit of the contributor, and of the eventual benefit at the contributor's death. Some calculations were done based on your age and the annual payment percentage, predicting when you would die, and how much at that point would be left. This amount was then present valued to the date of the contribution, and this value was allowed by the contributor to be taken against that year's taxes—even though the contribution to the charity was years away and the amount was, at best, a bit speculative.

Three benefits of this: (1) The stock can be sold and not reported as an insider transaction, which it is not. This was helpful as none of us at AES wanted to be seen as publicly selling the stock—it would look like a lack of faith in the company. (2) The annual income was a nice thing, although reported as ordinary income. (3) The immediate tax write-off of the future contribution was also valuable and could be carried forward if it exceeded that year's tax obligations.

Several of us at AES, once we learned of this, decided that this was a hell of a deal. I don't remember how much stock I put into it at the time, but the trust's value eventually grew to about $5 million. One more detail: If the contributor got tired of waiting around to die so he could give the rest of the value of the trust to the charity, he could liquidate the trust. Another calculation would be made, and the trust would get half, and the contributor would get half. The charity liked this. Money now was always better than the promise of money later, and what if I lived to be a hundred? It made sense to me.

This is a long way of saying that the trust was liquidated in 2022 and $2.6 million went to the Nature Conservancy. But nice as this was for them, and grateful as they were, I had no control whatsoever over what they did with the funds. Not my ideal way to give away a lot of money, but there were other reasons to do the liquidation.

Nature and Culture International: I have explained earlier (Chapter 14) about our $100K contribution to them to be used to purchase two properties in Ecuador and have them become bird preserves. For reasons never quite made clear, to me at least, only one of these "deals" ever closed but Matt Clark, the president, did return the "unused" $50K, and without any fuss. I confess to being quite surprised at the time. Good for him.

American Bird Conservancy: How I was introduced and how our first "deal" fell apart—land seller backed out, as frequently happens it turns out—are discussed above (Chapter 15). But all this didn't happen without a lot of conversation with Mike Parr, the CEO. We almost went to Ecuador to look at the timberland, and then Covid. I doubt that I have to explain more than that.

For a while after this, we discussed Jocotoco's change in strategy. The area they were after not only and most desirably had a big-ass piece of timberland in it, but the connecting piece was also in fragmented ownership, sixteen or twenty pieces if I recall correctly. The pieces weren't big—one hundred to five hundred acres—and they were beset with problems of lawlessness. The main problem was landless peasants moving in, cutting down all the trees, and selling them on the black market, then planting corn or beans. All illegally, as they didn't own the land, nor did they have the legal right to squat on it. Jocotoco decided that since they were already property owners in the area anyway, and for the moment they couldn't buy the big property from Botrosa, the lumber company, why not turn to a guerrilla approach, and pick off the small properties, one by one?

Why would the smallholders (I have always liked this word—does it refer to the weight or the stature of the landowners, or both?) wish to sell? Set aside the simplistic "everything has a price" mantra of radical capitalists. In this case, most of the landholders were not living on the land. It was a rainforest, for goodness' sake, and this means (drum roll) that it rains there a lot. These properties are not in downtown Dubuque, they're out on dirt roads (if any) with precious little law enforcement and damn sure no convenient 7-Elevens where you can stop for a Big Gulp before going out to view your beautiful property. Taking care of a property when you are an absentee landlord is not a walk on the beach.

Many years ago, I was living in a beautiful little row house on Capitol Hill and working in the Carter White House. We had just passed the National Energy Act of 1978. Well, the Congress passed it, but we felt proprietary about it. A whole team of us had been working on this for the first several years of the Carter administration, literally night and day. Arguing about what should be in the bill, how to draft it, when to send it to the Hill, drafting testimony to support the bill, answering the thousands of questions that the Hill staff sent to you, figuring out how to negotiate with the various staffs of the committee members, how to help line up votes, all the things at the lower level that need to be done before you get a bill across the finish line, and—voila!—it has become a law. And then there's the whole process of writing the regulations that implement the law, but let's leave that for now.

We had finished this key bill, an important part of President Carter's National Energy Program or some such grandiose name. I had been through a bunch of those names since Nixon so can be excused for being a tiny bit jaded as I had never seen any previous "energy independence strategies" ever get passed or implemented. But the sucker was done, I was pooped, and I remember distinctly coming home one night at about nine o'clock, which was when I had been coming home for the last three years, and thinking, "Goddam, we got it done." Then thinking, "I wonder what I should do now?"

I meditated on this for a while. We at the staff level had been working on energy policy under Nixon, Ford, and now Carter. We had written bills with all the ideas that we had that made any sense, and probably some that didn't, and some that had unexpected consequences, which is always what happens with legislation. Finally, I said to myself, "Goodness, I am out of policy." There wasn't anything that we still wanted to do and had been trying to do for five or six years, since the embargo in 1973. It was now 1979 and nothing, no good idea, was left on the legislative or policy to-do list. The fate of a policy analyst who is out of policy is not something that I studied in college. I assumed that I was to go back to being a GS-14 schlub somewhere in the government.

Shortly thereafter Dave Freeman called.

Dave Freeman was up to that point a Tennessean who had gone to law school at University of Tennessee, then made his way to Washington and somehow got a job as an assistant to the chairman of the Federal Power Commission, Joe Swidler. This agency, the predecessor to the Federal Energy Regulatory Commission (FERC), regulated the price of oil and gas and electricity if it moved across state lines. It was a powerful set of functions but appreciated only by those in the energy industry.

Dave spent his time well there, probably listening more than he talked—which was hard for him. He learned all there was to know about energy policy. Note: at this point, oil was two dollars a barrel except in Saudi Arabia where the lifting cost was probably ten cents a barrel. Dave eventually made his way to the Ford Foundation where he turned out a book called *Energy: The New Era*, which was not an especially catchy title. Except that it was published in early 1974 shortly after the Arab oil embargo, which began in November of 1973, and changed the energy landscape forever. Timing, timing, timing.

Dave hustled back to Washington and got a job as a senior staff guy on the Senate Committee on Energy and Natural Resources. That's where I met him as he was frequently on the other side of the table when we would go to the Hill and pitch our latest energy policy ideas. They were never really advanced enough for him, but we were working for Gerald Ford, after all.

When Jimmy Carter got elected in 1976, he put Dave in the White House as one of the senior staff people working on energy policy. We finally were on the same team, and we worked closely for three years to produce the energy legislation that finally passed.

Dave was better at political maneuvering than I was and had managed to get President Carter to appoint him to be chairman of the Tennessee Valley Authority. Dave got to return to his roots, although his roots weren't all that deep. His father had run an umbrella repair business in Chattanooga. He had gone to school at the University of Georgia, but law school at the University of Tennessee.

Never mind all that. Dave called me up after the bill passed and I was moping around. He said, "Come on down to Tennessee, we got a real electric utility to play with." I carefully considered this detailed employment offer for all of thirty seconds, said yes, and started packing.

I moved to Tennessee as fast as my elderly blue Ford Econoline van would carry me. I didn't have the time or the inclination to sell the small house on Capitol Hill that I owned. Instead, I found a real estate agency who would act as my agent in renting it out and managing the property. Thus began my experience with tenants.

They were awful. I only rented to people who worked on the Hill or in the government (better credit) and had college degrees (smarter, maybe—that was the theory). But they did all manner of dumb things, including signing leases for a year and then leaving after eight months without even a farewell and no hope of my collecting the remaining four months of rent that was clearly due to me.

My favorite was when my tenant, this time a smart young woman, sent me my monthly rent check. It was more or less on time, but it was two hundred dollars short. I called her up and said, in effect, WTF? She said that she had bought a new pot and charged it to the house. I explained that the house had been rented as "unfurnished" and that meant that it had no furniture, no bedding, no pictures on the walls, no plates and glasses, and no pots. She said that she needed a pot, so she bought one "for the house." I was dumfounded, but she also said she would be leaving in two months. It was not clear how this was related to the pot, and of course was before her lease ended. I hung up and thought about never again being a landlord.

The landlords in Ecuador had problems I never had, but when it was explained to me why they might want to sell, I was sympathetic. Mike Parr explained all this and suggested that I might consider funding Jocotoco as it found properties to buy in the target area. I pondered this for a while. I was not unsympathetic, and the numbers were smaller than the commitment that I had made to the larger project. But the due diligence problems were more significant. I suppose I could have gotten on a plane and flew to Ecuador every time there was a property to buy, but that would have added measurably to the money being spent on that small property, at least by me, and would not have been a charitable contribution. Besides, I still had never even set foot in the country. I had never met the president of Jocotoco, nor visited a couple of his existing reserves. Traveling was still dicey as it was still Covid time. I discussed all this with Mike and reluctantly said I would pass on this opportunity. He was remarkably gracious about it.

Time passed, and the significance of the disease as a bar to travel declined as vaccinations, at least mine, increased. My ability to find projects that fit our criteria was no better than it had been, i.e., lousy. I called Mike up to whine and cry on his shoulder. Mostly I bitched about what jerks Cornell Lab was for not being willing to do what I wanted with my ten grand. He listened sympathetically and then said, "I think we might have some projects that could fit your criteria and your interests." The "interests" part was easy since all his organization does is bird conservation, mostly by buying land and preserving it. But there's more. He described his ideas to me, then sent me an email with more clarity. Here's what he proposed:

Hawaiian Forest Bird Conservation

As you know [actually I didn't know, but didn't tell him], Hawai'i is on the precipice of the most significant modern bird extinction event, according to many observers, ABC included. The archipelago could lose 12 of the 17 remaining iconic Hawaiian honeycreepers in the next few years if we do not act quickly to address the threat of avian malaria transmitted by non-native mosquitoes. In 2023, ABC will continue to help spearhead the multi-stakeholder initiative Birds, Not Mosquitoes (BNM) to advance the Incompatible Insect Technique (IIT), a safe, effective, and proven strategy for suppressing mosquitoes across large spatial scales. Next year ABC anticipates completing the lab work necessary to initiate field trials in Maui and hopefully by the end of the year, Kauai as well. As ABC works to deploy technology to address avian malaria, ABC continues to work with partners throughout the state to mitigate other significant threats to Hawaiian forest birds. This includes predator control during the nesting season, habitat restoration and protection on Mauna Kea for Palila, and research on mosquito population dynamics to inform the strategy for BNM. In 2023, we will once again have a National Fish and Wildlife Foundation (NFWF) grant to cover a portion of this work, but ABC has the obligation to raise an additional $126,999 to match NFWF and ensure the field teams are funded. A grant of $25,000 would be a significant contribution towards helping ABC fill this funding gap.

Author's note: Back a million years ago when I was a mere GS-11 working in the Department of Health, Education, and Welfare, I managed to get myself into a group of analysts working for Fred Malek, the Deputy Under Secretary and thus third-ranking guy in the department.

I was hired in as part of a program called Management Interns, only we got paid and were actually employees. You had to take a civil service exam for this, which I did while I was at Fort Bragg being a second lieutenant of infantry and jumping out of airplanes and getting ready to go to Vietnam, which was the destiny of all infantry second lieutenants. But since I planned on surviving my year in the 'Nam, and I did NOT plan on making a career out of the infantry, I figured that I would need a job when I got back and my two-year commitment ended, which would be the same date. Some clever army planning since what would you do with a lieutenant back from Vietnam, with one and a half months of service time left, and no doubt a bad attitude?

I had an advanced degree in political science from UCLA to go along with my equally not useful undergraduate degree, again in political science from Yale. I was not an engineer, or a scientist, or a business guy. I was clearly destined for government service. I was at the time okay with that. Good thing, since I didn't seem to have a lot of other choices.

I arranged to take the civil service exam, which was a classic true/false/multiple choice exam of not very difficult words and a few math problems at the level of fourth-grade arithmetic. Ever since being schooled in such types of tests at the Air Force Academy, I had done well on these sorts of challenges. This one was no exception. I got a nice letter saying that I had qualified, and would I please let them (the Civil Service Commission) know when I could start, assuming it was as soon as I got out of school. Aha! But I had already gotten out of school a couple of years ago, and now was off to a different sort of learning experience. I explained that and told them I would be back in around fifteen months.

They were to my surprise quite reasonable about the delay, which meant that (1) I was a genius, and no one had ever scored this high on the management intern test before and they didn't want to lose me or (2) the Defense Department had made it clear that they needed all the infantry second lieutenants that they could get so the civil service people should not be an obstacle to this. Probably the latter.

Back safely from Vietnam in July of 1968, I put on one of my two suits and disappeared into the bowels of the Department of HEW. I was assigned to the Office of Field Coordination whose task was to deal with the ten regional offices of HEW. The office had no particular authority, and the field offices all reported to their various Washington bits of their parent agencies, of which HEW actually had six—like a conglomerate. The field offices didn't really think that they needed much help being "coordinated." This meant that there was literally very little for me, the most junior person in the office, to do. Every so often they let me write a memo of one or two pages but really we didn't do jack shit.

Then a memo went out indicating that the new Deputy Under Secretary needed an assistant and if you would like to apply, send a resume to his secretary, Judy Licata. One of my colleagues graciously pointed this out to me. Was I interested? Do a bear and the Pope both use bathroooms in the woods on occasion?

There was a small problem, however. I had never made a resume. I had never had to; all I had to do to get ahead in life was pass tests. But, I thought that old, classic rejoinder: "How hard can it be?" Somewhere in all my files I saved a copy. It doesn't have the correct format, it doesn't have the "job objective," it doesn't have the space at the bottom for "Other Interests" where you prove you're not a total loser, etc.

Judy called me and said that Fred wanted to interview me. Great! We picked a time several days out, and I duly showed up at this office. I didn't know much about him except that he was a young thirty-two-year-old millionaire who had started a company after graduating from business school, then got involved in politics, and was appointed to bring "business management skills" to the big, rambling, messy establishment that was HEW. I think I knew that he had been in the army, but since the internet hadn't been invented, that's about all I knew.

I walked into his office and sat down. Fred had my resume, and said, "I haven't seen a resume quite like this before." I beamed with pleasure since I thought this was a compliment. He first asked me about my military background, where I had been, etc. The subject of Vietnam came up pretty quickly. It turned out that he had served a tour there as an advisor.

"Were you ever at Lai Khe?" he asked.

"Oh God, yes, we flew over it a couple of times and I almost got my ass shot off."

"No shit, I was there as an advisor to a bunch of ruff puffs [Vietnamese regional forces and popular forces, sort of like militia but less effective]."

"Gosh," I said, "we worked with ruff puffs all the time, and it was always a crapshoot. They were forever losing their rifles."

"No, selling them to the local VC."

The conversation went on, for probably forty-five minutes, all Vietnam War stories.

Finally, Fred remembered the purpose of the interview. Besides the fact of having never had a resume, I also had never been to a job interview. I didn't know that there was a predictable format to it. One of the things that the candidate was always asked, and that he or she always had a prepared answer for, was the future question.

Fred said, predictably, "Where do you see yourself in ten years?"

I thought briefly, then said, "Lying on the beach in Hawaii drinking Primo beer."

This is not in the interview handbook as an example of a good answer to this question. You're supposed to say something like "Running a ten-million-dollar-a-year business as the CEO."

Before he went to Vietnam, Fred had been assigned to the 24th Infantry Division, headquartered in Schofield Barracks in Hawaii. His eyes lit up at my answer. I deduced that he had as a young officer done his share of lying on the beach in Hawaii drinking Primo beer.

The next day Judy called me and said that I was hired.

Several years later, Fred moved to the Nixon White House where he was the number two guy at the Office of Management and Budget, once again charged with bringing the well-known business management principles to the even larger and even more messy entire federal government. He took several of his cadre with him to OMB, including me.

One of my jobs was to help implement the new (for the government) system of Management by Objectives, frequently shortened to MBO. Each department or agency had to set down in measurable language its ten most important objectives to accomplish for the year. Each of us on Fred's team had a government agency or cabinet department to work with on this program, and I got the Department of Agriculture.

All I knew about agriculture was that farms were where food came from. To my surprise, the department was about this and much, much more. It ran the Forest Service, for example, and thus could be considered one of the government's top landowners. And then there are price supports and research and marketing orders and building small dams for farmers and all manner of other stuff.

My favorite was the group who were implementing this objective, one of the department's top ten: *Eliminate screwworm diseases by using irradiated sterile screwworm flies*. If you have any idea what any of that means, you are probably a rancher from Texas, which I decidedly was not.

Screwworms are nasty little larva that hatch from the eggs of the female screwworm fly. She has the bad habit of laying such eggs in any open sores, cuts, etc. she can find on a cow. Anyone who has been around cows (again not me) knows that cows are forever running into barbed wire fences, trees, and spikey bushes, and each other. Small wounds and open cuts serve as the home for the screwworm fly eggs, which subsequently hatch into nasty little larvae that eat into the cow and cause it to lose weight—do they kill it? I never did find out. The whole purpose of raising cows, I have subsequently determined, is to get them fat enough to (euphemistically) "harvest" and become steaks and hamburger.

Amazing in that this was 1972 and Rachel Carson was still alive and only a few people had really read and understood her book. However, attacking the screwworm larva didn't work because you couldn't get access to them, and you couldn't afford to spray DDT on the whole herd to kill the flies before they laid the eggs. This was a big problem. Some clever agriculture scientists had come up with the solution, which was to breed the flies in captivity, then irradiate them just before they were ready to mate and fly them in airplanes (the Screwworm Express?) over potentially affected areas and drop them by the literal millions out of the planes.

They were still perfectly interested in mating; they just weren't able to do it fertilely. Strange as all this sounds, it was a good and extremely cost-effective program, and Texas has a lot of electoral votes. Once we all got over our schoolboy giggles of dealing with the screwworm problem, we backed them and even commended them.

This is a long explanation for why, when the ABC proposed that we help fund something they called the Incompatible Insect Technique (IIT), I didn't need a lot of coaching.

Here's how it works: *Wolbachia* is a naturally occurring bacteria that is present in over half of all insect species worldwide. The bacteria are already present in many insects in Hawaii, including some mosquito species. Researchers have found that *Wolbachia* plays an important role in insect reproduction, because it can function like birth control. Male mosquitoes with one strain of *Wolbachia* can only reproduce with females with the same strain of *Wolbachia*. Conversely, males with one strain of *Wolbachia* cannot produce viable offspring with females with a different strain of *Wolbachia*, or females without *Wolbachia*.

In a laboratory setting, researchers can expose mosquitoes to a different strain of *Wolbachia* and then rear large numbers of them. The mosquitoes are then separated by sex and only male mosquitoes are released into the wild. Male mosquitoes do not feed on blood, only nectar.

Once released, the lab-raised male mosquitoes mate with wild female mosquitoes and those females lay eggs that never hatch. When such releases are completed consecutively, mosquito populations decrease because new generations are not produced in the wild. And don't ask about how the mosquitoes are separated in the lab by sex. It's a trade secret.

Here is the second ABC proposal:

> Motus Wildlife Tracking System Expansion across the Western Hemisphere
>
> Not long ago, scientists couldn't seriously consider tracking a bird smaller than a mourning dove through its migration. The typical tags were just too big and bulky. In the last decade, however, a new research network called the Motus Wildlife Tracking System—consisting of tiny "nanotags" and a collection of stations built specifically to pick up their signals—has revolutionized migratory bird tracking in North America. [Authors note: Motus is Latin for "movement."] This, in turn, is giving conservationists unprecedented insights into the habitat they need to protect and restore to help save struggling migratory bird populations. Hundreds of Motus stations have been placed on the landscape over the past decade, but there are still vast areas along major migratory flyways that lack coverage that could provide key information to manage and conserve vulnerable and endangered migratory species. To facilitate the placement of new stations to target these bird species, American Bird Conservancy, in partnership with Birds Canada, has hired a new Motus Director for the United States and in 2023 will be bringing on two regional coordinators for the Southeast and Northwest US. Next year we want to start installing Motus receiver stations in strategic locations to fill the gaps, and a grant of $25,000 would help fund the installation of 10 Motus stations.

More author's note: I have investigated this whole idea, to include looking into getting one of the antennas and putting it on my very own house and then tracking the birds that fly by. "Why would this be a good idea, you birdy crackpot?" some ask.

The current best practice for tracking birds is roughly equivalent to shipwrecked guys on small tropical islands throwing messages in bottles (where do they get the bottles, and how did they manage to bring pencil and paper with them to this desert island when their boat sank?) into the ocean and hoping that the current carries the bottles somewhere where someone walking on the beach will pick one up and read the message and then come rescue them. Assuming the beachgoing someone can speak English, of course, and doesn't just decide that either it's a scam or that he will keep the bottle on his mantel as a souvenir.

Here is how it currently works: The researcher who wants to track the activities of a bird or a clump of birds sets up something called a "mist net." This is like a volleyball net, but more finely woven. It is set up between two poles, hopefully in an area where birds will fly into it. There are folds in the net and when the bird hits the net, it then drops into one of the folds/pockets and then really cannot get disentangled no matter how much it tries.

The setting up of such a net is regulated by the Fish and Wildlife Service and you need a permit and, I suppose, a good reason for catching a bunch of birds in the first place. I also presume that you could set one up on your own property and catch some birds, maybe, but then what would you do with them? I also presume that this same technology is used by illegal trappers in the wild bird trade.

Step two is taking the net down and carefully disentangling the birds that you have caught. If you are looking for a particular species, then I guess that you disentangle and turn loose the other ones.

Once your target birds are all disentangled, the researcher than adds leg bands to the birds in question. These bands have identifying data on them and coded requests that anyone else who catches, or I guess shoots, the tagged bird is supposed to let the original researcher know where and when and how the bird was re-caught. The researcher can compile more accurate data on migration patterns or foraging patterns or whatever the research hypothesis is. It's allegedly better than just sitting in a bird blind for twelve hours and watching for your target species to show up. And even then, you just have Point A in the study, and no way to really acquire Point B.

There are several problems with this approach. First and perhaps most important is the mortality issue. Not all the caught birds survive the impact, the disentanglement, the banding, and the release. Then they have to be caught again, disentangled again, the bird band removed, the data forwarded to the original researcher, and the twice-caught bird released on his or her merry way. It is very difficult to find good data on this, but there is talk in ornithology circles of a mortality of 5%. My guess is that it's more, but no one will talk about that.

Since no one wants to have Fish and Wildlife crack down on mist netting and bird banding, no one keeps careful records and publishes results on netting mortality, at least none that I have been able to find. Why would you?

The other part is more straightforward. How many banded birds are re-caught, their bands read, and this data forwarded to the original researcher? The consensus seems to be 5%, but there is a more honest estimate from more conservation-minded scholars that the number is closer to 1%. All that effort and injury for a 1% data yield.

Some people point out that Audubon, the original bird guy, didn't get all those terrific pictures by sitting around in the cold for eight hours so he could get a glimpse of a lesser goldfinch. No, he shot all those birds, or he had associates shoot them, and then there wasn't that pesky problem of getting them to pose. It's not clear to me that previous bad behavior justifies current bad behavior, but we digress.

The wildlife tracking business has had radio collars for some time now, with dramatic increases in battery life, transmitter range, and receiver quality. But this has almost uniformly been applied to large mammals, and we don't mean squirrels. The reasons are obvious—the apparatus was big and clunky and expensive. You had to shoot the animal with a dart gun loaded with an anesthesia drug. This posed a nontrivial risk for the shooter, and a big risk for the target animal. Dosage was and is difficult to calculate accurately, and the consequences of miscalculation in either direction are obvious—either the animal dies and is thus no longer interested in being tracked by the big human things, or it doesn't and is interested in ripping out the throat of the shooter or shooters. Or anybody else who is standing around helping.

But technology has come to the rescue, and "tags" as they are called are now small but powerful, and batteries are the same so you can glue them even to songbirds and then track them if you have enough receiving stations.

Yes, you still have to catch and disentangle them, and someone has to hold the bird while somebody else applies the glue and tag, but they don't have to be caught again. This is clearly an improvement, and that's why we were excited to support it. That and the fact that the antennae don't really cost that much—the whole rig can be set up—antenna and base, data capture, and transmission—for around five grand.

Here is the final ABC proposal. As it is about habitat, we were especially interested.

> The Conservation Coast BirdScape of Guatemala
>
> The Caribbean coast of Guatemala provides important stopover and wintering habitat for at least 153 neotropical migratory birds. It is a vital link in the Mesoamerican Biological Corridor and the Caribbean migratory flyway of Central America. Unfortunately, more than 65% of the forests in the Conservation Coast BirdScape have been cleared for cattle ranching, banana and oil palm plantations, short cycle crops such as corn, and subsistence agriculture. ABC and our Guatemalan partner, FUNDAECO, have been working together since 2012 to create and expand five protected areas through land acquisition. In total, these lands account for more than 42,000 acres of core habit for migratory birds. FUNDAECO is now focused on completing the purchase of 164 acres of coastal forest in the BirdScape that is under significant threat of tourism development due to its location along the coastline and its scenic nature. This parcel has one of the last mangrove forests in the Guatemalan Caribbean, making it a particularly important site to protect for birds and

other wildlife, and there is the potential to purchase 113.5 acres of adjacent land in the future to expand this protected area. FUNDAECO has negotiated a long-term payment plan with the owner of the 164-acre parcel that has allowed FUNDAECO to take over management of the property while paying off the purchase price of $600,000. They have a $75,000 payment due by the end of the year (after this payment, they will have $300,000 left to pay over the next four years). ABC has already raised $60,500 toward this need, leaving a $14,500 gap.

I read this all carefully, plus the additional material Mike Parr sent me subsequently, and thought, "Dang, this is way more like what I had in mind, and it fits our current financial situation." I sat down and wrote him a check for $75,000 and sent it off, along with a note asking that he not spend the funds on anything else other than what he had proposed, and that he send me a quick paragraph or so while the projects were going, letting me know that the money had been spent and what progress had been made. One year was all the time I suggested for this. It didn't seem like much to ask. But then, I have thought that before.

22

A Final Note on Philanthropy

Warren Buffett is Right, Not Just on Business But Also on Philanthropy and the Causes of its Decay: Arrogance, Bureaucracy and Complacency.

I have now lots of evidence that this applies just as well to nonprofit organizations as to for-profit commercial enterprises, maybe more.

So what to do if you're still interested in using your excess resources to make some small difference in the world? Here is a remarkable example of what we believe is a foolish way to do philanthropy.

Four or five months ago a local entrepreneur named Jay Kahn died at the age of ninety-two. He had been successful in early investing on both Costco and Apple. Quite successful it turns out. He left $100 million to the San Diego Foundation. He left no instructions on what they were to do with the funds. The foundation was pleased, no surprise.

Here's what's wrong with that. First, he was dead, so he couldn't tell what they were doing with his money and whether he liked it or not. Second, he left no directions on how to spend it. Making a hundred million dollars is not easy, you have to be lucky but also smart and diligent. How he could have no idea what to do with this major charitable donation is, to say the least, surprising. Third, he left it to the San Diego Foundation. This is an organization that does not have a philanthropic mission. They manage money for people who leave them funds, doing more or less whatever the donor wants. I have tried to deal with them and found them unimpressive, to be charitable. I am pretty sure that the first thing they did with Jay's money was to go out and hire an assistant for everyone at the grade of manager or above. Great.

Here in contrast is what we think. You could call this "How to Do Philanthropy If You're Not Bill Gates, or Melinda Gates, or Jeff Bezos's Former Wife." If you really do have a foolishly large amount of money and wish to give it away to support worthy purposes or causes, it is not an easy task. It is particularly difficult if you wish to see results from your largess. But that is not a problem that will generate much sympathy in the population at large, and it is also not our problem.

Our approach, simply stated, is that we are fortunate enough and worked hard enough that we have a modest amount of money that we want to deploy effectively to help solve important problems. The option of leaving it to our relatives or the government when we die does not appeal. We want to be assured that our donations are accomplishing their intended purpose, effectively and efficiently. We do not in general find the nonprofit/charitable purpose world to be good at this. Perhaps we have not been clear, or we have not looked hard enough. But that is our challenge.

The backstory: We spent much of our professional lives developing and implementing projects in the energy industry, where we both worked successfully for thirty years. In that business, you spend money on a specific project, sometimes a lot of money and time. If you're good and lucky, you end up with a great asset (power plant, pipeline, transmission line, distribution business) or some other clear asset or set of assets that you own, and that will carry out their functions and make the investors reasonable returns. Or it doesn't go well and was all a spectacular waste of time and money. Then you got nothing but a tax write-off—and since we weren't working for companies with lots of other income, a "write-off" was hardly what we were striving for.

It was a tough but interesting business model. It made you eschew fancy ideas and focus on projects and activities that actually met a commercial need at a reasonable cost. If you were really good, and we both were, then maybe you had a hit rate of 50%. Usually less.

We always knew what we were spending the money and time and brainpower on. Once we succeeded, and the project got built or acquired, we could watch it operate and see if it performed in accordance with what we had projected to be its economics. Sometimes it did better, sometimes it did less well. As the Chinese proverb goes, "The art of prediction is difficult, especially when applied to the future."

The nonprofit world in general does not appear to us to operate in this fashion. The model seems to be: We do good works, give us some money and we'll do more good works. Maybe at the end of the year you'll get your name in the back of the annual report under "Donors."

We have developed a self-imposed rule as follows (which we reserve the right to violate as we please):

Donations $5,000 or less annually do not require anything other than the routine assurance of good intentions—fancy websites, great-looking pictures, famous board members, and a reasonable explanation of purposes, although more precision is better than less. But precision as to costs and benefits is quite hard to find in the philanthropic world.

Donations of more than $5,000 require three things ("P, T, A"):
- Purpose: What exactly will the money be spent on? Good examples all drawn from real life: buying more habitat in Montana to increase grizzly bear range, with names and costs of the habitat pieces in question. Or helping fund an innovative mosquito reduction effort in Hawaii to save Hawaiian endemic birds on a particular island. Or funding the work to add four ranches in San Diego County to the Audubon Ranching program. And what will this activity/acquisition cost, at least our piece of it?
- Transparency: Will we be informed as to when and how much of our donation has been spent, and what it has been spent on? Will we receive this on some regular and predictable basis? Same question on results achieved.

- Accountability: Will we receive information as to the results of our donation? Did it do what you said it would do? If not, why not? And what did the activity in question end up actually costing? Audited annual financials would also be nice, just in general.

There is a fourth thing, less easily quantifiable or expressed as one word: We need to know and like the people in the organization to whom we are entrusting our funds. We need to know the professionals who will be doing the actual work. We need to know and be comfortable with the leadership of the group. We need to know that this leadership understands what the project is upon which we are jointly embarking and supports the goal and the necessary implementing activity. We have tried activities without this set of relationships, and the results were not just unsatisfactory, they were terminal.

All of this is hardly revolutionary; it is nothing but the discipline that we lived under for our professional lives. We do not find these requirements/suggestions well received in the philanthropic community. To quote an Ivy League university head of development, "You're only giving us ten thousand dollars. It's too small a donation for us to provide you such information."

To sum it up: the "give us the money, trust us, and go away" model doesn't work for us. If that is what is required for any particular philanthropic activity, then we are not the right donors for the charity to waste its time on. And ours. Ten thousand dollars, or fifty thousand dollars, or one million dollars can have significant impact when applied to serious causes with good stewards and smart strategies. We have seen it from local grocery stores to conservation lands to international renewable energy programs. Careful philanthropy, smart philanthropy, rewards and benefits those dedicated nonprofits who are really building a better world for all of us, with good intent, with efficiency, and with transparency. We have enjoyed working with them and we hope they have enjoyed working with us.

Appendix

Cornell California Land Acquisition Grant Program
Bissonette & Hemphill Habitat Preservation Program

General Notes:

The value with most of these properties lies in maintaining oak woodland communities within a larger landscape context. Oak woodlands comprise some of the most extensive old growth stands left in California, but unfortunately regrowth and sapling density is low and the invasion of non-native grassesare high due to overgrazing by cattle and fire suppression. Sudden oak death caused by a species of fungus-like water mold (and triggered by wet conditions), also contributes to development of seeping cankers on the trunk, die back of foliage, and the eventual death of infected trees. It is believed to have been introduced from Asia and proliferated in plant nurseries.

California oak woodlands rank among the top three habitat types in North America for bird richness due to their ability to produce an ample food source such as acorns and provide cavities for nesting. This habitat type is also essential for water filtration, nutrient cycling, carbon storage, soil formation, and erosion prevention.

Yellow-billed magpie, oak titmouse, Lawrence's goldfinch are all of high importance in the top tier set of birds for concern scores in oak woodlands.

There are also riparian habitats and related restoration efforts mentioned in these projects. Wetlands, lakes, streams, sloughs, and flood irrigated pastures can provide crucial habitat during the migratory and breeding seasons of wetland-dependent bird species. Riparian corridors will become increasingly important for wildlife and birds as we work to mitigate climate change by helping to stabilize stream banks and resist the flow of floodwaters, recharge groundwater and alluvial aquifers, and provide food sources, nesting habitat, and cover for birds such as the yellow-billed cuckoo (endangered in CA) and willow flycatcher. Riparian habitats are under threat from activities that alter their hydrology including development, invasive species, and grazing.

Raptors, mentioned with these acquisitions, are increasing since their huge loss from DDT in the 1950s and '60s. There are now regulations against hunting raptors, which used to occur in large numbers. Raptors are also becoming urbanized and without human pressure through hunting are starting to live side by side with humans. We aren't sure if they are back to their historic numbers or are increasing but do know they are not as much of a concern as the smaller birds listed above. However, raptors are showy and easy to use to engage donors and members, thus they can be seen as important engagement tools for land protection efforts.

Mountains Restoration Trust: La Sierra Acquisition Project
Contact: Kevin Gaston
County: Los Angeles
Land Conservation Type: purchase in fee
Property Size: 75 acres
Total Price of Land Purchase: $2,100,000
Close or Close Date: August 2021

Use of Awarded Funds: $ used for stewardship funds; includes a bargain sale of $1.32M (seller giving difference in sale price and fair market value as a gift).

Property Use: Open space, habitat protection, and passive recreation; certain areas containing sensitive cultural or ecological resources will be protected by selective trail alignment.

Type of Ecosystem: Mixed-chaparral and interlaced with coast live oak and sycamore-willow riparian corridors (forest and riparian).

Ecological and Bird Value: Biodiversity hot spot in the La Sierra watershed. Noted birds = golden eagles, red-tailed hawks, red-shouldered hawks, Cooper's hawks, American kestrels, peregrine falcons, white-shouldered kites, barn owls, great horned owls, western screech owls, long-eared owls, burrowing owls, and turkey vultures.

Reviewer Comments: This project is funding stewardship requirements that go along with the acquisition, but there was no stewardship concept plan uploaded with the application. Note land trust acquisitions must be purchased with a stewardship fund and plan in place. Wish applicant gave a better explanation about why this property is important for birds. Much of the information is general to the area and not specific to the property, although this property may not have any baseline data currently. They do have monitoring experience with EQUIP.

Their application is fairly sparse, thus want more info about why parcel is special. Do like the connectivity angle as this property will link two other preserves and public land—adjacent to conserved land.

Nice piece of oak savannah and close to LA where more open space is needed and important. Don't list birds that are of unique value; raptors and other "big" birds are essential for engagement tools and garnering interest in protecting wildlife with the public but are not the most critical species in need of protection within this habitat type.

Liked the many different partners with relationships already in place that could help with outreach and restoration. Focused on a science-based approach to restoration plan. Excluding sensitive species areas from public use. Compelling effort and trying to engage community while still protecting space.

Save Mount Diablo: Saving Mount Diablo's "Missing Mile" of Conserved Land

Contact: Edward Sortwell Clement
County: Contra Costa
Land Conservation Type: conservation easement
Property Size: 154 acres
Total Price of Land Purchase: $1,040,000
Close or Close Date: 12/31/21

Use of Awarded Funds: $ to go toward purchase price of conservation easement, owned by Concord Mount Diablo Trail Ride Association (nonprofit).

Property Use: Draft conservation easement restricts use of the property to natural resource protection, equestrian, recreational, and educational uses. Existing trail systems already on property will be used, but land is private so not public access, just continued use of the land by the organization that owns the property.

Type of Ecosystem: Oak woodland and grasslands.

Ecological and Bird Value: California Floristic Province (one of world's thirty-five biodiversity hot spots), Forever Wild campaign, Missing Mile and peregrine videos, property includes missing mile of Mt. Diablo.

Because of proximity to the Bay Area, this region is also under severe threat of development. Working to protect this area for fifty years, piecing together mosaic of conserved property and this is the last "missing mile" of terrain remaining on the face of Diablo itself. Noted birds = northern harrier, white-tailed kite, golden eagle, western burrowing owl, and peregrine falcon.

Reviewer Comments: Appreciate that they took the time to draft a very thorough application. The LT does have unrestricted cash available in reserves and capital campaign (money for emergency access) to fill any funding gaps with this project if they can't raise enough fundraising dollars before it needs to close. Seems as if we are early in their Forever Wild fundraising campaign and there is still much to be raised. Cornell funds will be paired with individual gifts and foundation grants. The total budget to secure the CMDTRA conservation easement, including pre-acquisition costs, is $1,075,000. Save Mount Diablo received a grant of $35,000 from the Resources Legacy Fund toward pre-acquisition costs, leaving the purchase price of $1,040,000 to be raised from individuals, foundations, and government sources.

This property is owned by a nonprofit recreation group. Is the threat level or need for protection as high as for a property that was slated for development? Perhaps organization wouldn't be able to afford the property in the future without an easement in place (development rights sold and tax incentives) and thus there was a risk of development or natural resource extraction? LT does state that there is high pressure for development in this area due to its proximity to the Bay Area.

How will the stewardship change once the easement is purchased as they say the land is already being carefully cared for by landowner? What difference is the land trust making to the protection and conservation of the property? It will be permanently protected forever, and it is of high significance to the LT as they have been working to protect this area for fifty years.

Great that this property is already being monitored using eBird and Mount Diablo Audubon Society runs Christmas Bird Count on the property. They do seem to be serious about including birds as indicators and in stewardship plans. Do like that this is part of a larger landscape effort (connectivity) around saving this watershed and region around Mount Diablo. "Missing Mile" is the final piece of the puzzle in this special area, great story in video. DDT crash of peregrine falcons around 1970s. Historic peregrine nesting sites on Mount Diablo ('80s and '90s), was very high profile at the time following the biologists and their cross-fostering of peregrine chicks with prairie falcon chicks. Delisted in 1999, success story. Still a very active volunteer group, documenting peregrine breeding success. This land surely helps provision adults and fledgling peregrines.

The videos included in the additional information section helps one visualize the project area and its importance within the region and surrounding landscape. Smart way to generate interest around this campaign.

Value here is in maintaining oak woodland in the larger landscape, thus oak woodland restoration is very important. Raptors are doing well, some of smaller birds are priority species such as oak titmouse, which is not mentioned. Management plan is included with the application and specifically addresses birds of conservation concern including golden eagle, peregrine, and kestrels and plant communities that will support these birds and other wildlife.

The Land Conservancy of San Luis Obispo County: Santa Rita Ranch Fee Acquisition

    Contact: Kyle Walsh
    County: San Luis Obispo
    Land Conservation Type: purchase in fee—already purchased
    Property Size: 1,715 acres
    Total Price of Land Purchase: $7,600,000
    Close or Close Date: 12/29/20

    Use of Awarded Funds: $ to go toward reimbursement of programs and stewardship fund for acquisition's purchase.

    Property Use: Protecting wildlife habitat, long-term environmental restoration projects, sustainable livestock grazing, and nature education; perhaps limited, nonmotorized outdoor recreation informed by ecological assessment and potential impact of access; sustainable working ranch. Education programming would use buildings already in place on the property.

    Type of Ecosystem: Grasslands, oak savanna, and woodland.

    Ecological and Bird Value: Top of southern Santa Lucia Range, connects designated wilderness areas within the Los Padres National Forest. Without permanent protection, the property would remain threatened by intensive land use and could not be easily accessed for adaptive habitat restoration over time. They are changing farming practices on the property. Noted birds = peregrine falcon, Swainson's hawk, and burrowing owl (special status species); bank swallow, Lawrence's goldfinch, and California thrasher; perhaps California spotted owl (spotted on adjoining property). Tom Edell, an eBird reviewer, will be conducting bird surveys and assessments.

    Reviewer Comments: This project has already closed and provides security that the project is already protected and purchase won't fall through. They did tap into internal resources to complete purchase before end of

2020 to capitalize on CA state support. These funds are normally directed to general LT programs and stewardship and need to be recovered and replenished by land trust through fundraising.

They must raise money and replenish funds as could prevent LT from moving on another piece of property until they have raised the money. Our money won't go as far with this price tag but does give this land trust the opportunity to move toward additional land purchases with our funding in place to reimburse their programmatic and stewardship fund. Could think of it as a longer-term relationship with the land trust as our money will be tied to this Santa Rita Ranch purchase and enable them to move forward with other acquisitions in the future.

This is a huge property, unique in its size and was at risk of being developed and subdivided into six separate properties thus there was urgency for protection. High risk for development because of zoning laws and lack of enrollment in Williamson Act contract (incentive for land use protection/conservation of agricultural properties).

The main use of the ranch will be for nature education and they will convert one of the existing buildings into a nature center. Diverse habitat types = valley oak savannah, mixed hardwood forest, and riparian habitat along with 230-acre lake that is year-round waterfowl habitat. LT already incorporates birds into their planning—frequently uses avian indicators to evaluate the long-term success of restoration sites or those that undergo a change in land management practices.

Portions of the ranch suffer as a result of poorly managed agricultural practices that focused on production value rather than biological function and diversity. LT will not continue dry-land farming on the ranch and will revegetate areas with appropriate tree and herbaceous species. The restoration of natural land cover will help control sedimentation into the lake and enhance habitat for both resident and migratory avian species. Without permanent protection, the property would remain threatened by intensive land use change. Acquiring and protecting the property appears that it could stand to make a significant difference.

Property does contribute to a private and public protected wildlife corridor, protecting more lands closer to the coast within the Pacific Flyway.

Currently there is a large focus on ranches in CA and sustainable grazing programs. Yellow-billed magpie, oak titmouse, and Lawrence's goldfinch are an important part of the CA oak avifauna. Birds of high continental concern that are common in oak woodlands. Lawrence's goldfinch is mentioned as a bird observed on the property. Also potential for spotted owl habitat.

Elkhorn Slough Foundation: Securing the Future of a Globally Important Bird Area: Acquiring a Key Property Inholding in Elkhorn Slough, California
Contact: Mark Silberstein
County: Monterey
Land Conservation Type: purchase in fee—already purchased
Property Size: 2.4-acre inholding in 3,000 acres of surrounding protected lands
Total Price of Land Purchase: $375,000
Close or Close Date: 3/3/20

Use of Awarded Funds: Use funds to pay down $50,000 of the $375,000 promissory note loan from a private lender.

Property Use: Restoring and managing wildlife habitat by removing several buildings and debris left by previous owners and removal of invasive plant species. Completing the access trail from ESF's Outdoor Classroom to the Porter Community Center. Links Hall District Elementary School Outdoor Classroom with the Porter Ranch Community Center. Mile-long trail will be used by students from the school and be open for community events.

Type of Ecosystem: Riparian habitats along the creek are flanked by grasslands and upland habitats of oak woodlands and maritime chaparral.

Ecological and Bird Value: Advance protection of a globally important bird area and birding hot spot—Upper Elkhorn Slough. Elkhorn Highlands, lower Carneros Creek floodplain, trying to improve water quality in slough. Many protected areas with a diversity of designations reflects the tremendous diversity of habitats and species supported in the Elkhorn Slough watershed. Securing and rehabilitating this land buffers and protects the riparian corridor and important upland habitats. This acquisition eliminates one of the last three inholdings along three miles of the creek and watershed and adjoins the single other lower creek inholding that is an acquisition target. This is part of a thirty-year effort to protect the main drainage to the upper slough. Birds noted: endangered snowy plover, but at the mouth of the slough not at the head near this property.

Reviewer Comments: This transaction is a very small property, yet they stated that this property acquisition is a step to reaching the goal of protecting 30% of land and water by 2030. Trade-off between small acreage and really important area for global biodiversity and riparian habitat protection? Would have to look at the property in context with the larger ecosystem.

Since the property is very small, our award dollars would be a more significant portion of the purchase price, but the real ecological value of the property itself is not completely clear. There is certainly significance in the surrounding landscape, but maybe not as large of an impact? It does sound like this property was in bad shape so the purchase alone, even without restorative practices, will stand to make a difference.

The LT will use funds to pay down $50,000 of the $375,000 promissory note loan from a private lender as they borrowed funds to acquire this parcel before it came on the market. A donor has pledged $125,000 if they are successful in repaying the note; sounds like there are matching funds/pledge of donations that will be given based on successful repayment of loan. These funds will provide leverage to raise additional funds. One reviewer suggested perhaps neighbors are giving the land trust an added incentive to pay it off quickly so the land won't go back on the market or option other properties?

Trying to restore a habitat corridor and have already cleaned debris on the property to ready for habitat restoration. This land buffers and protects the riparian corridor, important upland habitats, and eliminates one of the last three inholdings along three miles of the creek and watershed and "tees up" the adjoining property for acquisition. This is part of a thirty-year effort to protect the main drainage to the upper slough, improve water quality, and increase connectivity in a globally important bird area with high biodiversity.

LT does a good job of describing the ecological value of the larger area and slough, but not of the specific parcel. They do discuss continuing bluebird box installation on this property with school groups in the future and initiating restoration of the uplands and the adjoining transition zone between the creek and the salt marshes that will enhance the value to migratory and resident bird populations. Could have done a better job looking at critical bird species on adjoining properties.

Does sound like this property was in bad shape upon purchase and has the potential to change greatly over time with some management and damaging activities removed.

California Rangeland Trust: Willow Creek Ranch Pacific Flyway Conservation Easement Project
Contact: Katie Schroeder
County: Lassen
Land Conservation Type: conservation easement
Property Size: 1,577 acres
Total Price of Land Purchase: $1,531,000 (fair market value of the ranch at $2,142,000.00 with an estimated easement value of $1,530,800.00)
Close or Close Date: 12/15/2022 or 01/15/2023 (currently out of our window, but could discuss)

Use of Awarded Funds: Purchase a conservation easement on a privately owned ranch that encompasses important habitat for birds (and other wildlife) within the Pacific Flyway as defined by the Intermountain West Joint Venture's SONEC priority conservation region.

Property Use: Active cattle ranch, therefore future land use is expected to continue to be agricultural grazing for both summer and fall followed by shallow spring irrigation on the summer and fall pastures. Family that owns the ranch has actively worked with local conservation groups including National Resources Conservation Service, Point Blue Conservation Science, and Ducks Unlimited to implement restoration and management practices that improve habitat on the property. The easement will be a capstone to past conservation accomplishments. Does not include a public access component, however the landowners will continue a variety of partnerships with public agencies such as Lassen County, University of California Agriculture and Natural Resources (UC ANR), NRCS, and others on weed abatement and plant management, water quality and riparian management, pasture and range management (rotational grazing), fuel reduction practices, timber management, as well as public land grazing concerns.

Type of Ecosystem: Rangelands, riparian areas, and flood-irrigated pastures.

Ecological and Bird Value: The ranch is positioned to connect two large expanses of public lands—the 2,700-acre Willow Creek Wildlife Area, and Bureau of Land Management that includes the 19,984-acre Tunnison Mountain Wilderness Study Area. These adjacent natural areas enhance the value and impact of the ranch for habitat. Flood irrigation within historic wetlands in SONEC replicates floodplain function that supports habitat for wetland-dependent birds. Willow Creek is a spring-fed system with water persisting year-round. Late season water during fall migration is extremely limiting in SONEC and is identified as a bottleneck for migrating birds returning to wintering areas. The ranch has rangeland uplands, flood-irrigated wet meadows, and riparian areas along Willow Creek. Birds noted: western meadowlark, Savannah sparrow, marsh wren, greater sandhill crane, yellow-headed blackbird, common yellowthroat, cliff swallow, willet, Canada goose, Gadwall, Brewer's blackbird, Wilson's snipe, horned lark, barn swallow, cinnamon teal, American white pelican, and white-faced ibis.

Reviewer Comments: Rangeland Trust will submit a proposal to NRCS's Agricultural Conservation Easement Program on March 5, 2021, seeking $765,400 toward the purchase of the conservation easement. On February 18, 2021, Rangeland Trust was invited to submit a full proposal to WCB's Pacific Flyway Conservation Program by April 8, 2021, and is seeking $715,400 toward the purchase of the conservation easement. With the Cornell land acquisition grant award of $50,000, the project will be fully funded. We anticipate notice of funding awards to be received no later than August 15, 2021. If needed, the project's landowners have confirmed their willingness to provide a partial landowner donation to ensure the project comes to fruition. This does mean that we will be one of a small number of partners and possibly more significant, even though our award is small compared to the other two partners.

The close date on the easement is not until late 2022, so technically out of our award window, but don't feel as if we're wedded to that window if project is really special. Even most seamless of transactions might take a year.

From the description it sounds as if this family has been managing this cattle farm with restorative practices in mind and this easement will ensure the same practices continue so there will be little if any change in land use due to the easement protection. This is an active cattle farm—how much is actively grazed versus ungrazed? What BMPs are already being used?

They don't describe the value to birds in excessive detail, but do make a case for the importance of the water on the landscape for migrating birds. Would like more thoughtful detail about the bird conservation value specific to property protection and how they might enhance the practices once the easement is in place, if it will change at all. There are regular bird surveys on the property and a nice write-up about the birds seen on property. If they were going to do major riparian restoration to the creek, it could attract yellow-billed cuckoos, chats, and Bell's vireos. Not much truly outstanding bird value according to what they listed.

Why the sense of urgency to protect the property right now? Does the landowner need to put it under easement to be able to maintain the ranch—decrease property taxes as value of land would be less and taxed at lowest or lower tax value?

One of few locations in the area that has water in the wetlands year-round and since migratory birds are dependent on wetlands it could be very important in this landscape. Intense irrigated agriculture is restricted to 10% of land, what impact will this have on habitat for birds? Like that they have a thorough plan for use, conservation, and stewardship values and that the owners are engaging with other partners.

Putting an easement on this property will protect it in perpetuity, but might not make as big of a conservation impact as the other ranch property (Santa Rita), which will be owned in fee and will be managed by a conservation organization. This property does have a path to closure with just three parties (CLO funds, Pacific Coastal Flyway program, and NRCS).

About Robert Hemphill

Robert Hemphill was an OMB senior manager in Washington when in 1973 he was thrown into the energy business, thanks to the Arab oil embargo. He worked on fuel efficiency standards for cars and trucks and ran the program that set national appliance energy efficiency standards. He moved to TVA in 1978 and managed the utility's conservation and solar programs. In 1981, he joined with two other executives who started AES, a $1 million start-up focusing on cogeneration that has grown into a $7 billion global electric power-generating and distribution company. While at AES he initiated the company's wind generation program and started a utility-scale battery effort, which is now the largest in the world. In 2008, he founded and served as CEO of AES Solar, which designed and constructed fifty-one solar plants in seven countries, growing from a start-up venture to $2.5 billion in assets in six years.

Mr. Hemphill holds a BA from Yale University, an MA from UCLA, and an MBA from George Washington University. He served as an airborne infantry officer in the US Army in Vietnam and in the Special Forces, and was awarded a combat infantryman's badge and Senior Parachutist wings.

He has been on the board of several nonprofits including the Smithsonian National Museum of American History, the US Botanic Garden, the Museum of Contemporary Art San Diego, and Counterpart International. Mr. Hemphill has published three books about his energy, international, and business experience: *Dust Tea, Dingoes and Dragons*; *Stories from the Middle Seat*; and *Goats Ate Our Wires*.

Acknowledgments

The art for this cover was done by Alice Lemon, an Encinitas artist of great talent. She also provided the art for the cover of book three, *Goats Ate Our Wires*.

Shelley Chung provided masterful and careful editing of this entire manuscript, as she has with all my previous books. She is a joy to work with.

Victoria Vinton did the book design work with consummate skill and care. She too has done such things for all my previous books.

I am deeply in the debt of all these women for making this book attractive and readable.

www.ingramcontent.com/pod-product-compliance
Lightning Source LLC
LaVergne TN
LVHW041657060526
838201LV00043B/461